Ground Attack Aircraft
OF WORLD WAR II

Ground Attack Aircraft
OF WORLD WAR II
Christopher Shores

A Macdonald Illustrated War Study

MACDONALD AND JANE'S • LONDON

First published in 1977 by
Macdonald and Jane's (Publishers) Limited
Paulton House, 8 Shepherdess Walk
London N1 7LW

Drawings and diagrams : T. Brittain

Printed in Great Britain by
REDWOOD BURN LIMITED
Trowbridge & Esher

ISBN 0356 08338 1

Contents

Introduction 9

1 Development 11
2 The First Year of War 39
3 War in the Mediterranean Area 51
4 Eastern Front 67
5 Western Developments 101
6 Sicily, Italy and the Balkans 113
7 The Conquest of Western Europe 136
8 The Pacific 160
  Appendix 184
  Bibliography 187
  Index 188

Introduction

To be called upon to prepare a study of ground attack aircraft raises many problems of interpretation and of boundaries. The question "when is a military aircraft a ground-attack aircraft, and when does it cease to be one?" remains foremost in the mind. Due consideration had to be given to other titles in this series — Alfred Price has dealt with the fighter in its specific role of combatting opposing aircraft; David Brown has dealt concisely with the carrier-based fighter in all its aspects, whilst Roger Freeman and Alfred Price have covered the topic of level bombing — in the latter case some space also having been given to dive-bombing, though basically by twin-engined types.

The guidelines introduced have therefore been as follows. Ground attack aircraft have been deemed to be those operating at low level to employ fixed gun armament and/or other weapons against ground targets, mainly (though not exclusively) in support of military operations taking place below. Linked to this concept are two facets which, though not entirely, are closely connected. These are, firstly, the specialist dive-bomber, and secondly the fighter aircraft carrying out firing attacks on ground targets as a secondary adjunct to its primary air combat duties.

In order to provide a rounded picture, both dive-bombers and 'strafing' fighters are dealt with here, though not it must be stressed at the start, as exhaustively as those types considered to be 'ground attack aircraft' in the purest sense to which this very generalized term can be viewed. This 'pure' category is considered to relate to 'assault' aircraft (heavily armed and armoured aircraft specifically designed or modified for low-level attack on and around the battlefield in direct support of the ground forces), anti-tank aircraft (a more specialized offshoot of the latter), and fighter-bombers (those fighter aircraft modified to carry bombs, rockets, or other non-fixed armament, the primary duty of which has been assigned as the attack of targets on the ground, air combat having become a secondary function only).

While the ultimate in ground support aviation probably occurred on the Eastern Front, in the West the activities of the rocket-firing Typhoons of the Royal Air Force are probably pre-eminent in many minds. Controversy has arisen in recent years regarding the effectiveness of these particular exponents of ground attack, and I am deeply grateful to Col. Raymond 'Cheval' Lallemant — himself one of the 'leading lights' of the rocket-Typhoon pilots — for providing a detailed and illuminating exposition on the subject. I would also like to record my profound thanks to my good friends David Brown and Alfred Price for their unstinted help and advice, to Waclaw Klepacki, and to other friends who have provided photographs from their files for use herein, including Bill Hess, Kenn Rust, Frank Smith, Malcolm Passingham, Franz Seliger, Jerry Campbell, Richard Hill, Barrett Tillman, Robert Mikesh, and Chris Ehrengardt. A special "thank you" is due to Ted Hine and the staff of the Photographic Department of the Imperial War Museum.

C.F.S. 1977

1. Development

It is the purpose of many types of military aircraft to attack targets on the ground, yet despite this general commonality of *purpose*, the term 'ground attack' has become associated with one particular aspect. This description has come to apply to those aircraft specifically designed or modified for low-altitude attack with guns, frequently augmented by other weapons, against targets generally of a tactical nature.

The concept of ground attack is almost as old as that of military aviation itself, and certainly preceded that of combat between opposing aircraft. Indeed the first experimental fitting of machine gun armament to early aircraft, undertaken before the outbreak of war in 1914, was specifically with a view to the use of these weapons against objectives on the ground.

Hostilities in 1914 however, found aircraft in service still unarmed in the main, their duties being envisaged as reconnaissance, together with aerial bombing. The explosive force of the bomb at this stage offered a greater destructive possibility than a single rifle-calibre machine gun. The latter were also in short supply and in great demand by the ground forces at this stage in any event. The bomb also offered the advantage that it could be delivered from an altitude above the effective height of small calibre fire from the ground. To descend to a level at which a gunner might with advantage engage enemy forces with his machine gun, put the slow and vulnerable machines of 1914 into a position where they were in grave danger of being shot down themselves by a greater volume of return fire from the ground.

Consequently for the first three years of the war such attacks were rare, and were made only at the impulse of the individual pilot. The rapid development of stronger, faster and more heavily-armed aircraft which resulted from the protracted struggle for control of the air above the trenches, reopened the possibilities of low-level ground attack, and after some impromptu support of advancing British troops by fighter aircraft during the Messines offensive of June 1917, such support of the infantry became a matter of established practice as the year wore on.

Realizing the potential of aircraft for attacking entrenched troops, the Germans at once began experimenting with specialized aircraft for this duty, featuring a degree of armour protection around the engine and pilot. The British on the other hand decided to rely upon the speed and manoeuvrability of the standard fighting scout, which offered a far greater versatility of use than the specially-constructed machine. It then became increasingly common practice for scout pilots of the Royal Flying Corps and Royal Naval Air Service to undertake their offensive patrols over enemy territory with six 20 lb. Cooper bombs carried beneath the wings of their aircraft. These could then be dropped either on targets of opportunity, or on specified objectives. During bomber escort sorties, bombs were frequently carried to augment the striking power of the actual bombing aircraft. Thus at this stage were born both the armoured specialized ground attack aircraft, and the versatile general-purpose fighter-bomber, the two basic types of aircraft with which this work is concerned.

When the first massed tank attack was launched by the British Army at Cambrai in November 1917, it was supported by a considerable force of bomb-carrying DH 5 and Sopwith Camel fighters, but it was during the following spring that the fighter-bomber first really came into its own. During March 1918 the final great German offensive was launched on the Western Front, the massed German infantry receiving considerable support from low-flying attack aircraft of the *Schlachtstaffeln*, which had been formed specifically for such duties. They also received a certain amount of support from German fighting scouts, which made machine gun attacks on ground targets when conditions above allowed.

As the Allied armies fell back before the onslaught, their air forces were thrown in in great strength in an effort to slow down the momentum of the advance. Going out again and again to attack infantry, cavalry, artillery and supply columns at very low level, the aircraft played a major part in allowing the advance to be brought to a halt after several weeks of extremely hard fighting. Severe casualties and much confusion were inflicted by the constant harrying machine gun attacks of the scouts (soon to be known as 'strafing'), while the sharp explosions of the deadly little Cooper bombs added further to the chaos.

Losses during these operations proved to be heavy. Flying at such low level the aircraft were a prime target for every determined rifleman or machine gunner who felt inclined to hit back, and most of the aircraft which returned featured numerous bullet holes in their fabric covering. Also air supremacy had not been wrested from the Germans at this stage, and flying at low altitude, concentrating on the search for suitable ground targets, the Allied aircraft proved easier-than-usual targets for the patrolling German fighters.

The effectiveness of these operations had not gone unnoticed on either side of the lines, such attacks on ground targets remaining an important, though little-publicized feature of the air war throughout the remainder of the period of hostilities. Because of their increasingly great numerical inferiority in the air, German fighters were less able to be spared for such duties however, and it was on the newly-formed Royal Air Force in particular that the bulk of such activity devolved. With the opposing forces once more dug in to more static positions after the Spring offensive, the problems of more accurate bomb delivery by fighter aircraft raised the need for revised tactics. It was at this stage that a number of units equipped with Sopwith Camel fighters attempted to attack trench targets by making an approach in a steep dive, aiming with the gunsight, and releasing the bombs at low level as the pull-out from the dive commenced. Thus was born the first concept of the dive-bomber.

With the final Allied offensives of Autumn 1918, fighters operated in great numbers in close support of advancing troops and tanks, undertaking low-level strafing and bombing attacks on German concentrations, convoys etc., very similar to those flown during the spring, but on an even larger scale.

In the Middle East too, ground attack by low-flying aircraft had been developed to something approaching an art. Here the situation was even more favourable, since the British Empire air forces supporting General Allenby's forces in Mesopotamia enjoyed virtually total air supremacy. Following Allenby's great offensive of September 1918, RAF fighter aircraft played havoc with retreating Turkish Army columns, inflicting great casualties.

The climax came on 21 September when the Turkish 7th Army was caught on an exposed road to the north-east of Nablus, flanked on both sides by steep ravines. In a classic initial attack, the strafing aircraft blocked the head of the column. Thereafter there was no escape, and the trapped, practically helpless column was cut to pieces. Over scenes of appalling carnage, SE 5As and Bristol Fighters swept in again and again, pouring bursts of fire from their Vickers and Lewis machine guns into the seething targets below. Ground crews worked flat out to refuel and rearm the aircraft, while the aircrews flew themselves to the point of exhaustion. So many sorties did the small number of aircraft available make, that throughout the day at least two aircraft appeared over the target every three minutes.

When darkness brought these attacks to an end, the 7th Army had for all practical purposes ceased to exist, and advancing ground forces had only to round up the prisoners. This most successful of all ground attack operations of World War I coincided with the signing of an Armistice with Turkey, and the end of the war in the area.

DEVELOPMENT CEASES WITH THE RETURN OF PEACE

As has often been the case, the lessons learned in the later stages of a long war are often the first to be forgotten, and after the final Armistice of November 1918 ground attack aviation suffered greatly in this manner. There were a number of reasons for this, which may best be summed up by dealing with the various major nations separately.

Germany and the Central Powers had been defeated, and by the terms of the Treaty of Versailles were to be forbidden air forces in the future. For the time being therefore development of military aviation in those states was at a virtual standstill. Russia and her smaller neighbours in Eastern Europe were still in various stages of armed conflict and utter chaos following the Bolshevik Revolution of 1917, and were more concerned with the establishment of stability of some form or another, than with the development of highly-specialized concepts of military aviation. It should be mentioned however, that during 1919 and 1920 Red Army units — particularly the Russian cavalry armies — were to experience damaging strafing attacks on several occasions, firstly in the Caucasus by British fighters supporting the White forces, and then in Poland, where the fledgling Polish air force played a major part in turning a massive Bolshevik offensive into a crushing defeat.

Among the Western democracies the reasons for the failure to develop further the tactics which had been basically of their own inovation, were somewhat more complex. Sickened by the waste and cost of war, popular pressure in these countries was for disarmament, reliance on the new League of Nations, and the belief that the war had been one "to end all wars".

Against this background the British, French and Italians also had other problems and priorities — notably colonial ones. The advantages of the aircraft for policing and pacification of dissidents in colonial territories had been realized at an early date, together with he great cost-saving in manpower thaat accompanied these.

With the end of the war most development work had been cut back, particularly of such specialized types as trench-strafers, while large supplies of surplus wartime production remained to hand, which was perfectly adequate for the colonial role. By the time that it became necessary to consider replacements for these aircraft, the stringent times of the Great Depression were arriving, and in a period of general economy, governmental allocations for military aircraft development and production were cut to the bone.

Apart from small numbers of the primary types — bombers and fighters — for the metropolitan air forces, main requirement was for a cheap 'maid-of-all-work', which would undertake the maximum of colonial duties for the minimum of cost. Designed for conditions where serious opposition was unlikely, these aircraft lacked the performance to have any real practical application in a full-scale war.

These 'general purpose' aircraft undoubtedly did frequently undertake ground-attack sorties against hostile tribesmen in many areas from the deserts of Morocco to the mountainous wastes of the North-West Frontier of India. They were however not in the true sense ground attack aircraft, coupling their activities with normal bombing, reconnaissance and such duties.

At home, the British and French based their military policies purely on the concept of defence. In line with the theorists of the inter-war period, the bomber was seen as the main instrument of air power — to strike strategically at a potential enemy's war industries and thus deprive him of the capability to continue to wage war. Fighters were retained in service mainly as defensive interceptors, to protect against an aggressor's bombers. In order to have the maximum performance for this role they were short of range and unequipped for the carriage of offensive weapons other than their machine guns.

Britain alone among the major nations had formed her air force into a separate and independent arm of equal standing with the army and navy — a position in which considerable resentment and jealousy from the older services had swiftly forced the young newcomer onto the defensive. As chance would have it, those who had gained early ascendancy in the RAF had been (not surprisingly) officers dedicated to the idea of independent air power, and notably those who had been involved with the RAF's strategic bombing arm, the Independent Air Force. Few of these men had any direct experience of the ground attack activities of 1918, and most evinced little interest — ground attack smacked too much of subservience to the Army!

Clearly co-operation with the army could not be totally overlooked, but the requirement to do so was kept very much in the background, and the army co-operation units became the 'Cinderellas' of the service, their duties being most narrowly defined as tactical reconnaissance, artillery spotting and message dropping.

While in France the air force remained under army control, the French had not developed ground attack to nearly the same degree during the war as had their British allies, while their espousal of strategic bombing had predated the similar enthusiasm of the latter. The French took the possibilities of multi-duty economy even further than the other Western nations, developing a family of '*multiplace de combat*' aircraft for he metropolitan air force, designed to undertake bombing, fighting and reconnaissance duties. Generally however, development and employment of bomber, fighter and army co-operation types closely followed that of the RAF. In Italy too the situation was little different, though the advent of Benito Mussolini's Fascist regime did result in a swifter expansion and modernisation of the air force during the thirties than was the case with any of the other old European Allies of 1918.

While a member of the Allies during the First War, Japan had played but little part in the fighting, and military aviation remained in a relatively undeveloped state at the close of hostilities. Consequently advisory teams from the victor nations were subsequently employed to aid in the development of Japanese air power, these of course incorporating many of the ideas and prejudices of those advisers. As a result no early development of ground attack aviation was undertaken in Japan either.

It was in the United States however, that the seeds of the early experience were nurtured and allowed to grow — even if this development was at first slow and faltering. Surprisingly, the Americans were not only to keep alive the ground attack concept, but were to develop independently both its manifestations — the low-flying 'attack' or 'assault' aircraft, and the plunging dive-bomber.

DEVELOPMENT IN THE UNITED STATES

While the United States enjoyed many of the same disarmament sympathies as did the European democracies, the First World War had cost her less, and she was less war-weary. Further, her air force remained basically under Army command, whilst both Navy and Marine Corps were developing their own air arms, albeit initially on a relatively small scale.

The US Air Service had been a late participator in the European war as an independent service, but many Americans had served with both British and French units, and the command had enjoyed adequate opportunities to observe all aspects of the war in the air. To the Army command, the prospect of a heavily armed and armoured aircraft to give low-level support to the troops virtually as a flying machine gun nest, was an attractive one. Consequently during the early twenties a number of experimental 'strafers' were tested, but with rather disappointing results. It was not found that the concept itself was necessarily at fault, but that with the powerplants and airframes then available, the substantial lowering of performance occasioned by the weight of a sufficient quantity of guns and armour, took away the viability of the whole proposition.

The idea was shelved but not forgotten, awaiting the development of more suitable machines. In 1926 a two-seater observation and light-bombing biplane, the Douglas O-2 appeared to offer the necessary power-to-weight ratio with its 433 hp Liberty V-1410 engine. One was converted for the attack role by the addition of armour protection for the engine, cooling system and crew, together with the extremely heavy armament for that time of six forward-firing .30 in. Browning machine guns, as well as two flexible Lewis guns in the rear cockpit for the observer/gunner.

First US aircraft designed from the start for ground attack purposes to enter service was the Curtiss A-12 Shrike. This graceless, heavily braced and strutted monoplane is seen here carrying the insignia of the 13th Attack Squadron, which was based at Barksdale Field, Louisiana. *USAF via W.N.Hess*

This time results were much more promising, and after further development work by Douglas and Curtiss, a similar observation biplane, the Curtiss Falcon, was ordered into production in modified form as the A-3 — the first aircraft to enter squadron service with the US Army Air Corps in the new 'Attack' category. Powered by a 435 hp Curtiss D-12D engine, the A-3 was seen only as an interim type to introduce the attack aircraft into service, although 76 were ordered, followed by 78 improved A-3Bs. These were quite large orders at the time. Weighing 4,378 lb. gross, the A-3 reached a top speed of 141 mph at low level, but differed from the earlier Douglas test aircraft in having only four forward-firing Brownings.

The day of the biplane in the USAAC was fast approaching its end however, and by the early thirties the first all-metal monoplanes designed specifically in the US for the attack role were under test. Two very similar types, the Fokker XA-7 and the Curtiss XA-8, were both powered by the new 600 hp Curtiss Conqueror engine, and both armed with four fixed wing-mounted Brownings, together with a fifth flexible gun in the rear cockpit for defence.

The contest was won by the Curtiss machine, but only a batch of 13 for test purposes were ordered in 1931. Undoubtedly one of the ugliest aircraft ever to enter service, the Shrike as it became known, featured a braced and strutted low wing, and enormous streamlined 'spats' for its fixed main undercarriage members. These spats each housed a machine gun in production aircraft, in place of one of the pair fitted in each wing. Tests proved satisfactory and a more substantial order for 46 A-8 aircraft to replace the A-3s was just about to be placed in 1933 when Army policy was revised with regard to powerplants. Radial engines were proving less difficult and costly to maintain, while for aircraft involved in low-altitude operations such as the Shrike, they were less susceptible to ground fire, having no coolant liquid and associated radiators to fall foul of the odd bullet. The order was in consequence modified to specify that the aircraft be powered by the 670 hp Wright R-1820-21 Cyclone engine. In this guise it was re-designated A-12, entering service during 1934. The extra drag imposed by the radial engine resulted in a maximum speed of 177 mph, 20 mph below that of the original XA-8. However it now had provision to carry 488 lb of bombs in addition to its five Brownings.

At this stage development of the single-engined attack bomber in the US moved from Curtiss to two other manufacturers, neither so far noted for their production of military aircraft. During the early thirties both the Northrop and Vultee Corporations had developed highly successful low-wing all-metal cantilever monoplanes of extremely advanced design, construction and performance. The possibilities of these aircraft for modification for the new attack role attracted both manufacturers, and work on these developments began as the A-12 was being readied for service. Development was spurred considerably by a ban on the use of any further single-engined aircraft by commercial airlines imposed in the States due to the greater safety factor afforded by the additional powerplants in multi-engined aircraft.

Northrop was first on the scene with its Model 2, a development of the civilian Gamma and Delta aircraft, featuring a heavily-spatted undercarriage similar to that on the Shrike, and a 712 hp Wright Cyclone engine. One was tested by the USAAC as the XA-13 during 1934, the biggest attack ircraft order yet placed being given for 110 examples. This was followed by an even bigger order from China in 1935 for 150 aircraft of the slightly-improved Model 2E type. This latter nation had previously acquired a small export batch of Shrikes.

The Air Corps order specified a more powerful Pratt and Whitney R-1830 engine of 950 hp however, and a test installation showed this to be beyond the airframe limitations without redesign of the

Probably the most successful of all attack aircraft types of the 1930s was the sleek Northrop A-17A. Exported to seven other nations in its various forms as the Northrop Model 8A, the aircraft was however completely outmoded by the outbreak of World War II, and saw only very limited peripheral service. This particular machine is serving with the 90th Sqn/3rd Attack Group of the USAAC.
USAF via W.N.Hess

tailplane. Consequently the order was changed to incorporate the 750 hp Pratt and Whitney R-1535, while the delay allowed a redesign of the undercarriage spats, a much neater and more compact open-sided fairing being substituted. Delivered during 1936 under the designation A-17, this aircraft was the classic US attack type of the thirties, and was as aesthetically pleasing as the Shrike had been ugly.

It was followed on the production line by 129 A-17As, a development of the design featuring a retractable undercarriage and a more powerful version of the R-1535, producing 825 hp. These improvements raised maximum speed from 206 mph to 220 mph. Both versions were armed with four wing-mounted .30 in Brownings for strafing, a single gun for rear defence, and twenty 30 lb fragmentation bombs carried in special internal chutes, or alternatively 650 lb of bombs carried externally.

Following the order from China for the Model 2E, Northrop became for a time the world's leading exporter of attack aircraft, providing the initial equipment in this role for several of the world's smaller air forces. The Model 8A-1 and 8A-2 — both basically similar to the USAAC's A-17 — were exported to Sweden and the Argentine respectively, the Swedes also undertaking the licence production of the aircraft re-engined with a British Bristol Hercules engine. Of the more advanced A-17A-type aircraft, ten 8A-3Ps were sold to Peru, and 20 8A-3Ns to Holland during 1939, while in 1940 15 8A-4s went to Iraq and 36 8A-5s for Norway were delivered to the Free Norwegian forces in Canada, following the occupation of . Norway by the Germans. 31 more export aircraft of the 8A-5 model were subsequently taken over by the USAAC as the A-33.

Meanwhile Vultee had produced their V-11 model in 1935, too late to have a chance of gaining a substantial US order. Powered by an 850 hp Wright Cyclone, the aircraft achieved 229 mph top speed. Armed with the usual four wing-mounted Brownings, it featured an additional rear defence gun firing through a hatch in the underside of the rear fuselage. While augmenting this armament with 600 lb of bombs in its attack configuration, it could also carry significantly heavier loads when employed as a conventional medium-altitude light bomber.

Like the Northrop aircraft, it won immediate favour on the export market, 30 going to China and others to the Soviet Union where it was also reportedly tobe built under licence in small numbers. More orders followed from Turkey for 40 and Brazil for 26. An up-engined version was produced in 1939 as the V-12C with 1,050 hp or V-12D with 1,600 hp. These versions also featured a slightly heavier armament, two of the .30 in Brownings being replaced by .50 in guns; without doubt the more powerful engines gave them the best performance of any American attack aircraft of the decade. 78 were built for China, but although both the V-11 and V-12 were tested by the USAAC, no orders were forthcoming, for Army thinking regarding the attack aircraft was already undergoing a change.

THE APPEARANCE OF THE TWIN-ENGINED ATTACK AIRCRAFT

This new thinking was directed at the development of a larger aircraft for attack purposes, carrying a greater offensive load, and thus requiring more than one engine. This line of thinking had been communicated to Curtiss following the order for the Shrike, and while Northrop and Vultee were capturing the single-engined market in attack aviation, Curtiss were breaking new ground. Their design, the XA-14, was an exceptionally clean little cantilever monoplane powered by two 775 hp Cyclones, and offering a top speed of 254 mph. With uprated engines and four nose-mounted .30 in Brownings, plus one rear gun, the production aircraft as the A-18 was 1,000 lb heavier and slightly slower. 654 lb of bombs could be carried internally, thus not inflicting the same drag penalty suffered by the A-17A when carrying a similar load. Only 13 test examples were ordered however, for the basic idea, and recent developments in Europe, offered possibilities to advance this concept even further.

War was now threatening in Europe, where most air forces were introducing to service high-performance light bombers such as the Bristol Blenheim, Dornier Do 17 and Potez 63, to which the USAAC currently had no counterpart. Development of the A-18-type aircraft appeared to offer the best chance of producing an American equivalent of such an aircraft, and consequently a specification was written for a somewhat larger twin-engined aircraft with an increased bombload. This led to the appearance during 1938-39 of a number of prototypes from Douglas, Martin, North American, Stearman and

With the Curtiss A-18 US attack aircraft development was getting very close to the traditional light bomber. Only a test batch of some 13 of these aircraft would be built; they were operated by the 3rd Attack Group. *USAF via W.N.Hess*

Bell. Of these the Douglas machine proved the most attractive to the USAAC and was ordered into production as the A-20. The North American offering was somewhat larger than the other aircraft, and was subsequently developed into the highly successful B-25 Mitchell medium bomber.

Export orders were also forthcoming from France for both the Douglas DB-7 and the Martin 167 aircraft, and subsequently after the fall of France in June 1940 many of these aircraft would be delivered to the United Kingdom, where they were issued to the RAF as the Boston and Maryland respectively. However although these aircraft featured a fixed forward-firing machine gun armament well in excess of the normal defensive armament requirements of contemporary bombers of that time, they had in reality left the attack category behind and become in all but name fast light bombers, more suited to medium altitude bombing duties. Indeed it was in this role that they would be employed by both the French and British. When the US entered the war, the A-20s were also employed mainly in the light bomber role, although some examples were fitted with increased armament in the nose for strafing purposes, of which more later.

Thus by 1939 the initial US line of attack aircraft had developed almost full circle, beyond the original concept and out of it into a new category, which is considered in another volume of this series dealing with bomber aircraft. The last generation of the true attack category were still in service, both in the US and elsewhere in the world when war broke out in September 1939.

DEVELOPMENT OF THE DIVE-BOMBER

During the twenties the US Marine Corps was called upon to assist a number of Central American governments in subduing rebel elements threatening national stability. Expeditionary forces were sent to both Haiti and Nicaragua during this period, where long and savage jungle campaigns were fought. The Marines received a modicum of air support, mainly from De Havilland DH 4B aircraft, purchased from the Army Air Corps.

Finding the encampments of the dissidents difficult targets to destroy by conventional level bombing methods with the small numbers of aircraft available, and in the enclosed jungle areas in which operations took place, the Marines resorted to dive-bombing for accuracy and economy of effort, using small 50 lb bombs for this purpose.

The success of these tactics led the Corps to set up a requirement for a general purpose aircraft which could undertake reconnaissance, dive-bombing and other duties in such a colonial-type situation. Curtiss had just developed from the Army's O-1 and A-3 Falcon observation and attack aircraft, a two-seater biplane fighter, the F8C,

The true parent of the dive-bomber in US Navy service was the Curtiss F11C Goshawk fighter, which was adapted for use as a dive-bomber, the designation subsequently being changed to BFC-1. It was two aircraft of this type which were purchased for Germany by Ernst Udet in order to develop work on the *Stuka* theory. *USN*

which seemed to fit the bill, and during 1928 a small quantity of these aircraft were ordered. Suitably equipped for their multifarious duties, they were redesignated OC-1, and named Helldivers — a name which was subsequently to be carried by all Curtiss dive-bomber types.

The Navy had been impressed by Marine experience with dive-bombing for anti-personnel purposes, incorporating a light dive-bombing capability in their order for the new Boeing F4B shipboard biplane fighter forthwith, and in all their subsequent fighters of the period. These aircraft entered service at the turn of the decade, fitted to carry a pair of 116 lb bombs beneath the wings, and with a telescopic sight to aid in aiming these.

Up to this time the Navy's main offensive striking power aboard its new aircraft carriers had rested on the torpedo-bomber, which could double when necessary as a level-bombing machine. However the Navy was unimpressed with this latter mode of attack insofar as accuracy against small, moving targets such as warships were concerned. Damaging test attacks on elderly warships which had been carried out by Army bombers at the instigation of Col. William Mitchell, had been undertaken in unrealistically favourable circumstances. The targets had been at anchor and not attempting to offer any form of defence; even then, the bombers had had to descend well below their assigned bombing height in order to achieve decisive results.

If the Helldiver offered greatly increased accuracy against small land targets it was reasoned, then a larger and more powerful aircraft capable of carrying a much heavier bomb, could well be the answer against a moving ship. Orders for the construction of prototype aircraft were given, and a production order was placed for the Martin BM-1 in 1931. This aircraft was the first capable of pulling out of a dive while carrying a 1,000 lb bomb, and was to introduce the dive-

Half way to modernity; the last biplane dive-bomber to enter service with the USN was the Curtiss SBC Helldiver, which featured such inovations as a fully enclosed cockpit and a retractable undercarriage. Although the British took over a number of French orders in summer 1940, the machines saw no action. *J.Christie via W.N.Hess*

bomber to service as the Fleet's second major form of air attack.

The BM-1, was followed into production in 1934 by the Great Lakes BG-1, a tough biplane which was to serve with both Navy and Marine units. The following year a new requirement was framed for an aircraft capable of both scouting and dive-bombing, the first such design to enter service being the Vought SBU-1, developed from the O3U Corsair reconnaissance biplane. An exellent and versatile machine, the SBU was to see long service, and was also to achieve export orders from countries such as Thailand and China.

As a replacement, the last of the US biplane dive-bombers was developed by Curtiss during 1936, 83 SBC-3s being delivered in 1937, followed in 1939 by 89 SBC-4s. These aircraft were a compromise with modern design techniques married to the shipboard advantages of the biplane configuration — good lift, short wingspan (for below-decks stowage) and manoeuvreability. As such they featured enclosed cockpits and retractable undercarriages; they carried a single 500 lb bomb beneath the fuselage.

Meanwhile the concept of the fighter/dive-bomber had also been progressed further. During 1932 28 Curtiss F11C-2 Goshawk single-seater biplane fighters had been ordered, these being capable of carrying either four underwing 116 lb bombs, or a single 474 pounder partially recessed beneath the fuselage. Two years later an order for 27 examples of the F11C-3 followed. This aircraft differed from its predecessor in having aretractable undercarriage and a partially-enclosed cockpit. With their increased bombloads, these fighter Helldivers undertook a great deal of the Navy's development of dive-bombing tactics, bringing accuracy to a high level. Their increased bombing capabilities were recognised during 1934 when the F11C-2 was redesignated BFC-2 (Bomber-Fighter Curtiss), and the F11C-3 became the BF2C-1. Examples of these fighters were also widely

A contemporary of the Northrop A-17A and the British Blackburn Skua, the Vought SB2U Vindicator was a clean and attractive shipboard scout/dive-bomber, used by the US Navy and Marine Corps 1936-42. Export versions saw action with the French in 1940, whilst late model SB2U-3s were employed briefly at the Battle of Midway by the USMC in June 1942. *American Official via IWM*

exported, seeing particularly large-scale service in China.

Even as the more modern Curtiss SBC-3 was entering service, so too were fighters of similar configuration. Designed from the start to incorporate retractable undercarriages and enclosed cockpits, the Grumman F2F and F3F biplane series began to enter service from 1935, eventually replacing all other fighter types in service with both the Navy and Marine units. These aircraft however reverted to a bomb-carrying capacity of only two underwing 116 lb missiles.

By this time it had become clear to the Navy that its next generation of aircraft would have to be monoplanes, improvements in technology allowing wing-folding mechanisms to overcome one of the major objections to this more advanced configuration. In 1936 a new scout-bomber was ordered to supplement the SBC, this coming from the Vought stable. A clean and rather attractive aircraft, the SB2U-1 was similar in general appearance to its contemporary, the Army's Northrop A-17A. The same 825 hp Pratt and Whitney R-1535 engine, driving a two-bladed propeller, imparted a somewhat superior top speed of 250 mph, while forward firing armament also noted an advance, with a pair of .50 in Brownings for the pilot, the observer having a single flexible .30 in. The aircraft could carry either a 500 lb or a 1,000 lb bomb. 54 were ordered in 1937, 58 SB2U-2s the following year and 57 SB2U-3s in 1939.

Just before the SB2U was put into production, a pure dive-bomber from the Northrop organization was also ordered to replace the last of the BG-1s and 2s. The BT-1 was again powered by the R-1535, enjoying a performance very similar to that of the A-17A. It featured a main undercarriage which partially retracted into underwing 'bathtubs', and forward-firing armament comprised only a single fixed .50 in gun for the pilot; one batch of 54 was ordered. A cleaned-

up development with a fully retractable undercarriage and a pair of forward-firing .30 in guns was produced as the XBT-2, but at this stage the Northrop Corporation was acquired by Douglas, becoming that concern's El Segundo Division. With the designation changed to SBD, the aircraft received orders in April 1939 for 57 SBD-1s and 87 long-range SBD-2s — the first of the famous Dauntlesses, and at the time probably the best all-round dive-bomber in the world.

The development of monoplane fighters — the Brewster F2A-1 in 1938 and Grumman F4F-3 the following year — continued to incorporate provision for underwing bombs. These were the only fighters in the world at this time which had bomb-carrying provision built in from initial design.

THE REST OF THE WORLD BEGINS TO FOLLOW GERMANY

Despite the restrictions put upon the development of military aviation in Germany by the Treaty of Versailles, it was to be that nation which was to most closely shadow the USA in the development of ground attack aircraft. Greatly impressed by the effects of Allied air power in disrupting ground operations during 1918, development of aircraft for support of the army was considered as a priority by the German High Command when the first secret measures were put afoot to rebuilt a military air arm.

Provided with clandestine training facilities in Soviet Russia during the 1920s, the German authorities began a series of trials during the latter part of that decade, which culminated in a requirement being framed for an aircraft capable of dive-bombing attacks. The Germans were by then convinced of the value of armoured fighting vehicles; against such targets, or against well dug-

At the outbreak of World War II only US Navy fighters were fitted at production line level for the carriage of bombs. The main US carrier fighter at that time was the Grumman F4F-3 Wildcat, several of which are seen being readied for take-off from USS *Ranger* in December 1941, carrying a 100 lb bomb under each wing. These fighters are serving with Fighting Sqn VF-41. *Smithsonian Institute via R.M.Hill*

in artillery or machine gun positions, the value of strafing aircraft, possibly carrying a few small bombs, was questionable at the least. A relatively heavy bomb would undoubtedly be necessary to ensure at least the disablement of the target, but with small targets of this nature level bombing could in no way be relied upon to provide a sufficient degree of accuracy. Level bombers were also considered to be of limited use in attacking supply targets well behind the battlefield — a role which adherents of the theorist Italian General Douhet believed to be the more important one. Delivery in a dive was therefore deemed to be the answer to the problem.

During 1928 the Swedish factory of the Junkers organization, set up outside Germany so that development and production might continue, produced a two-seater fighter of braced monoplane configuration, the K-47. When fitted to carry bombs on underwing racks, this proved a suitable type with which to progress the trials, although of too limited a performance to order into production.

Full formulation of requirements resulted in a specification being written during 1933. This year also saw a visit to the United States by Ernst Udet, who attended a demonstration of US naval dive-bombing techniques. Following his recommendation on return, two examples of the Curtiss F11C-2 dive-bomber/fighter were acquired for evaluation and further development, pending availability of the home-built product.

The first German dive-bomber built to an official specification was essentially similar to the F11C-2. A single-seat biplane with a fixed, spatted undercarriage, the Henschel Hs 123 was a rugged and practical aircraft powered by an 880 hp BMW 132 radial engine, which offered a maximum speed of 212 mph. Its fixed armament of

First German dive-bomber to enter full scale production was the Henschel Hs 123, which provided the initial equipment for most of the newly-formed *Stukageschwadern* from 1936 onwards. When superseded by the Junkers Ju 87A, the Hs 123s were passed to the new Schlacht-staffeln for ground attack development. *Bundesarchiv*

only two nose-mounted 7.9 mm MG 17 machine guns was augmented by a single 551 lb SC 250 bomb carried beneath the fuselage, or by four 110 lb SC 50 bombs on racks underwing.

Ordered into production at once, the Hs 123 began to flow from the production lines early in 1936, entering service straight away. With the new aircraft in prospect, the first service unit had been formed the previous October, equipped initially with elderly Arado Ar 65 and Heinkel He 50 biplanes. With the arrival of the Henschel, I *Gruppe*, *Stukageschwader* 162(I/StG 162) was formed in April 1936, swiftly followed by two further *Gruppen*.

Despite this early enthusiasm for the Hs 123, it was seen by the recently-formed Luftwaffe as at best an interim type. Its successor was already being prepared for production, and was of far more advanced aerodynamic design. Destined to become probably the most famous dive-bomber of all time, the Junkers Ju 87 had been designed in the light of experience gained with the earlier K-47. Of all-metal construction, it was a low wing cantilever monoplane, featuring a cranked gull wing configuration, which allowed for the inclusion of relatively short main undercarriage members, whilst still allowing adequate ground clearance for the carriage of a large under-fuselage bomb. This undercarriage, fixed and heavily 'trousered', was tough enough for rough field operations and relatively adverse weather conditions.

The aircraft differed considerably from the Hs 123 in other ways too. It carried a crew of two in an enclosed cockpit, and featured a liquid-cooled inline Junkers Jumo 210 engine of 635 hp. Although its 199 mph top speed was below that of the biplane, it enjoyed the advantage of a substantially greater range. To prevent too great a build-up of speed during its dive, it featured underwing dive brakes, which when extended made good the loss of drag occasioned by the greater aerodynamic 'cleanness' of the monoplane design. Its greatest advantage over the Henschel however, was its much heavier bombload — 1,000 lbs. Fixed armament comprised a single MG 17 in the starboard wing, and one flexible 7.9 mm MG 15 in the rear cockpit, manned by the radio operator to provide an element of rear defence.

While these two production types swiftly became the mainstay of the Luftwaffe dive-bomber units, they were not the first dive-bombers to gain production status in Germany, nor by any means the only ones to be built. Ernst Heinkel A.G. had developed the He 50, a two-seat biplane dive-bomber for the Japanese Navy in 1932, powered by an uncowled radial engine. Its performance was low, and in the event it was not ordered by the Japanese. However a small batch was purchased by the Luftwaffe as interim equipment until supplies of the Hs 123 became available.

The Hs 123 had been in competition with another aircraft, the Fieseler Fi 98, but had proved to be superior on all counts. The Ju 87 encountered much stiffer opposition however, from three other manufacturers — the Arado Ar 81, Blohm und Voss Ha 137, and Heinkel He 118. The He 118 was undoubtedly the most advanced aircraft in the competition, owing much to the Heinkel concern's earlier He 70 monoplane. It featured an extremely clean design, enclosed cockpit and fully retracting undercarriage. Unfortunately it proved more mechanically complicated, and hence less reliable than the more robust Ju 87, this last factor outweighing the better performance offered, and carrying the competition in Junkers' favour.

THE TEST OF ACTION

The outbreak of civil war in Spain during summer 1936 offered the opportunity to those nations prepared to become involved, to test equipment and theories in the crucible of actual combat conditions. It was initially the fact that the fighter equipment sent to Spain by the Germans was obsolescent, that opened an entirely new concept of ground support aviation to the Luftwaffe.

When Soviet Polikarpov I-15 and I-16 fighters began to operate over Spain late in 1936, these proved to have a definite edge over the Heinkel He 51 biplane. The German and Spanish Nationalist pilots flying this latter aircraft were forced increasingly to avoid combat, leaving the bulk of the air fighting to those units equipped with the superior Fiat CR 32 fighter of Italian manufacture. While more up to date equipmen was awaited, the He 51s were employed instead in making strafing attacks on Republican trenches and columns. While such attacks were carried out at first only with machine guns, their immediate and obvious success was soon augmented by the carriage of small anti-personnel bombs beneath the wings.

So successful was the He 51 in this fighter-bomber role, that even after the arrival of the Messerschmitt Bf 109 to replace it in the fighter role, the Germans formed a further *Staffel* within their Legion Condor to continue operating these aircraft. Not until much later in the war would they finally replace them. Meanwhile the availability of further He 51s as the Legion Condor replaced them with Bf 109s in the *Jagdstaffeln* (fighter squadrons), allowed the Nationalists to expand their own units specifically for such ground attack duties.

When a small batch of Hs 123s reached the Legion Condor in early 1937, the Germans in Spain had become so enamoured with the ground attack tactics devised for the He 51, that they employed the Hs 123 almost entirely in this role (known to the Germans, as in the First War, by the generic description *'Schlacht'* or 'Battle'). The Spanish Nationalists were also impressed, requesting the supply of a batch of

Hs 123s. They eventually received sufficient to equip a single unit during the closing months of the war.

In Germany meanwhile the number of *Stukagruppen* was increasing rapidly during 1937, though all but two were now equipped with the Ju 87A. At the very end of the year a small detachment of three of these aircraft were sent to Spain on test, crews then being sent from Germany in rotation to fly the aircraft under war conditions. Switched from front to front, but always operating with the advantage of local aerial supremacy, the dive-bombers achieved a high degree of success.

Although convinced of the superiority of the Stuka over the *Schlacht* aircraft, the glowing reports from Spain regarding the latter led the *Oberkommando der Luftwaffe* to agree to the setting up in Germany for test purposes of a number of provisional *Schlachtstaffeln*. The Hs 123 was obviously a much more suitable aircraft for this duty than was the Ju 87, and as a result these biplanes made up the main equipment of the new units, supplemented by older fighter types, such as the He 51. Five *Staffeln* were formed by 1938, and were employed during the occupation of the Sudetenland during that year, when a Luftwaffe 'show of force' was made by stretching the relatively slim resources available at that time to the very limit.

1938 was also marked by the appearance of the Ju 87B however, and this improved version of the dive-bomber seemed to spell the end for the Hs 123 in no uncertain terms. Cleaned up, with much neater and smaller 'spats' replacing the heavy 'trousers' encasing the main undercarriage legs, the aircraft was powered by a 900 hp Jumo 211 engine, which raised maximum speed to 217 mph, and allowed an even greater bombload to be carried. Now a 1,100 lb SC 500 bomb could be slung beneath the fuselage, supplemented by four SC 50s beneath the wings. Forward-firing armament was also doubled to two wing-mounted MG 17s. Tests in Spain early in 1939 proved most successful — particularly against Republican shipping. With such an aircraft available there seemed no reason to continue with production of the Hs 123, or to develop any replacement for it. Four of the *Schlachtstaffeln* were disbanded, the fifth forming the nucleus of a new unit which was retained for development purposes.

Two *Lehrgeschwadern* were in the process of formation at this time, these incorporating *Gruppen* of aircraft of different types. Frequently incorrectly considered as advanced training units, these *Geschwadern* were in fact operational test and development units, usually crewed by extremely experienced personnel. The remaining *Schlachtflieger* were now incorporated into II (Schlacht)/LG 2. Even this unit was scheduled for eventual re-equipment with the Ju 87. Meanwhile the latter aircraft equipped no less than ten *Gruppen* by mid

1939, eight of them within *Stukageschwadern*, one in *Lehrgeschwader* 1, and one was *Trägergruppe* 186. This latter *Gruppe* had been formed as the shipboard complement of the new aircraft carrier *Graf Zeppelin*, which was still under construction. In the interim it was available for land-based operations, with naval targets as a priority.

Thus the outbreak of World War II found the Luftwaffe heavily committed to close support aviation, but concentrated almost entirely upon the dive-bomber. The single *Schlachtgruppe* received little official interest or encouragement, and was equipped in its entirety with obsolescent aircraft.

SOVIET UNION

Until the 1930s, the aviation industry in the Soviet Union was in no position to develop numerous types of specialized aircraft. At first all efforts were concentrated on the formation of an industry capable of mass production, and on the setting up of a number of viable design bureaux. Once this primary aim had been achieved, the Russians were not slow in perceiving the possibilities of attack aviation, since their air arm was still basically an adjunct to the land forces, designed to assist and supplement the soldier in the field.

A sound single-engined, two-seater reconnaissance-bomber biplane, the Polikarpov R-5, had entered production at the start of the

The first Soviet *Shturmovik* aircraft to see service were all developments of the Polikarpov R-5 light bomber/-reconnaissance biplane. The more powerful, better-armed R-SSS saw fairly wide-scale service during the late 1930s, and three of these aircraft are seen making a simulated low-level attack at this time. *Passingham/-Klepacki Collec.*

new decade. For ground assault (*Shturmovik*) duties this aircraft could be fitted with an additional four machine guns below the wings. The R-5 proved to be a sturdy and dependable aircraft, development soon producing an improved version, the R-SSS. This designation, *Skorostnoi, Skorostrel'ny, Skoropodyomny* translated literally as 'Faster, Faster-firing, Faster-climbing'; the aircraft was cleaned up generally, and featured streamlined wheelspats, together with an uprated M-17 engine, and with machine gun armament replaced by the new faster-firing ShKAS guns — at the time the best aviation machine guns in the world. Following this came a version with a completely redesigned, shortened fuselage with a partially-enclosed cockpit, this being designated R-Z. The basic R-SSS and R-Z armament equalled in numbers that of the R-5, but both versions were also built or converted for the *Shturmovik* role with four additional ShKAS guns under the wings. Bomb loads on all variants could include eight 110 lb, four 220 lb, or two 550 lb bombs, maximum speeds varying from 180 mph to just under 200 mph.

All three versions remained in service for several years, although the R-SSS was built in smaller numbers than the other types, seeing service only in the Soviet Union. Both R-5 and R-Z saw action in Spain, against the Japanese in Mongolia, and over Finland. In the event the older R-5 was to outlast the R-Z, as it proved a somewhat stronger aircraft in service. By mid-1941 most aircraft of these types had been withdrawn from active service, but many were still available in the second-line reserve.

A full replacement for the R-5 family was a long time in coming. During 1936 Polikarpov and Nyeman produced the R-10, a two-seater monoplane attack bomber, powered by a 750 hp M-25V radial engine. Of very similar concept to the attack bombers then being produced in the United States, the R-10 offered little advance over the biplane. Fixed armament was reduced to two forward-firing 7.62 mm machine guns, and one flexible gun in the rear cockpit, whilst maximum bomb load fell to 880 lbs. Only in maximum speed was it slightly superior, reaching 224 mph. Built only in limited numbers, the R-10 did not see widespread service, although later versions powered by a 750 hp M-63 engine, reached a more realistic speed of 272 mph.

Shortly after the R-10 had entered service, the Soviet Union purchased a small quantity of Vultee V-11GB attack bombers from the United States. It was subsequently rumoured that these were being built under licence in Russia, but no confirmation of this exists. Probably the R-10, which bore a passing resemblance to the Vultee machine, was mistaken for the latter in squadron service. 1938 was the year of change on the Soviet scene, for during that year development was begun on three aircraft which would make up the bulk of Red Air Force ground attack aviation for some time.

From the Sukhoi bureau came a light attack bomber of absolutely standard design, known initially as the BB-1, and later as the Su-2. A low-wing two-seater monoplane, powered initially by a 1,000 hp M-88 radial engine, the type entered service during 1940. It was armed with four wing-mounted 7.62 mm ShKAS machine guns, with one more (later increased to two) in a manually-operated dorsal turret for defence; 1,322 lb of bombs could be carried internally. The crew were protected by 9 mm armour to the front and rear, and below. After the outbreak of war in the East in 1941, these aircraft would subsequently be modified to carry six 82 mm RS-82 rocket projectiles on rails fitted beneath the wings, and during that year an improved version began to flow from the factory, featuring a 1,100 hp M-88B engine, six wing guns, and provision for ten underwing RS-82s. About 100 Su-2s were in service by summer 1941.

While rocket projectiles were not new to aviation, the first effective ones had been developed in the Soviet Union, initially as air-to-air weapons. The RS-82 (82 mm diameter), tested in 1937, was to be fitted to all main fighter types, which were to carry six or eight of these missiles beneath the wings, while the following year the larger RS-132 (132 mm diameter) was developed to be fitted to bombers for attacks on ground targets, though this later weapon was much slower in being introduced to service. The RS-82 was used for the first time during the Nomonkhan Incident in Mongolia in 1939, but while some successes against Japanese aircraft were claimed, its oprational debut in reality seems to have proved rather disappointing, for little use in the air fighting role was made of these weapons after the opening weeks of the war with Germany. Of more immediate interest was the development of a more specialised ground attack version during 1941, the RBS-82. This was followed by the ROFS-132, an armour-piercing missile with an increased propellant charge to improve velocity, and the big BETAB-150DS for use against concret defensive emplacements.

The obvious shortcomings of such aircraft as the R-10 and Su-2 for close battlefield support of troops, had led to the development of a very specialized aircraft, the BSh-2 (*Bronirovanny Shturmovik* — light Armoured Assaulter). Specifically required to carry out low-level strafing and rocket attacks on front line targets in the face of sustained ground fire, the aircraft had to be very heavily armoured. The weight this imposed required an unusually powerful engine, if performance was not to be unacceptably low.

Initially envisaged as a two-seater, on Stalin's insistence the aircraft was designed by the Ilyushin bureau as a single-seater, and was ordered into production at the start of 1941 as the Il-2. While the wings, rear fuselage, tail section and forward portion of the nose were of standard metal construction, the central portion of the aircraft including the engine, water and oil radiators, pilot and fuel tank, were encased in armour. This was mainly of 7 mm thickness, though it was increased to 12 mm to the rear of the pilot.

Armament was originally envisaged as four wing-mounted 7.62 mm ShKAS guns, but before production began two of these were replaced by 20 mm ShVAK cannon, with 100 rounds per gun. To augment this fixed punch, eight RS-82 rockets could be carried on rails beneath the wings, or 1,100-1,320 lb of bombs, partly internally in the wing centre section bomb bays. The main undercarriage members retracted backwards into streamlined fairings under the wings, the wheels remaining partly exposed.

To power this heavy monster, the 1,600 hp AM-38 inline was fitted, providing a respectable top speed, varying between 260-270 mph, depending upon thhe armament load carried. On similar considerations range varied from 370-465 miles.

While the ground support aircraft were under development, reports from Spain indicated the success of the German dive-bombers, and thought was given to the possibility of acquiring aircraft of this type. The rearmament programme was well-advanced, and the need too pressing to attempt a new design from scratch. However a twin-engined high altitude heavy fighter design was in the process of modification as a high altitude light bomber, and this offered the promise of a possible further adaptation.

The result was the Petlyakov Pe-2, an extremely advanced machine with a very high performance. The prototype of the dive-bomber version (PB-100) flew in 1940, and was immediately ordered into production. A sleek twin-engined aircraft with twin fins and rudders, the Pe-2 was powered by two M-105R inline engines of 1,100 hp. Carrying a crew of three, it featured a fixed nose armament of two 7.62 mm ShKAS, with one more of each on flexible mounts for rear defence above and below the fuselage. Either or both nose guns were replaceable by larger calibre BS guns if required. Bomb load included six 220 lb bombs in the fuselage bomb bay, one more in the rear of each engine nacelle, and two carried externally under each wing centre section, for a total load of 2,640 lb.

Fitted with dive brakes for use during the attack, this very fast aircraft (335 mph) could nearly equal the speed of the Messerschmitt Bf 109E, then the standard Luftwaffe fighter. In concept it was very similar to the German Junkers Ju 88, and was to be employed both as a level and dive-bomber, and as a fast long-range reconnaissance aircraft.

When war broke out in September 1939 however, neither Su-2, Il-2 nor Pe-2 was in production, although in the event all three types would be available, albeit in relatively small numbers, when the Soviet Union became embroiled in the conflict in June 1941.

THE HEAVY FIGHTER SYNDROME

During the mid and late thirties the majority of countries with their own aircraft industries began development of twin-engined heavy fighters. The desirability of providing escort to bomber formations in the face of the new high-performance interceptors that were appearing at the time had not escaped several air ministries. Others felt that the speed of the modern bomber would allow only one swift attack; in consequence the need for the power of two engines to lift a very heavy armament for this purpose was also given deep consideration.

First to appear were two conversions of light bombers — the Bristol Blenheim IF in England, and the Potez 631 in France. Small quantities of each type subsequently saw service as night fighters. It was in 1936-37 that the first purpose-built machines appeared however, the Messerschmitt Bf 110 escort fighter and interceptor, and the single-seat Focke-Wulf Fw 187 interceptor appearing in Germany, whilst the twin-boom Fokker G-1 was produced in Holland. In France the Hanriot NC 600 and the Bréguet 690 appeared to fill a similar role to that of the Bf 110. In the United States a most unusual twin-engined long-range interceptor, the Bell FM-1 Airacuda took the air, followed in 1939 by the single-seat, twin-boom Lockheed P-38 Lightning interceptor.

A design for similar duties, the Westland Whirlwind, had flown a year earlier in England, followed during 1939 by the longer-range Gloster F9/37 single-seater, and the heavy two-seat Bristol Beaufighter. The Germans meanwhile were experimenting with a long-range heavy fighter versin of their sensational new Junkers Ju 88 bomber, while the Italians had produced the Fiat CR 25 long range fighter and the Breda Ba 88, designed specifically as a ground attack aircraft. In Japan the Kawasaki Ki 45 heavy escort fighter made its first flight during 1939, as did the SE 100 in France, designed to replace the Potez 631. This glut of twin-engined types was rounded off in 1940 with the appearance in the United States of a single-seat interceptor for the Navy, the Grumman XF5F-1. This was later developed as an Army Air Force prototype, the XP-50, as well.

From the start, the potential of the long-range escort fighter to carry out a secondary ground strafing role had been foreseen. Indeed their heavy armament, added security of two engines, and longer endurance rendered them near-ideal for this purpose, coupled with the fact that their main armament was concentrated in the nose, for the maximum concentration and accuracy of fire. The same applied in several respects to the interceptors, but with these, this was not to be exploited for some longer time.

By 1939 and the outbreak of war, the Bf 110 and Fokker G-1 had already entered service with their respective national air forces. In

Britain the Whirlwind and Beaufighter had both been ordered into production, as had the Ki 45 in Japan and the P-38 in the United States. The Ju 88C (initially known as the Ju 88Z — Zerstörer — was also being produced in small numbers, while in Italy a limited batch of CR 25s were on order, together with the Ba 88.

The French had perceived the possibilities of the heavy fighter as a ground strafer to such an extent that the Breguet had been developed for this specific role; the Br 693 and 695 were in production to equip newly-formed *Groupes de Bombardement d'Assault*. The NC 600, Fw 187, FM-1, XF5F, XP-50 and F9/37 all failed to achieve production status, whilst the SE 100 was too late to do so before France capitulated in June 1940.

FRANCE

In September 1939 the new Br 693 attack aircraft had not yet entered service, although six *Groupes de Bombardement* equipped with obsolescent bomber types had been earmarked for conversion to the new role. As interim equipment until sufficient numbers of the new aircraft were available, a number of Potez 633 twin-engined fighters from an export order for Greece and Rumania had been taken over. These were capable of carrying a pair of 441 lb bombs for dive-bombing attack, but were fitted with only one fixed 7.5 mm MAC 1934 machine gun, and one flexible weapon for rear defence.

Meanwhile the *Aeronavale*, France's naval air force, had decided to emulate the US Navy in acquiring dive-bombers. Consequently sufficient Vought V-156F scout-bombers (the export version of the USN's SB2U) were purchased to equip two *escadrilles*, whilst two more were equipped with Loire-Nieuport LN 411s.

The latter was a single-seat dive-bomber of French design and construction, developed from an earlier two-seater of very similar configuration to the Ju 87A. Like the Ju 87, the LN 411 featured an inverted gull wing, but differed in having a partially-retracting undercarriage. Powered by an Hispano-Suiza 12Xcrs inline engine of 690 hp, the aircraft had a top speed of 236 mph and carried a bombload of one 496 lb BEA 1938, or 331 lb I2 bomb beneath the fuselage; alternatively ten 22 or 33 lb light bombs could be carried. Fixed armament comprised an engine-mounted 20 mm Hispano-Suiza cannon, firing through the propeller boss, and two wing-mounted 7.5 mm Darne machine guns. An improved version, the LN 42, was under development in summer 1940, but failed to reach production before the French surrender.

ITALY

Having provided a very substantial air force, as well as large ground forces for service in the Spanish Civil War, the Italians were fully alive to the desirability of assault aviation for the support of the army, and had expended considerable effort developing aircraft and forming units. Th Breda Ba 88 has already been mentioned; powered by two 1,000 hp Piaggio P.XI R.C.40 radial engines, it was armed with three fixed 12.7 mm Breda-SAFAT machine guns in the nose, and a flexible 7.7 mm gun for rear defence. It could carry two 550 lb, three 220 lb or three 100 lb bombs up to a range of 1,019 miles. Maximum speed was 304 mph. On paper it was a formidable aircraft.

The same manufacturer had also produced the single-engined Ba 65, developed from an earlier fighter/light bomber, the Ba 64. First flown in 1935, this aircraft had been tested late in the Spanish war, and had been issued to several units of the *Regia Aeronautica* by 1939. It was difficult to fly however, and by June 1940 had been withdrawn, although it was due to be re-issued, this time to two *Gruppi d'Assalto* in Libya. The latter had in the meantime been equipped with Caproni Ca 310 light bombers, and a fighter-bomber conversion of

Destined for failure, the Breda Ba 88 Lince appeared to be a very advanced and promising aircraft on its introduction to service with Italy's *Regia Aeronautica*. Appalling serviceability rates proved its main downfall. *Stato Maggiore*

Italy's attempt at designing a dive-bomber proved even more disastrous than the Ba 88: the Savoia SM 85 was grotesquely underpowered. Seeing service with only one unit, a single aircraft made just one operational sortie during the opening days of World War II in the Mediterranean, before the type was withdrawn in favour of Junkers Ju 87Bs purchased from Germany. *G.Pini*

the now-elderly Fiat CR 32 biplane fighter. Although a two-seater version of the Ba 65 was built, and exported to Iraq, among other countries, the Italian service models were all single-seaters. Armed with two 12.7 mm and two 7.7 mm machine guns in the wings the Ba 65 reached 267 mph.

By June 1940, when Italy entered the war, single *Gruppi* of Ba 88s were based in Central Italy and on the island of Sardinia, while on Pantelleria, an island to the South of Sicily, was a *Gruppo* of Savoia SM 85s. These were twin-engined, single-seat dive-bombers, which had already proved to be grossly underpowered by their pair of 500 hp Piaggio P.VII R.C.35 engines, which imparted a top speed of only 228 mph.

THE UNITED KINGDOM

In September 1939 the RAF had no ground attack aircraft and no dive-bombers. An attack bomber, the Hawker Henley, had been developed from the Hurricane fighter, but had not been put into production for front-line use to avoid disrupting work on the urgently-needed fighter. The Beaufighter was in the process of being ordered, but would not appear in service r at least another year, while the position was the same with regard to the Whirlwind. The only aircraft available for such duties was the Blenheim IF, which equipped a few day fighter squadrons at this stage, as well as the night interceptor units.

There were substantial quantities of Fairey Battles in service, but these single-engined light bombers in no way filled either category. Designed specifically for level bombing, they were not equipped to undertake steep diving attacks, nor did they possess sufficient forward-firing armament or defensive armour to be employed in the strafing role.

A number of other air forces employed single-engined light bombers of this kind during the early years of the war, and these might on cursory examination be mistaken for attack types. However, like the Battle, the Polish PZL P.43 Karas, Dutch Fokker C.X, and a variety of Japanese Army light bombers are strictly outside the scope of this work.

In the Royal Navy the position was somewhat different. The original developer of the aircraft carrier, the RN had relied for many years on the torpedo-bomber as its main striking air weapon. The American development of the dive-bomber had been observed however, and eventually an aircraft had been ordered to fulfil the joint Fleet requirement of fighter, dive-bomber and scout. The short, but action-packed service life of this aircraft, the Blackburn Skua, has already been fully chronicled in David Brown's 'Carrier Fighters' in his series.

JAPAN

The Japanese had seen attack and dive-bomber aircraft in action by 1939. During 1937 an undeclared war with the Chinese had broken out in the Shanghai area, and gradually spread to the whole country. In the early months of fighting the Chinese employed their Northrop, Curtiss and Vought attack bombers against Japanese troops and shipping around Shanghai, supported by Curtiss Hawk biplane fighters. The latter were export versions of the US Navy's BFC and BF2C fighter/dive-bombers, and were also employed in this role by the Chinese when opportunity permitted.

Against superior Japanese Naval fighter aircraft, the Chinese units suffered severe losses, and obviously failed to impress upon the Japanese the need for such types. Thus in 1939 the Japanese Army Air Force was in a very similar position to the RAF, possessing light medium and heavy bombers, fighters and reconnaissance aircraft, but no specialized dive-bombers or attack aircraft. Like the Royal Navy the Japanese Naval Air Force had previously relied upon the torpedo bomber, but following observation of the US experience, had developed and begun introducing to service its own dive-bomber, the Aichi D3A. This single-engined, fixed-undercarriage monoplane was an excellent and highly-manoeuvreable aircraft, powered by a 1,000 hp Mitsubishi Kinsei 43 engine. The aircraft was armed with two 7.7 mm Type 97 machine guns in the nose, firing forward, and a similar calibre flexible Type 92 gun in the rear cockpit. Bomb load comprised a single 551 lb bomb beneath the fuselage and a 132 lb missile beneath each wing.

2.The First Year of War

With the experience of Spain and Munich behind him, Adolf Hitler was ready to risk all at the end of August 1939 by attacking Poland. Somewhat behind the original schedule, and following a carefully fabricated border 'incident', his forces moved across the Polish border during the early hours of 1 September. The advance was spearheaded by the new Panzer divisions, and closely supported by the Luftwaffe. The very first strikes were undertaken by Ju 87s of StG 1, which actually attacked a quarter of an hour ahead of the set time.

Ten full *Gruppen* of Stukas were available, together with the sole surviving *Schlachtgruppe* — still awaiting re-equipment with Ju 87s. Initial dive-bomber attacks were directed against demolition settings around bridges over the Vistula. These attacks were designed to prevent the destruction of these bridges, to allow the Wehrmacht columns to pass straight over them into the heart of Poland. Other attacks were directed at airfields around Warsaw, in an unsuccessful effort to destroy the Polish air force on the ground. More Ju 87s — notably from the *Kriegsmarine* 4 (Stuka)/186 — attacked Polish naval units in Hela on 3 September, sinking a large destroyer and a minesweeper.

Thereafter the Ju 87s were everywhere in support of the Panzers, acting as airborne artillery to blast Polish troops concentrations, strong point and supply columns, and to attack their cavalry formations with the most devastating effect. Operating generally with little interference in the air, the Stuka exceeded expectations, proving to be one of the decisive weapons of the campaign. For psychological purposes, the bombs carried by the dive-bombers had been fitted with wailing sirens. Coupled with the pinpoint accuracy and overbearing appearance of the ugly, crank-wing aircraft diving directly at the target, the overall effect could paralyze resistance and create both panic and confusion.

When the Polish Army gathered itself sufficiently to launch a surprise counter-attack, which caught the Germans off balance, and brought their main thrust on Warsaw to a temporary halt, it was the Stukas which saved the situation, playing a major part in turning a near-victory for the Poles into a defeat.

The Henschel Hs 123s of II(*Schlacht*)-/LG 2 were active both in Poland in September 1939, and over France during the 'Blitzkrieg' offensive of May/June 1940. Three of the unit's aircraft are seen here on an operational airfield during this period, with a number of Messerchmitt Bf 109E fighters in the background. *Smithsonian Institution via Squadron/Signal*

With the dive-bombers carrying all before them, the elderly Henschels were forced into something of a back seat — mainly because of their small numbers. However, II (Schlacht)/LG 2 played an extremely active part from the first day. Carrying light incendiary bombs known as '*Flambos*', the Hs 123s strafed in direct support of the Army, the raucous, uneven note of their BMW engines adding in no small way to the general effect of the onslaught. One *Staffelkapitän* of this unit during the Polish Campaign was *Oberleutnant* Adolf Galland, who had led the He 51 *Schlachtstaffel* of the Legion Condor in Spain, and who would later become famous as a great fighter ace, and General of the Luftwaffe's fighter force. Despite the fact that the *Stukagruppen* seized most of the limelight, the good results obtained by the single *Schlachtgruppe* had not gone unnoticed in the right quarters, and the plans to convert the unit to the former role were abandoned.

Although the Polish air force had not been destroyed on the ground at the opening of hostilities, and had put up a valiant defence against the attackers, it had been vastly outnumbered and outperformed by the Luftwaffe's aircraft. In consequence the close-support units had suffered little interference with their operations. The efficacy of dive bombers and ground-attack aircraft in the face of sustained aerial opposition had yet to be tested.

In the West Britain and France had entered the war following the German invasion of Poland, but here the stalemate period which became known as the 'Phoney War' saw no major action, and hence no operations of a close support nature. For the first eight months of the war, operations in the West involved mainly only fighter and reconnaissance aircraft.

THE SHOOTING WAR BEGINS
OPERATION 'WESERÜBUNG'

It was in Scandinavia that Germany next struck, air and seaborne forces invading Norway in the early hours of 8 April 1940, whilst other elements occupied Denmark virtually without a fight. British and French assistance to the hard-pressed Norwegians was swiftly despatched, although with the range involved, and the early German initiative, it proved a vain effort which did little more than prolong the inevitable.

However the war in Norway certainly did much to further the prestige of the dive-bomber. As soon as airfields in Southern Norway were available, the Luftwaffe moved in a *Gruppe* of Ju 87s (I/StG 1) with great despatch. These aircraft were employed in attacking Allied troops in Central Norway, and in bombing British and French shipping off the coast. They were joined in the latter duty by the first fully-operational Ju 88 unit, *Kampfgeschwader* 30. (The Junkers Ju 88 is not dealt with in any detail here, as its use is covered in the companion volume on Bomber Aircraft by Alfred Price).

Fighter opposition to these activities was mainly remarkable by its absence, the dive-bombers managing to enjoy considerable success both against land and sea targets. It was at this time that the Royal Navy Skuas were used regularly in their dive-bombing capacity also, gaining considerable acclaim for sinking the German cruiser *Königsberg* in Bergen fjord with 500 lb bombs. This was a considerable achievement for the British, the *Königsberg* being the largest vessel so far sunk by air attack. As such it remains a landmark in naval/air history. Later in the campaign — after the withdrawal of the last British troops during early June — the Skuas, this time operating from aircraft carriers rather than from land bases in the Orkneys, returned to Norway to attack German capital ships at Trondheim. The results on this occasion were not so readily publicized. Fighters were by then available for the defence of the area, and these savagely mauled the British dive-bombers, shooting down more than half of the formation. The survivors returned without having achieved any success. The message of this defeat was not lost on the Royal Navy.

By this time however, the dive-bombers' star was already past its zenith, for events of major import had been taking place elsewhere in Western Europe.

THE 'BLITZKRIEG'

On 10 May 1940 the great German armoured offensive in the West was launched with air-landing assaults on specified targets in Holland and Belgium, air attacks on Allied airfields, and a massive invasion of the Low Countries, spearheaded by the tanks of a large

Main Luftwaffe close-support aircraft during the campaigns of 1939-40 was the famous Junkers Ju 87B — the aircraft for ever linked with the generic name 'Stuka'. Carrying all before them in Poland and France, the Ju 87s were very vulnerable to determined fighter attack, and suffered such heavy losses during the opening phases of the attack on South-Eastern England in summer 1940, that they were withdrawn from operations over the Channel front. *Bundesarchiv*

number of Panzer divisions. The assault was closely supported by the Luftwaffe once more; whilst medium bombers raided airfields, rail and road targets, and other communications objectives, the Stuka and *Schlacht* units attacked strongpoints, convoys, concentration areas, and other similar targets standing in the way of the advancing Wehrmacht.

For this new venture the Germans had available nine *Gruppen* of Ju 87s — mainly Ju 87Bs, but including a few long-range Ju 87Rs. There was still only the single *Gruppe* of Hs 123s, but these were to play an extremely active part in operations, and to cement firmly the future of *Schlacht* aviation within the Luftwaffe. II/(Schlacht)/LG 2 supported the airborne troops in the capture of the major Belgian fortress of Eben Emael on the first day of the offensive, and subsequently flew many low level strafing missions in aid of the Panzers.

Their greatest moment of the campaign for the Henschels arrived on 22 May, as the main Panzer thrust headed across North-Western France towards the Channel coast, to split the Allied Northern Army Group from the rest of the French armies in the South and Centre. An Allied counter-attack, mounted by some 40 tanks and 150 lorries loaded with infantry — one of the few Allied mobile concentrations achieved — was spotted from the air advancing to launch a surprise attack on the weak and lightly-protected flank of the Panzers, which were by then well ahead of the following infantry.

At once the Hs 123s were thrown in, attacking with SC 50 (110 lb) bombs and machine gun fire. They were joined in their strafing attacks by the Messerschmitt Bf 109Es of their escort, which added the fire of their 20mm cannons to the weight of assault. This air attack did much to disrupt and slow down the Allied thrust, which was subsequently held, and turned back.

The Ju 87s had again enjoyed great success, their steep diving attacks, and fearsome scream of the sirens attached to their bombs often severely damaging the morale of the Allied troops. The latter, unprepared and untrained to meet such attacks, felt helpless and vulnerable in the face of such attacks, and as a result were often left in no state to meet the tank and infantry attacks which followed.

It was in the area of Sedan that the dive-bombers gained perhaps their greatest effect. Believing a major armoured attack through the Ardennes Forest to be impractical, the French High Command had manned the line here rather weakly, with their 2nd Army, which was one of the least highly trained and well-equipped units; it was composed mainly of elderly reservists and raw young conscripts. When the main German thrust was launched here on May 12, after the bulk of the Allied Northern Armies had been drawn into Belgium by the attacks there, the Stukas fell in all their fury on the hapless 2nd Army. Utterly demoralized, these second line troops cowered in their dugouts, or even fled, offering little resistance as the German tanks appeared from amongst the trees, smashing their way across the frontier, and swiftly achieving a crossing of the Meuse.

It was here however that the first signs appeared that the all-conquering Stuka had its 'Achille's Heel'. On that very first day of the action at Sedan, a formation of five Curtiss Hawk fighters from the 'crack' French fighter group, GC I/5, encountered a large unescorted body of Ju 87s over the Ardennes, claiming no less than 16 of them shot down without loss. While this claim was undoubtedly an over-estimate, it did show convincingly that the dive-bomber was extremely vulnerable to determined fighter attack. This was particularly so at the point where the aircraft recovered from its bombing dive. The pull-out was automatic, since the gravity forces involved caused the crew to 'grey-out', as the blood drained from the upper parts of their bodies. At this moment, as the aircraft wallowed along at low speed, its crew temporarily out of action, it was for the fighter pilot a prime 'sitting duck'.

Such events were rare however. While the Allied aircrews were flying continually, and with great determination, they were in more cases than not fighting for their lives. Every available offensive aircraft was thrown in to attack bridges and columns in an effort to slow down the German advance, fearsome losses being suffered to Luftwaffe fighters, and to the concentrated and highly-efficient German light flak defences. French fighters particularly were used on strafing attacks because of their cannon armament, only the machine

The Vought V-156F
dive-bomber of the
French *Aeronavale*
(the export version
of the US Navy's
SB2U) was
probably as good as
the Ju 87B.
Operated in small
numbers against an
overwhelming op-
position of fighters
and flak, the air-
craft had no chance
however, and these
machines suffered
extremely heavy
losses in operations
during late May
1940.
via C-J.Ehrengardt

gun-armed Hawks being spared this precarious duty. Substantial
numbers of Morane 406 and Dewoitine 520 fighters were lost in this
way to groundfire when the vulnerable cooling systems of their inline
engines were hit. Defensive flights were usually made by only small
sections of fighters, which generally found the German formations
heavily escorted by large numbers of Bf 109s and Bf 110s. Only on rare
occasions, as on May 12, were bombers or dive-bombers encountered
without overwhelming escorts.

What then of the Allied ground attack types? Those employed by
the Dutch had been extremely short-lived. On May 10 the
Douglas/Northrop 8A-3N attack bombers were scrambled at dawn in
the face of an incoming raid, to be employed as makeshift fighters.
Almost before they were airborne, they were attacked by Bf 110s and
wiped out in detail. The powerful Fokker G-1s were mainly
employed whilst they lasted for interceptor duties. Some did manage
a few effective strafing attacks with their eight nose-mounted rifle-
calibre machine guns against numbers of Junkers Ju 52/3m transport
aircraft which had landed on beaches along the Dutch coast. However
the G-1s were small in number, and after the first few days no more
remained airworthy.

From England the RAF sent a formation of its Blenheim IF long-
range fighters to strafe these same Ju 52s, but this was engaged by Bf
110s, and suffered very severe losses. No further use of the Blenheim as
an offensive strafer during the hours of daylight was made in that
campaign.

The French, with their greater number of these types, first made use
of the new Bréguet 693s on May 12 — not at Sedan, but against
columns advancing into Belgium in the Tongeren area. Already
subject to much Allied air attack, the German defences were ready and
waiting, and it proved an inauspicious start for GBA I/54. Eleven

Bréguets 'hedge-hopped' in to strafe, but met a veritable blizzard of light flak, which sent seven of them crashing to the ground. One more crash-landed before it could regain its base, whilst another suffered a similar fate on return to its home airfield. A similar attack by the sister unit, GBA II/54, proved much less costly, only one of the seven aircraft employed failing to return. Thereafter, when attacks were subsequently made on columns that were not so fully prepared to face an assault, the Bréguets operated with some considerable success, and without again facing such disastrous losses.

The same cannot be said for the dive-bombers of the Aeronavale however. These suffered badly on the very first day of the 'Blitzkrieg', when German air attack wrecked a dozen Vought V-156Fs and two Loire-Nieuport LN 411s on the ground. However, as German forces approached the Calais area, coming close to the Navy's area of jurisdiction along the coast, the dive-bombers first went into action against the advancing columns on May 17.

Thereafter attacks were made almost daily, but tragedy was in the offing. Twenty LN 411s struck on May 19 — 10 failed to return, while the rest were all damaged. Next day 12 V-156Fs and three LN 411s repeated the attack, five Voughts and an LN being shot down. Thereafter only small raids were made, generally with fighter escorts, but on practically every occasion one or two losses were suffered. Royal Navy Skuas flown over from England on a similar mission also suffered losses to Luftwaffe fighters.

At this stage however a third *Armee de l'Air* ground attack unit, GBA II/35, equipped with a mixture of Bréguet 691s and Potez 633s, also entered action. While the three GBAs continued to operate effectively until the Armistice in June, they were too few in number to have more than a harrassing effect. Meanwhile the dive-bombers were withdrawn to the South of France early in June, where they undertook some limited action following the Italian declaration of war on 10th of that month.

Breguet Br 693 assault aircraft of *Groupe de Bombardement d'Assaut* I/54. This unit suffered very heavy losses to ground fire during its first sorties on 12 May 1940.

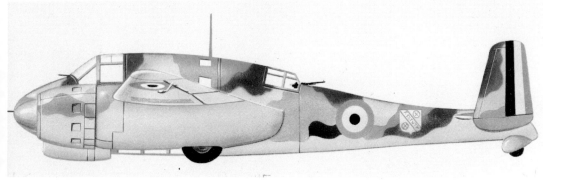

The first fighter to be pressed into service as a fighter-bomber during World War II was the Luftwaffe's Messerschmitt Bf 109E. Serving initially with a *Staffel* of the special *Erprobungsgruppe* 210, they supplemented the Hs 123s of II(Sch)-/LG 2 during the late summer of 1940. By the autumn of that year most *Jagdgeschwardern* had formed a special '*Jabostaffel*' to undertake these operations. Here a Bf 109E-7 of III/-JG1 is seen in flight carrying a 551 lb SC250 bomb beneath the fuselage centre section.
Bundesarchiv

The first really serious opposition to be met by the Luftwaffe was encountered during the last four days of May, as the British sought to evacuate their Expeditionary Force and as many of their French allies as possible, from their positions along the Channel coast around Dunkirk on the Franco-Belgian border, to which they had been driven by the German advance. The Luftwaffe was given the task of reducing the trapped Allied force, while the Panzers were held back for maintenance ad supply.

This was a real dive-bombers' target — the packed, confused British and French troops and their equipment, jammed into a small area; the mass of shipping offshore, trying desperately to take them all off. Fortunately for the Allies, cloud did much to protect the troops on the ground from the worst of the Luftwaffe's depredations, whilst RAF fighters from South-Eastern England fought a savage battle to wrest temporary local air superiority from the Germans. Whilst the Stukas managed to inflict massive damage to installations, troops and shipping, they were constantly harried by Hurricanes, Spitfires, and Defiant turret fighters. Even patrolling Lockheed Hudson coastal reconnaissance/bombers proved capable of taking the measure of the Ju 87 at times, and losses amongst the *Stukagruppen* rose sharply.

THE ATTACK TURNS ON ENGLAND

As the fighting in France drew to a close, the British prepared for an immediate invasion of the southern part of their country. The Germans were exhausted temporarily however, and were unprepared for such an exercise. Every arm, Luftwaffe included, was in need of rest and re-equipment, while it was clear that control of all the English Channel area against interference by the Royal Navy would first be necessary before any invasion could be launched.

In the interim the British were to be harried by limited attacks on their coastal shipping, which was still operating around the South-East coast, despite the perils involved. A single *Stukageschwader* (StG 51) and a fighter unit (JG 51) were allocated to carry out this duty during July 1940, on occasions aided by elements of StG 2 and IV (Stuka)/LG 1, whilst reconnaissance of South and East coast installations was carried out by other units. These operations led to some very fierce fighting during the month, in which both sides suffered some sharp casualties. Activities at this time nonetheless remained on a relatively small scale.

The effectiveness of the *Schlacht* unit in France had given rise to further consideration of this form of attack by the Luftwaffe, particularly in view of recent experience of the vulnerability of the Ju 87 to fighter attack. The high speed and adequate range of the Messerschmitt Bf 110 seemed to offer itself well for low level pinpoint attacks on heavily defended targets, and the necessary arrangements were made for this possibility to be tested. V(Z)/LG 1 was re-equipped with Bf 110C-4B aircraft, fitted to carry two SC 250 (551 lb) bombs beneath the wings, while a special new operational test unit, *Erprobungsgruppe* 210, was formed to apply the fighter-bomber concept to special strategic targets. This was a completely new appliation for the fighter-bomber, and the unit under *Hauptmann* Walter Rubensdorffer, a Swiss-born officer, was manned by picked experienced crews from the *Zerstörergeschwadern*. It incorporated two *Staffeln* of Bf 110C-4Bs, and one of Bf 109E-4Bs, the latter fitted to carry a single SC 250 bomb beneath the fuselage, or four SC 50s. Meanwhile the well-blooded II(Schlacht)/LG 2 had been withdrawn at the end of the French campaign, and was also re-equipping with Bf 109E-4Bs.

Late in July a number of Luftwaffe attacks were made on targets along the South coast of England, mainly around the Portsmouth area, where major naval dockyards were situated. During these, the first fighter-bomber attack on English soil was undertaken on 21st by Bf 110s of V(Z)/LG 1. Eight days later a similar raid marked the first operational mission by the new ErpGr.210.

By early August the Luftwaffe was ready to launch a pre-invasion 'Blitz' on England, the major initial objectives being the radar chain, airfields and naval installations. The assault was to be carried out by all available medium and dive-bombers, escorted mainly by Bf 110s, while the Bf 109Es ranged ahead and around the main attack formations to bring the British fighters to battle and destroy them.

Apart from a small force based in Norway, the main Luftwaffe strength was concentrated in two air fleets, *Luftflotte* 2 in Northern France, Belgium and Holland, and *Luftflotte* 3 in France. The former included in its establishment only two *Stukagruppen*, together with the special ErpGr.210. The latter, in which V(Z)/LG 1, still the only *Zerstörergruppe* equipped for fighter-bombing, was serving, boasted seven *Stukagruppen*, all under the command of Gen.Wolfram von Richthofen's VIII *Fliegerkorps*.

The first attacks of what became known as the Battle of Britain commenced on August 11, but from the start the Stukas found themselves in trouble whenever the aggressive British fighters could break through the escort to them. The fast, low-flying formations of ErpGr.210 proved extremely difficult to detect and intercept however, and initially they achieved some quite outstanding successes.

Their method of attack was to come in low and fast, approaching the target in a shallow dive to release their bombs. By these methods on August 12 three radar stations at Dover, Rye and Pevensey were put out of action — albeit only temporarily — by the unit for the loss of only one aircraft. Two days later, under cover of a Stuka attack, the *Gruppe* hit Manston airfield, which was extremely badly damaged. Again losses were light, only two Bf 110s failing to return.

The euphoria was short-lived however. After another successful attack during the morning of August 15, this time on Martlesham, the whole *Gruppe* set out in the afternoon to attack Kenley. Missing their escort, the fighter-bombers got slightly off course, and attacked Croydon instead by mistake. Once again their attack was very damaging, but before they could turn for home, they were hit by the airfield's Hurricanes, which had scrambled in time. Six Bf 110s, including that flown by Rubensdorffer, and one Bf 109, were shot down. Following such losses, the unit was temporarily withdrawn.

By the end of August the *Stukagruppen* had suffered such severe losses that they were withdrawn permanently from the Battle, considerably reducing the Luftwaffe's striking power. However

Messerschmitt Bf 109E-4/B fighter-bomber as used during the later stages of the Battle of Britain, and subsequently in the Balkans, Mediterranean area, and over the Eastern Front. (Bottom) fitted with 1 x 551 lb SC 250 and (*right*) with 4 x 110 lb SC 50 bombs on underfuselage rack.

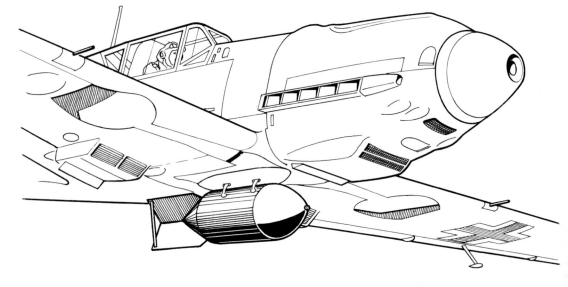

V(Z)/LG 1, which had been employed solely in the escort role during August, began occasional fighter-bomber attacks again at the start of September, while II(Schlacht)/LG 2, equipped with its new Bf 109E-4Bs, returned to action during the month, also operating over England with *Luftflotte* 2.

Mid-September saw the return to operations of ErpGr.210, with an attack on the Spitfire factory at Woolaston, near Southampton, on 15th. Further attacks followed, but almost always losses were now suffered. Towards the end of September the Bf 110s of II/ZG 76 were also modified for bomb-carrying. However the strength of the defending fighters was now growing rather than diminishing. Heavy losses to the medium bombers had forced their transfer to night raids by the end of the month, so that any attacks by Bf 110s could usually be intercepted in strength. During this period ErpGr.210 lost two more commanding officers and an acting commander, and by the end of November the whole business had become too hazardous. No more daylight operations over England by Bf 110s were to be made. In its brief but eventful period of action, ErpGr.210 had received the award of no less than five *Ritterkreuze* (Knights' Crosses) to its pilots.

This left only II(Schlacht)/LG 2 still operational as a trained ground attack unit over England. However, in an effort to maintain the pressure on the British defences, as soon as the medium bomber force had been obliged to cease daylight attacks, each *Jagdgeschwader* had been ordered to form a fighter-bomber *(Jabo) Staffel*. Unlike the pilots of II(Schlacht)/LG 2 and ErpGr.210, these pilots enjoyed no specialized training, time allowing only the briefest of instruction before it was necessary for them to begin operations.

These attacks were in no way intended — or capable — of inflicting serious damage. Their main intention was to cause a sufficient degree

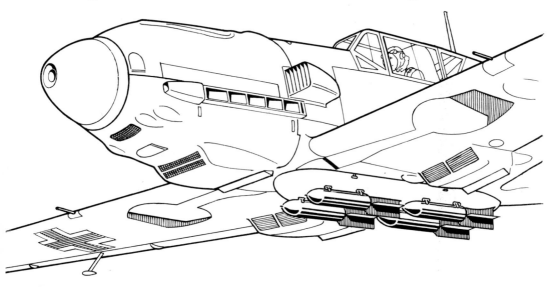

of annoyance and inconvenience to bring up the RAF's fighters to be engaged by large formations of high-flying Bf 109s. The approved method of attack was a 45 degree dive, the bomb being aimed with the standard Revi reflector gunsight. As a rudimentary aid to pilots, a red line was painted on the glazing on one side of the cockpit canopy at this angle. When the pilot had this line parallel with the horizon, he knew he was diving at approximately the correct angle! Nonetheless the German fighter pilots disliked this new duty, which burdened down their aircraft with drag-inducing bombs and bomb-racks, and on many occasions the bombs were simply released haphazardly in level flight.

During November 1940 Ju 87s were briefly re-introduced in attacks on British shipping. Substantial casualties inflicted by defending fighters swiftly proved the correctness of the earlier decision to withdraw them, and they did not appear again. Thereafter the onset of winter, and preparations for momentous events elsewhere led to a virtual end for the time being of daylight incursions.

3. War in the Mediterranean Area

During the early months of World War II the Mediterranean area remained quiet while the Italians played a waiting game. When in June 1940 Benito Mussolini finally decided to throw in his lot with Germany in the hope of sharing in the spoils, his relatively large *Regia Aeronautica* was faced by little in the way of serious opposition in the air. As already mentioned, considerable efforts had been made to set up assault units, and to develop aircraft for them — aircraft which were without exception to prove a disappointment.

During the first days of war the new Breda Ba 88s from their base in Sardinia made strafing attacks on the French island of Corsica. These were to be virtually the only operations undertaken by these aircraft, for which much had been hoped, their appalling serviceability rate making it impossible to maintain them in front line service thereafter.

So disappointing was the performance of the SM 85 dive-bombers that they were never directly committed to action as a force. Shortly after the Italian entry into the war, Germany agreed to the sale of Ju 87Bs to their new ally, and the first of these were collected during August 1940. The following month they were introduced into service with the *Regia Aeronautica* in Sicily, making initial attacks on British naval units, and on targets on Malta. Facing only limited opposition, their performance proved satisfactory to the Italians, and in October they were moved to Albania to support the Italian army's invasion of Greece.

In the North African colony of Libya meanwhile, the elderly Fiat CR 32 was still in use with 50° *Stormo Assalto*, awaiting the arrival of the Breda Ba 65 fighter-bomber attack aircraft. The first of the new aircraft arrived within days of the outbreak of war, but the *Stormo* was to operate both types throughout the rest of 1940. However operations in Africa were fairly limited at this time, and only a relatively few strafing attacks on British forces were made by these aircraft, which were also occasionally engaged by Gladiator biplane fighters of the RAF.

As elsewhere, the British had no attack aircraft or fighter-bombers at their Middle Eastern bases. However, experience in the

"The answer to the Stuka!" Pressed into service during General Wavell's First Libyan Campaign of December 1940, elderly Gloster Gauntlet biplanes undertook dive-bombing operations with underwing 40 lb bombs while serving with one flight of 3 Sqn, RAAF in the Western Desert. *via F.F.Smith*

Sudan, where a handful of elderly Gloster Gauntlet fighters were employed for army co-operation purposes, fitted to carry eight 25 lb incendiary or 20 lb fragmentation bombs beneath the wings, demonstrated the possibilities inherent in this concept. In Egypt a limited offensive was planned to retake territory occupied by the Italians during September 1940, but the small number of Gladiators and Hurricanes available to support this in the face of considerable Italian numerical fighter strength, did not allow any of these to be so modified.

However an Australian unit, 3 RAAF Squadron, had arrived recently, and while now mainly equipped with Gladiators as a fighter unit, had originally been intended for army co-operation duties, and as such still had an additional flight equipped with Gauntlets. Fitted to carry bombs, these aircraft were employed as dive-bombers at the start of General Wavell's highly-successful First Libyan Campaign, which began on December 9, 1940. Known somewhat sarcastically as the "Answer to the Stuka" by their pilots, these old aircraft gave stalwart service nonetheless, operating in this role during the first days of the offensive. When withdrawn later in the month, they had not suffered a single loss in combat. This was to be an isolated interlude however, for it was many months before the RAF was again able to operate aircraft in the fighter-bomber role. However the associated ground strafing was becoming more widely practiced. During the First Libyan Campaign Hurricane pilots were ordered to use any ammunition they had left for their battery of eight .303 in machine guns to attack any suitable ground targets during their return flight, in a general effort to lower their enemy's morale.

This campaign saw the end of the Ba 65 and CR 32 in the assault role, 50° *Stormo Assalto* being virtually denuded of aircraft by February 1941. Many of these were destroyed or damaged on the ground, or were abandoned due to unserviceability. No effort was made to re-equip the unit with the Breda aircraft, more potent equipment being sought in due course.

GERMAN INTERVENTION

With Italy in trouble in Libya and Greece, the Germans decided to intervene in the Mediterranean at the start of 1941 in order to secure their Southern flank before launching their attack in the East against Russia. Initially dive-bombers played an important role in this intervention, which began with the arrival of units of X *Fliegerkorps* in Sicily during January. The initial task of the units of this command was the neutralization of the British air and naval bases on Malta. However opportunity provided the first of a string of striking victories against the Royal Navy, which established the dive-bombers' mastery over shipping which lacked fighter protection.

On January 9, 1941 Ju 87Bs of II/StG 2 attacked and badly damaged the aircraft carrier *Illustrious*, which was forced to limp into the shelter of Malta's Valetta harbour. Next day the same unit sank the cruiser *Southampton*. For the rest of the month attacks were made on Malta, on airfields and on the damaged carrier.

A part of the dive-bomber force moved to Libya from Sicily in February, where, supported by Bf 110s, they aided newly-arrived German Panzers to drive the British back into Egypt the following month. Only the vital port of Tobruk remained in British hands, and as this fell into a state of siege, the Stukas struck daily both at the defences, and at shipping carrying supplies and reinforcements from Egypt.

The arrival of the Luftwaffe in the Mediterranean meant the introduction of dive-bombers and fighter-bombers on a large scale. The first use of the Bf 109E '*Jabo*' in this area occurred over Greece and Yugoslavia during April 1941. Here groundcrew bring up an SC 250 bomb for an aircraft of the *Jabostaffel* of III/JG 27 on an airfield in Greece. *Bundesarchiv*

Meanwhile in the Balkans, where things were still not going well for the Italians in Greece, the Yugoslavians had repudiated their pact with the Axis. Consequently, on April 6, 1941 a major German 'Blitzkrieg' was launched to occupy Yugoslavia and push on to help the Italians clear up the situation in Greece. This attack was aided by a substantial Luftwaffe component, including two *Stukagruppen* II/ZG 26 which would operate its Bf 110s frequently in the ground attack role, II (Schlacht)/LG 2, flying both Bf 109Es and Hs 123s, and several *Jagdgruppen*. Several of the latter were still equipped with Bf 109Es, others using the newer Bf 109F. The former — notably from JG 27 and JG 77 — had several *Staffeln* fitted for *Jabo* duties.

The campaign proceeded similarly to those in Poland and France, although bad weather at times limited aerial activity. Whilst the Ju 87s were active against targets holding up the army, the *Jabos* made attacks on targets behind the front, and on Allied airfields. A particularly notable attack was made on Araxos airfield, Southern Greece, on April 23 by Bf 110s of II/ZG 26. All remaining fighters had been gathered here by the RAF when the Messerschmitts swept in low and with almost complete surprise. 13 Hurricanes and a number of Greek aircraft succumbed to the heavy and concentrated fire of the Zerstörer, which brought to an end in this one blow further British aerial resistance in Greece.

The following month under the codename Operation 'Mercury' an ambitious major airborne assault on the island of Crete was launched by the Germans. Bf 110s of I and II/ZG 26 strafed airfields and AA defences, whilst two *Gruppen* of Ju 87s and one of Ju 88 dive-bombed other targets. Attempts by British naval flotillas to prevent a back-up sea landing on May 22 led to sustained air attack being laid on. Ju 88s of I/LG 1 in a dive-bombing attack badly damaged the cruiser *Naiad*, whilst bomb-carrying Bf 109Es of III/JG 77 obtained a hit on the battleship *Warspite*. Subsequently StG 2 Ju 87s sank the destroyer *Greyhound*, these aircraft joined by Ju 88s, then sinking the cruiser *Gloucester*. A single Bf 109E of I(Jagd)/LG 2 dropped its SC 250 bomb alongside the destroyer *Fiji* bringing the badly damaged vessel to a halt. The pilot radioed for help, and other Bf 109s arrived to accomplish the first sinking of a warship by fighter-bombers.

This was only the beginning, for next morning I/StG 2 accomplished the sinking of the destroyers *Kelly* and *Kashmir*. By chance on 26th Ju 87s of II/StG 2 flying from Libya spotted the carrier *Formidable* withdrawing from an attack on an Axis island base in the Aegean, and inflicted severe damage. Thereafter Bf 109F *Jabos* of JG 77, I(J)/LG 2 and II(Schlacht)/LG 2, together with Ju 87s and 88s, hunted shipping south of Crete as the British withdrew from the island. Over the next few days several more warships were sunk and others damaged, but as soon as the evacuation of the island had been completed so far as was possible, these units all withdrew northwards to take part in the forthcoming invasion of the Soviet Union.

BRITISH DEVELOPMENTS

In England during 1941 quantities of Bristol Beaufighters were now being delivered. After going initially to the night fighter units, deliveries were made to the long-range fighter squadrons of Coastal Command. The potential of this heavily-armed aircraft for ground attack purposes was obvious, but against targets in Western Europe the aircraft did not possess sufficient performance to face the potent German interceptors based here. While it would frequently be used to strafe German shipping convoys along the European coast (and later to attack them with bombs, torpedoes and rockets), it was clear that it could be put to very good use in the Middle East.

The first batch reached Malta in the early Summer of 1941, from where they made attacks on Axis shipping crossing from Europe to Africa, but soon a few filtered across to Egypt. After a brief employment on a couple of occasions during the occupation of Syria, they were prepared for action over the Libyan Desert.

During June and early July the RAF had been involved in supporting the Allied action in Syria, finding itself faced by well-equipped and determined opponents in the French. During the latter

The aircraft which was to become the backbone of Allied ground attack strength in the Mediterranean was the Curtiss Kittyhawk — at that time also the main air superiority fighter in the area. Able to carry a wide variety of bomb loads, this particular Kittyhawk IA of 112 Sqn is shown with two 250 lb bombs side-by-side beneath the fuselage, and two 40 lb bombs beneath each wing. *IWM*

part of the brief campaign the RAF instituted a series of low-level massed strafing attacks by Hurricanes and Tomahawks on the French airfields, similar to those they had themselves recently suffered in Greece. The results were similarly impressive, the ability of the French air force to fight back swiftly being dissipated.

Initially during the later summer of 1941 the Beaufighters of 272 Squadron were employed against convoys along the Libyan coast road, and other similar communications targets, against which their heavy battery of cannons and machine guns proved most effective. It was planned to use them for airfield attack when the British army was able to launch a new offensive, in the hope that the Syrian success might be repeated.

As the RAF in Africa was steadily built up, another new element was also introduced. While most fighter squadrons were by then equipped with Hurricane IIs or Tomahawks, 80 Squadron was re-equipped with rather elderly Hurricane Is fitted to carry eight 40 lb fragmentation bombs beneath the wings — a full RAF fighter-bomber squadron at last!

The biggest British offensive of the war so far, Operation 'Crusader', opened on November 18, 1941 with the primary aim of raising the siege of Tobruk. On the first day the Beaufighters went out to make a number of damaging surprise strafing attacks on Axis airfields, while two days later 80 Squadron flew its first fighter-bomber sorties against Axis vehicles. On that same date the Beaufighters of 272 Squadron enjoyed a success comparable with that of II/ZG 26 at Araxos the previous April. Arriving over Tmimi airfield, they found it packed with Ju 87s dispersed on the ground, while others were landing or taking off. In one damaging attack the British fighters claimed four shot down, 14 destroyed on the ground, and a number of other aircraft also destroyed. During this period the Beaufighters also received assistance from a number of specially-converted Blenheim IV 'strafers' of 113 Squadron, while on the other side of the lines, it was during this offensive that the Bf 110s of III/ZG 26, which had previously been employed on long-range escort duties across the Mediterranean, were ordered to undertake strafing sorties in support of Rommel's Panzers.

GROWTH OF FIGHTER-BOMBER ACTIVITIES IN AFRICA

Throughout the 'Crusader' offensive, which lasted until early January 1942, British fighters strafed troop or transport targets on occasions, but were generally too involved in air superiority sweeps and bomber escorts to indulge in these activities other than on the odd occasion. During January a reinforced Rommel struck back, forcing the British to give up about half the territory they had gained, the line

stabilizing around the Gazala area, about midway between Benghazi and Tobruk.

At the end of that month 80 Squadron exchanged its Hurricane Is for cannon-armed Mark IICs, and once again for the time being the RAF in Africa was without fighter-bombers. Meanwhile however, due to the activities of the RAF in Malta, and of destroyers and submarines which were based there, in raiding the Axis supply lines across the Mediterranean, the Luftwaffe returned to Sicily during December 1941 for a renewed 'Blitz' on the island. This time the units involved included III/JG 53, which boasted a *Jabostaffel* of Bf 109Es fitted for fighter-bombing. Initially these aircraft attacked British airfields on Malta, but in January 1942 they moved to Africa to support Rommel's counter-offensive, and here they were joined by the *Jabostaffel* of JG 27, when that unit's III *Gruppe* arrived from Russia. At this time, with more fuel available as shipping convoys crossed the Mediteranean freed from the lash of Malta's scourge, the Bf 109F fighters of JG 27 were also on occasion pressed into service for fighter-bombing duties.

The other combatants were also preparing to introduce more fighter-bombers however. Early in 1942 the RAF had brought into service in Africa the Curtiss Kittyhawk (P-40E), and unlike the earlier Tomahawk this aircraft could be equipped for bomb carrying. The first test drop of a 250 lb bomb carried beneath the fuselage was made by the famous Australian fighter pilot, Sqn Ldr Clive R. Caldwell, on March 10, but it was to be mid May before his unit, 112 Squadron, became the first 'Kittybomber' unit.

More was afoot however, for a new weapon had been developed in England, and was to see its first service use in Africa. This was the Hurricane IID anti-tank aircraft, supplies of which reached 6 Squadron during early May. Armament tests in England with the Hurricane II had given rise to the development of this aircraft,

The most accurate anti-tank aircraft to see service with the RAF was the Hawker Hurricane IID. Armed with two 40mm Vickers 'S' guns beneath the wings, the aircraft proved very effective against *Afrika Korps* armoured units. However it lacked armour protection for engine and pilot, and in consequence losses to ground fire were intolerably high. In addition, the heavy gun fairings had a very adverse effect on the aircraft's performance, limiting its use to conditions of complete air superiority.
IWM

following the availability of two relatively light-weight 40 mm anti-tank guns, which could operate semi-automatically, and be carried by a single-engined aircraft. Initial production aircraft supplied to a squadron in England featured Rolls Royce BF guns, each with a 12-round magazine, but those sent to the Middle East all featured Vickers 'S' guns, which carried 15 rounds each.

The guns were fitted beneath the wings in quite neat fairings, while only one .303 in Browning was retained in each wing. Firing tracers, the machine guns were employed for aiming purposes. Despite this reduction in standard armament, the increased weight and drag of the big underwing weapons substantially reduced top speed to 316 mph, and greatly reduced the aircraft's agility. The one big omission — for obvious weight reasons — was that no additional armour protection was fitted to this aircraft to protect the engine, cooling system and pilot from the high volume of ground fire it was likely to encounter.

Since their disastrous retreat of December 1940, the Italians had deployed only fighters and dive-bombers to Libya, although *Regia Aeronautica* Fiat G-50bis and Macchi C.200 fighters frequently made strafing attacks on British airfields and other targets during the latter part of 1941, before the opening rounds of the 'Crusader' offensive. Activities at this time were constantly hampered by lack of fuel however. At home efforts were being made to introduce a fighter-bomber version of the CR 42 biplane fighter into service with the *Assalto* units, and during Spring 1942 the first such *squadriglia* arrived in Africa, soon followed by 2° *Stormo C.T.* This latter was a fighter unit, but had been equipped with MC 200s similarly modified to carry bombs in the ground attack role.

After the failure of their specialized ground attack types, the Italians equipped the majority of their ground assault units with fighter-bomber versions of the Fiat CR 42 biplane fighter. Loaded with bombs and shrouded against the Desert sands, an aircraft of the 238° *Sqdr.*, 101° Gruppo Assalto is seen on a somewhat damp Lybian airfield.
Bundesarchiv

Fiat CR 42 fighter-bomber of the *Regia Aeronautica's* 387 *Squadriglia*, 158° *Gruppe*, 50° *Stormo Assalto*. These aircraft were employed in quite large numbers in the North African desert during 1942, particularly during the period of the fighting at El Alamain.

During May 1942 both sides were preparing for a new offensive in Africa, but it was the Axis who struck first late in the month, in what became the Battle of Gazala. While the *Jabostaffeln* were to operate in conjunction with the fighters, striking at British airfields and similar targets, the Germans had on this occasion formed a special tactical command to aid the Panzers of the *Afrika Korps* with direct air support. Known as the *'Gefechtsverband Sigel'*, it was commanded by *Hauptmann* Walter Sigel, Kommodore of *Stukageschwader* 3, and included the three *Gruppen* of his unit, mainly re-equipped with Ju 87Ds, the Bf 110s of III/ZG 26, and the Junkers Ju 88C heavy fighters of 12 Staffel, LG 1.

As Axis armour swept round the Southern end of the front to outflank the British, the RAF's fighters were thrown in to strafe the transport columns supporting the drive — a task in which they suffered very severe losses to patrolling German fighters. By this time the Kittyhawks of two squadrons of 239 Wing (112 and 3 RAF) were carrying bombs, while 274 Squadron was just about to enter action with its Hurricane IIs fitted with racks for a 250 lb bomb beneath each wing.

On June 6, 1942 alone the Kittyhawks of 239 Wing claimed 70 vehicles destroyed, while next day the Hurricane IIDs of 6 Squadron entered action, and within ten days had flown 37 sorties, claiming 31 tanks immobilized and 28 large vehicles destroyed or badly damaged. MC 200s were also extremely active at this time, attacking British transport columns.

The German offensive was a success despite desperate British resistance, the latter force's armour being destroyed whilst other units were forced into headlong retreat. Fighter-bombers and strafing fighters joined Beaufighters and light bombers in repeated attacks on the advancing Axis columns, playing a major role in slowing them down and allowing the British army to withdraw in good order. On June 21 however, *'Gefechtsverband Sigel'* and Italian *Assalto* CR 42s were closely involved in supporting the Panzers which burst through the Tobruk perimeter and at last captured the port.

As the *Afrika Korps* pressed on towards Alexandria more units were thrown into the attack against them. Kittyhawks of the mainly-South African 233 Wing also undertook fighter-bomber duties, whilst 274 Squadron was joined by 7 SAAF Squadron, which initially dropped small missiles from elderly Hurricane Is, but soon converted to Mark IIBs, then carrying two 250 pounders underwing. To obtain the maximum blast effect these latter bombs were frequently fitted with extension rods to the nose fuses, these causing the explosion to take place just above the ground, rather than after the weapon had buried itself deeply in the muffling depths of the desert sand. Supplies of American-made 500 lb bombs were now becoming available, and the Kittyhawks were soon carrying these beneath the fuselage as an alternative to the 250 pounder. Alternatively two of the latter weapons were frequently carried, either mounted in tandem, or side by side.

The fighter-bomber was still a weapon for attacking lines of communication targets as far as the RAF was concerned, and its use outside periods of movement such as were occaioned by an offensive, were strictly limited. As soon as the lines stabilized the majority of fighters returned to bomber-escort, offensive patrolling and defensive sorties, leaving interdiction work against Axis convoys to the longer-ranging Beaufighters with their heavy armament for strafing. Even at this stage the number of squadrons whose aircraft were even fitted for bomb-carrying was still only a small proportion of the total number of fighter units involved. The only direct battlefield support aircraft was still the Hurricane IID, and so few in number were these aircraft that the moment offensive operations on the ground ceased, 6 Squadron was withdrawn for rest and further training. Meanwhile

By late 1942 the vulnerability of the Ju 87 had led the Luftwaffe to form more specialized ground attack fighter-bomber units. The first of these to see service in North Africa was formed as '*Jabogruppe Afrika*' from the *Jabostaffeln* of JG27 and JG 53, and from elements of newly-formed II-I/ZG 1. This unit saw action during the period of the Alamain battle, and the German retreat from Libya. ZG1 had been reformed in the Soviet Union the previous year from the Bf 110-equipped I and II/SKG 210 (ex ErpGr.210). For this reason, the unit carried, the S9 code letters previously used by the earlier units, which has led to the mis-identification of Bf 109Es of this unit (like that seen here) as serving with SKG 210.
IWM

however, Kittyhawks of 239 and 233 Wings still carried bombs on occasions whilst escorting Boston and Baltimore light bombers, diving down after the latter had dropped their load to attack any obvious targets which they had missed.

On the other side of the lines the Luftwaffe carried on in much the same way with regard to their *Jabo* and *Zerstörer* units. All but one *Staffel* of III/ZG 26 were moved to Crete when mobile operations ceased, but a new 10 *Staffel* was formed with Do 17s and Ju 88Cs for long-range strafing. Late in August the two *Jabostaffeln* were detached from III/JG 27 and III/JG 53, becoming *Jabogruppe Afrika* under *Oberleutnant* Langermann. At the same time they were joined by a new Bf 109E ground-attack unit from Germany, III/ZG 1, under the command of which they now came. The new unit got off to a bad start, losing its commanding officer, Major Roland Bohrt, on the very first day of operations.

At the end of September these units all withdrew to Italy, where the *Jabogruppe Afrika*, with additional personnel and aircraft from III/ZG 1, formed a new unit, I/*Schlachtgeschwader* 2, which returned to Africa in mid-October. III/ZG 1 meanwhile began equipping with Messerschmitt Me 210 *Zerstörer* aircraft.

The Junkers Ju 88C-6 heavy fighter was used as a ground-strafer in North Africa by a single special *Staffel* of III/ZG 26. It played an important part in supporting the Panzer columns which captured Torbruk during June 1942. *Bundesarchiv*

MALTA

During the spring of 1942 Bf 109F and G aircraft of JG 53 from Sicily had frequently made small fighter-bomber attacks on Maltese airfields between the main bombing raids. Approaching with a substantial escort at zero feet, they climbed to 3-4,000 feet when about ten miles out from the island, then diving at 25-40 degrees over the

Hurricane IID anti-tank aircraft of 6 Squadron attack German Pzkw III and IV tanks on a typical North African landscape. After early 1943 gun-armed anti-tank aircraft were rapidly phased out in the air forces of the Western Allies in favour of aircraft fitted with the more versatile if less accurate rocket projectile.
IWM

airfields to drop a single SC 250 bomb each. As soon as the bomb was released they remained in their dive, reaching zero feet again as they crossed the southern coast of the island, before making a fast low level flight back to base.

During the summer most Luftwaffe units left Sicily once more for the Eastern Front, and during the lull which followed the RAF retaliated. On Malta 126 Squadron devised a bomb rack for its Spitfire Vs, employing these aircraft in a limited and unofficial role during September as the first Spitbombers against airfields in Southern Sicily. At the same time a small number of Hurricanes were used officially as fighter-bombers on similar duties. In both cases the weapons used were the faithful 250 lb bombs. A return of the Luftwaffe for a new assault on the island early in October put an end for the time being to any more such activities.

EL ALAMEIN

At the end of August Rommel launched an offensive against the southern end of the line at Alamein, but the new British commander, General Bernard Montgomery, was ready for him, and the Battle of Alem el Halfa was a complete failure for the Axis, no progress being made and heavy losses suffered. Fighter-bombers and strafers of the RAF's Western Desert Air Force were much in evidence, including the Kittybombers of both Wings, and a new 7 SAAF Hurribomber Wing

This latter unit had four squadrons, including 6 Squadron with its 'tank-busters', 274 and 7 SAAF Squadrons as bomb-carriers, and 127 Squadron to provide escorts.

With the battle over, 7 SAAF Squadron was withdrawn after heavy losses to become the second Hurricane IID unit, joining 6 Squadron in a new independent role to operate directly under Headquarters control during the next offensive, rather than as part of a Wing. 7 SAAF Wing was reformed with 80, 127, 274 and 335 Squadrons, 80 and 274 being the unit's bomb-carriers.

As dawn broke on October 24, 1942 the Battle of El Alamein was in full swing, the Hurricanes and Kittyhawks now being joined by USAAF P-40F Warhawks. Having arrived earlier in the year and become acclimatized to operations, the Americans now also began fighter-bombing at this time. The *Regia Aeronautica* had by now greatly increased its ground attack complement, the MC 200 fighter-bombers of 2° *Stormo C.T.* being joined by two full *Stormi Assalti* of CR 42s with four *Gruppi* available in total, together with a single *Gruppo* of Ju 87s. The Luftwaffe had 10/ZG 26, I/SchG 2 and two *Gruppen* of StG 3, II *Gruppe* having moved to Sicily earlier in the month to take part in the renewed assault on Malta.

Early in November the Axis line was pierced and a full retreat across North Africa began. During the month the Me 210s of III/ZG 1 were sent over, together with a *Staffel* of Henschel Hs 129B anti-tank aircraft (see Chapter 4 for the development of these aircraft). With unreliable engines adversely affected by North African sand, the latter never even got into action, and were withdrawn to Germany the following January.

As the British advance into Western Libya progressed the Hurricane units were left behind, the main fighter-bomber support then being provided by 239 Wing and the 57th Fighter Group USAAF, and by two squadrons of Beaufighters. The South Africans also withdrew to receive replacement Kittyhawks of more recent manufacture, at the same time taking on the mantle of 7 SAAF Wing.

TUNISIA

Even as the Axis retreat from Alamein was beginning, Anglo-American troops landed in French North-West Africa on November 8, pressing on towards Tunisia to take Rommel's forces in the rear. Large numbers of aircraft were swiftly flown in to support these landings, initially most units being equipped with Spitfires. However two RAF army co-operation units accompanied the wings operating over the front. These were both equipped with Hurricane IIs fitted with bomb-racks to undertake the joint duties of tactical reconnaissance and bombing.

Axis reaction was swift, and forces were poured into Tunisia,

Late in the North African fighting, the Luftwaffe despatched two Staffeln of new anti-tank Henschel Hs 129B aircraft to the area. The fortunes of these heavily-armoured aircraft were varied. Those of 8(Pz)/ SG 2 in Tunisia saw quite a lot of action over the front, but those of 4(Pz)/SG2, which went to the Tripoli area of Western Libya, were crippled by unserviceability caused mainly by dust ingestion into their unreliable Gnôme-Rhône engines. These aircraft are believed to be from the latter unit, and are seen here on a dusty airstrip, with a Fieseler Fi 156 Storch liaison aircraft in the background. *Smithsonian Institute via Squadron/Signal*

including the *Gruppe* of Ju 87s from StG 3 in Sicily and the firs elements of another new *Zerstörergeschwader* that had arrived ir Italy, III/ZG 2. In December this *Gruppe*, which was just converting from Bf 109Es to Fw 190s, became III/SKG 10. Meanwhile a I *Gruppe* of SchG 2 was forming, also with Bf 109Es as initia equipment, giving way to Fw 190s as quickly as possible. This uni also sent across its first *Staffel* to Tunisia before the end of 1942 together with newly-formed 8(Panzer)/SchG 2 with more Hs 129Bs The *Regia Aeronautica* sent in a *squadriglia* each of MC 200 anc G-50bis fighter-bombers, while a *Gruppo* of Reggiane Re 2001 made fighter-bomber attacks on the port of Bone — newly-capturec by the British — from bases in Sardinia. This latter aircraft hac entered service as a fighter over Malta during the early summer, anc had first seen action as a fighter-bomber against British shipping during the famous Operation 'Pedestal' convoy to Malta in August

The two squadrons of Hurricanes were soon fully engaged ir supporting British troops in the mountains of Northern Tunisia while further south the USAAF employed its newly-arrivec Lockheed P-38s for strafing Axis convoys and troop movements, a well as for air fighting. These aircraft were soon joined by a group o P-40Fs, which were engaged in fighter-bomber activities wheneve they could be spared from the air defence role. However early in 194 the first of two groups of Bell P-39 Airacobras arrived, and these were employed exclusively for ground strafing throughout the rest of the campaign.

During January 1943, with Tripoli about to fall, and Axis troops from Libya already falling back into Southern Tunisia, the *Regia Aeronautica* withdrew all its Libyan-based ground attack and fighter-bomber units from Africa, leaving only the remaining Luftwaffe units to support the ground forces of the *Afrika Korps*. In the north however the Ju 87s and the Bf 109E and Fw 190A *Jabos* were extremely active against the Allied forces, frequently enjoying periods of local air superiority due to their having bases in much closer proximity to the front than the RAF and USAAF possessed at the time.

In the south the Western Desert Air Force fighter-bombers now regulary attacked Axis communications and airfields. This was possible as the Allies now enjoyed considerable numerical superiority, together with adequate numbers of Spitfires for the air fighting role, leaving the Kittyhawks and P-40s free to concentrate on the former task. This they did throughout early 1943 until the 8th Army was ready to launch an attack on the Mareth Line — the main Axis defensive position in Southern Tunisia.

While a frontal attack on the line was launched, the fighter-bombers performed their usual function of attacking the supply lines and vehicles as they tried to bring up ammunition, food and fuel; they also hit Axis airfields to keep down the level of German and Italian aerial activity. The initial attack failed to break through, and a major outflanking move to the south was made. To reach El Hamma and take the Mareth defences in the rear, the British columns had to pass through a gap between two mountains, known as the Tebaga Gap. This was heavily defended by dug-in German 88 mm anti-tank guns, which promised to make such an assault most costly. It was here therefore that Allied fighter-bombers were for the first time called upon to take a direct part in the main land battle.

In the late afternoon of March 26, 1943 no less than 18 squadrons of fighter-bombers, including the Hurricane IIDs of 6 Squadron, the Kittyhawks of 239 and 7 SAAF Wings, and the P-40s of the 57th and the recently-arrived 79th Fighter Groups, swept in in waves to attack the German gun positions. Infantry followed close behind the attack (an essential prerequisite of such an exercise), the result of which was more the keeping down of the gun crews' heads than the actual destruction of the guns in most cases. As they appeared from their dugouts the infantry were already upon them, silencing the guns and allowing the British armour to pour through the gap towards El Hamma almost unscathed.

Losses were not light, and at least 15 fighter-bombers were lost, most of them to concentrated small calibre fire from the ground. In the peculiar circumstances of this particular action however, the intervention of tactical air power had been the crucial factor in its immediate success. It was however almost the end for the Hurricane 'tank-busters'.

After Alamein 6 Squadron and 7 SAAF Squadron had been rested again, available remaining Hurricane IIDs then being concentrated in the former unit for the Mareth battle. Re-entering action on March 21, the unit suffered very heavily to ground fire, losing 16 aircraft in five days, six of them during one mission on 25th. The relatively slow aircraft lacked any protective armour to the underside of the engine or fuselage — so vital for an anti-tank machine — and as a result proved very vulnerable to the highly efficient German light Flak. Rested again immediately after the success at the Tebaga Gap, 6 Squadron returned to action briefly during April, but with similar results.

Efforts were made to provide armour for the Hurricane IID in England, but this was never to reach units in the Mediterranean, and the 'tank-buster' disappeared from Allied service here during May 1943. The British and Americans were unwilling to direct effort to the production of an armoured ground attack aircraft of this nature, as the new rocket projectile was at that time offering promise as a viable anti-tank weapon, while the flexibility of the fighter-bomber appealed more to Allied thinking. However the Hurricane IID was to prove the most accurate aerial anti-tank weapon of the war for the RAF, and the failure of the Anglo-American aviation industry to produce an equivalent of the Il-2 or Hs 129B was to be a matter of some regret to a fair proportion of high-ranking Army opinion.

As the campaign in North Africa moved inexorably to its climax, Allied ground attack formations continued to increase, whilst the remaining Axis elements were progressivey withdrawn. In Northern Tunisia, following tests with a Spitfire carrying a 250 lb bomb beneath each wing, 152 Squadron became the first *official* Spitbomber unit. During the final Allied offensive of April and May three USAAF P-40 groups with attached elements of a fourth, two P-39 groups, two RAF/SAAF Kittyhawk wings, plus one Spitfire and one Hurricane squadron, were engaged in almost continuous fighter bomber operations against remaining Axis transport, troop concentrations, gun positions, airfields etc., and against any shipping attempting to carry supplies to Africa, or evacuate men from that continent. They operated almost completely immune from air attack, beneath an umbrella of patrolling Spitfires and P-38s though they suffered an ever-growing number of losses to ground fire. For the Allies the tactical ground attack fighter-bomber was no longer an interim 'lash-up', but a major element of air power in offensive tactical operations.

4 Eastern Front

When in mid-1941 the Luftwaffe amassed a major offensive force for the fifth time (Poland, September 1939; France and the Low Countries, May 1940; Britain, August 1940; Yugoslavia and Greece, April 1941), its composition and size differed but little from those earlier occasions. Three *Luftflotten* were to support the main offensive against the Soviet Union, which would begin at dawn on June 22, while a fourth, based in Norway, would operate on a smaller scale both to East and West. *Luftflotten* 1 and 4, supporting the Northern and Southern Army Groups, contained no Stuka or *Schlacht* units, being composed of only conventional level bomber *Gruppen* (including the multi-purpose Ju 88s), fighter *Gruppen*, and reconnaissance and army co-operation units.

The bulk of the Luftwaffe's close support strength was available to the largest of the formations, *Luftflotte* 2, which was to support the major drive on Moscow by Army Group Centre. Once again, Stukas made up the bulk of this force, seven *Gruppen* of Ju 87Bs being available, together with the faithful II(Schlacht)/LG 2, still equipped with Bf 109Es and Hs 123s. There was one major difference however. Many of the *Zerstörergruppen* had now gone after the 1940 debacle, either to become night fighter units, or disbanded. Those that remained were now available almost in their entirety to *Luftflotte* 2, to double as ground attack aircraft. These units included I and II/ZG 26, fresh from their exploits over Greece and Crete, together with the rejuvenated ErpGr.210. This unit, now fully equipped with Bf 110s, was now I/SKG 210 (*Schnellkampfgeschwader* — Fast Bomber Wing). It was joined by II/ZG 1, which had been redesignated II/SKG 210, these Gruppen having been brought up to strength with crews from the now-defunct III/ZG 76.

There remained one *Gruppe* each of Stukas and *Zerstörer* in Norway, but all other available units of these aircraft were occupied in the Mediterranean area.

From the moment that Operation 'Barbarossa' was launched, the Luftwaffe achieved a succession of smashing victories. For the first time air liaison officers accompanied the Panzer spearheads, calling in the Stukas by radio to attack targets in direct support of the ground

While the main Luftwaffe close-support element was again the Ju 87B-equipped *Stukageschwadern* at the time of the invasion of Soviet Union in June 1941, these aircraft were supported by substantial numbers of Messerschmitt Bf 110C and D *Zerstörern*, which now operated mainly in the ground attack role. These aircraft are from ZG 1, which was reformed from SKG 210 during 1942, then operating over Southern Russia. All carry the unit's *Wespen* (Wasp) insignia on their noses. *Bundesarchiv*

In June 1941 II(Sch)/LG 2 was still the only *Schlacht* unit in the Luftwaffe. Despite deliveries of Bf 109Es, the unit also still operated a number of the elderly Hs 123s, and these were to remain in service for many months to come, forming part of the equipment of the first full *Schlachtgeschwader* — SchG 1 — when it was formed late in 1942. This aircraft carries the 'Infantry assault badge' on the forward fuselage, together with four SC50 bombs beneath the wings. *Franz Selinger*

forces' advance. The Bf 110s were particularly active in attacks on Soviet airfields, where many hundreds of aircraft were destroyed during the first days of the assault. With Soviet aircraft appearing in massed formations to oppose the lightning thrusts of the Wehrmacht, the *Jagdgeschwadern* were generally too busy to undertake fighter-bomber sorties, but with opposition in the air limited, and with adequate escort usually forthcoming from the Bf 109s, the Ju 87s once more had things all their own way, achieving the same devastating effects on the harrassed and unprepared Russians that they had achieved in Poland, France and Yugoslavia

Due to shortage of suitable *Shturmovik* aircraft, the Red Air Force had to press into service in 1941 large numbers of Polikarpov biplane fighters in this role. An I-15bis is seen here at dispersal, armed with a hollow-charge anti-tank bomb and a normal blast bomb of about 50kg weight, under each wing. *Passingham/-Klepacki Coll.*

The dive-bombers achieved one of their greatest successes of the war on September 23, 1941. German forces of the Northern Army Group were investing Leningrad, the defenders of this city receiving fire support from the guns of the Red Fleet, which operated from its main base at Kronshtadt. Moved to the area specially to attack these warships, StG 2 launched a series of attacks, during one of which on this date *Oberleutnant* Hans-Ulrich Rudel planted his PC 1000 (2,204 lb) armour-piercing bomb directly on the 'A' turret of the 26,170 ton battleship *Marat*, destroying the whole bow. This vessel had already been damaged by the same pilot a few days earlier; it now sank in shallow water — the first capital ship sunk by air attack during the war.

Meanwhile the Bf 110s, and the single-engined fighter-bombers of I(Schlacht)/LG 2, were employed against Soviet convoys, gun positions etc., attacking with gunfire and bombs. Against tanks their 20 mm cannon generally proved ineffective, and only a direct hit by a relatively heavy bomb could hope to disable one of these armoured vehicles in all but the most exceptional circumstances. The launching of bombs by fighter-bomber aircraft in level, or near-level, flight was, as we have already seen, a relatively haphazard and inaccurate business against such small and specific targets, particularly when they were moving. Only with considerable practice and skill could any degree of success be achieved.

An indication of the variety of targets attacked by the Bf 110 units during the first year of the war can be gained from a study of the achievements of one of the leading *Zerstörer* pilots. Major Eduard Tratt had flown with ErpGr.210 during the Battle of Britain, where as well as engaging in the low level bombing attacks, he was the unit's

most successful pilot in aerial combat, claiming 12 intercepting
fighters shot down. In Russia he had increased this score to 20 by
April 1942, for the Bf 110s achieved a fair degree of success in this role
against the elderly Soviet aircraft usually encountered during the
war's earlier months in the East. When he returned to Germany in
1943, he had also destroyed 26 aircraft on the ground during strafing
attacks, on top of which he personally claimed the destruction of 24
tanks, 190 covered lorries, 112 open lorries, 33 light anti-aircraft or
anti-tank guns, four anti-aircraft batteries and eight heavy machine
gun nests.

This time however, the Germans were not having it all their own
way. The Red Air Force was almost entirely a tactical arm, its main
'raison d'etre' being the support of the army. As such it was equipped
to a far greater degree than the Luftwaffe's previous opponents with
this in mind. At the outbreak of fighting few of the new Il-2 and Pe-2
aircraft were yet available, but those that were quickly showed
considerable promise. The initially more numerous Su-2, even in its
up-engined, up-armoured form, proved an easy quarry for German

A Soviet armourer
completes the fit-
ting of an anti-tank
bomb beneath the
wing of a Polikar-
pov I-153. A blast,
or general purpose,
bomb lies ready to
go on the adjoining
shackle.
IWM

fighters when fully loaded, and suffered heavy losses. With its all-machine gun armament the amount of damage it was able to inflict was strictly limited. Once the aircraft had released its bombload however, it was reportedly very manoeuvrable, and had a fair chance of holding its own with opposing fighters. On one occasion an Su-2 in the hands of a woman pilot, Z.Zelenska, was attacked by four Bf 109s after it had bombed troops concentrating in the Rovny area. Zelenska was reported to have shot down two of her attackers before ramming a third with her stricken bomber, the two aircraft falling locked together.

The Pe-2 on the other hand had so high a performance that it could only just be caught by the best German fighter, the Bf 109F, and at some altitudes could outrun the earlier Bf 109E, many of which were still in service in 1941. When used as a dive-bomber its attacks were every bit as accurate as those of the Ju 87, whilst its far heavier bombload made it a more effective proposition. Its greatest disadvantage in the early stages of the war was its extremely limited availability. Such of these aircraft as were in service were frequently retained for reconnaissance purposes, and when acting as a bomber, it had to double in the level bombing role as other types available such as the SB-2*bis* and DB-3F, had soon proved too vulnerable to fighter attack to operate at reasonable cost by day.

Indeed at first the aircraft was underutilized in its diving role, principally because it was supplied to re-equip units which had previously flown the standard medium bomber types, whose personnel did not appreciate how to take full advantage of this new capability without further training. One unit which did much to pioneer use of the aircraft as a dive-bomber was the 150th Bomber

This captured Polikarpov I-153 shows well the launching racks for four RS-82 rocket projectiles fitted beneath the wings of many of these aircraft as an alternative to bomb-racks.
Carson Seeley via Passingham/- Klepacki Coll.

Standard light bomber and ground attack aircraft in service with the Red Air Force in summer 1941 was the Sukhoi Su-2. Although a handy and manoeuvrable aircraft, the Su-2 was not well armed or armoured, and suffered heavily at the hands of German fighters. *Jean Alexander via Passingham/- Klepacki Coll.*

German personnel inspect a captured Sukhoi Su-2. This photo shows well the hinged dorsal turret, and the wing panel for re-arming the guns. *Passingham/- Klepacki Coll.*

Regiment, led by Colonel Ivan S. Polbin, who was to become to the Soviet dive-bombers, what Hans-Ulrich Rudel became to the German Stukas. Polbin's Pe-2s were active during the winter of 1941/42 during the first major Soviet offensive of the war, and by the middle of 1942, as a result of the experience gained by Polbin and others, most units were becoming proficient in the new role.

Polbin it was who early in 1942 developed the classic Soviet dive bomber attack, the *'Vertushka'* ('Dipping wheel'). Approaching the target in a 'Vee of Vees' formation, the dive-bombers went into line astern, with about 2,000 feet between each aircraft. Circling the target

each then attacked in a 70 degree dive, thus keeping the target area under constant attack until the formation had run out of bombs, or completed its work of destruction. In four days during the German summer offensive of July 1942, the 150th Regiment claimed 40 tanks and 50 other vehicles destroyed by this method.

Probably the most unpleasant surprises for the Germans in 1941 were the appearance — albeit in small numbers — of T-34 tanks, Il-2 *Shturmoviks* and the 'Katyusha' artillery rocket batteries. The T-34 proved superior in many respects to all German tanks then at the front, whilst the low-flying Il-2 seemed impervious to smallarms fire and light flak. Its massive quantities of protective armour also made it a difficult aircraft for fighters to shoot down. Its weak spot soon turned out to be its lack of rear defence, which allowed German fighters to close to minimum range, where the fire from their 20 mm cannons could achieve maximum penetrative and destructive effect. Like the Bf 110s and Bf 109s of the Luftwaffe close support units however, the Il-2's 20 mm main armament was to prove relatively ineffective against armoured vehicles.

The first use of the Il-2 had been made on 26 June 1941 over the Berezina River front, only days after the war began. The aircraft was introduced into action by the 4th ShAP (*Shturmovoi Aviapolk* = Ground Attack Air Rgt). This unit had previously been a light bomber formation which had flown R-Zs in Finland during 1939-40. So new was the Il-2 to this unit that the pilots had received no instructions in the flight characteristics or the tactics to be employed, while the ground staff still did not know how to service or re-arm the aircraft properly. Not surprisingly, losses were considerable and by 10 July the five *eskadrilyi* of the regiment were down to a strength of 16 pilots from an initial 65. When withdrawn to rest after one and a half months of continual combat flying, only three Il-2s remained to be handed over to the relieving 215th ShAP.

The Petlyakov Pe-2 was the main Soviet dive-bomber of the war, also doubling as one of the most widely-used light bombers and reconnaissance aircraft. This sleek and remarkably fast aircraft was to serve throughout the war, and was to prove difficult to intercept for the Bf 109E and F fighters with which the Luftwaffe was equipped during the early stages of the war. *Passingham/ Klepacki Coll.*

Although in service in only very small numbers at the start of the German invasion, the Ilyushin Il-2 — the archetypal *Shturmovik* — came as an unpleasant surprise to the Germans. One of the early single-seat examples of this aircraft is seen here, fitted with batteries of RS-82 rockets beneath each wing. *Passingham/ Klepacki Coll.*

Most Soviet Air Regiments had comprised five *eskadrilyi* at the outbreak of war but early losses forced the reformation of most on a two *eskadrilyi* basis — only 24 aircraft instead of 65. While production allowed an increase to three or four *eskadrilyi* later in the war, Air Regiments seldom reached their prewar strengths before 1945.

It must be said that when first introduced to Soviet pilots, the Il-2 raised little enthusiasm. In an age of superlatives for aircraft the Il-2 was unexceptional, and was a relatively unimpressive aircraft to fly. It was not particularly fast, did not have a long range or high altitude ceiling, and was not very manoeuvrable. Certainly the 4th ShAP found their initial tactics unsatisfactory; flying at low level to avoid Luftwaffe fighters and surprise the enemy columns, they were unable to see the explosions of their RS-82 rockets or of their bombs, and thus had little opportunity to check on, or improve upon the results of their attacks.

When employed against undispersed targets, or troops unprepared for such attacks the RS-82 could be most effective — not least in their effect upon morale. A hit from one of these weapons could destroy a substantial armoured vehicle without difficulty, but like all such unguided missiles, they suffered from an extreme lack of accuracy, due in large part to trajectory drop. Very considerable practice and experience was necessary to attain any degree of accuracy, and this was a luxury denied to the Soviets to a very great degree during the first two-three years of fighting.

The Luftwaffe was relatively unimpressed with the result obtained by the Soviets with the RS-82, and little attempt was made to produce a similar weapon for German use. During 1942 JG 54 undertook some operational tests against Soviet shipping which was supplying Leningrad across Lake Ladoga. Army-type 210 mm rocket shells were slung beneath the wings of Bf 109Fs, but these proved to have so great a trajectory drop due to their relatively low velocity, that they were discarded as next best to useless.

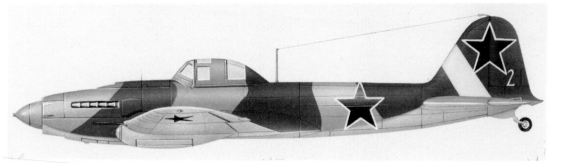

Combat in the Soviet Union, due to its inherently tactical nature, generally took place at a much lower altitude than in Western Europe, and Soviet fighter pilots were employed in ground strafing whenever possible. Few Soviet fighters carried bombs during the war, but most were equipped with underwing launching rails for RS-82s. With the early lack of sufficient *Shturmovik* aircraft however, numbers of Polikarpov I-153 *Chaika* biplane fighters were pressed into this role, joined by smaller quantities of their older sisters, the I-15*bis*. Fitted with either eight RS-82s or up to 440 lb of bombs beneath the lower wings, these little aircraft carried the main weight of ground attack duties during the first six or eight months of the war, and indeed it was these aircraft which devised the 'Dipping Wheel' (also known as 'Circle of Death') tactics later adopted by the Il-2s. So desperate did the situation become however, that during late 1941 authority was given for the formation of 27 regiments to be equipped with R-5s from the reserve, and five more with R-Zs. These aircraft were to be used mainly by night, but were soon very active, the 606th Air Regiment for instance undertaking some 800 sorties in one month during the battle for Moscow that winter.

Production was greatly increased once the pre-arranged plans to withdraw the war industries east of the Ural mountains had been carried out, and during the second half of 1941 twice as many aircraft were produced (8,000) as in the first half of the year (3,950). At the same time rationalization and mass production methods reduced labour time on each Il-2 by up to 80%.

Like the Germans however, the Soviets relied in the main on the use of the aircraft's fixed gun armament, and considerable effort was expended in improving this both in calibre and muzzle velocity. By early 1942 Lend-Lease equipment from the United States and Great Britain was beginning to reach the Soviet Union in appreciable quantities, including numbers of aircraft. Among these were Bell P-39 Airacobras; the P-39 was destined to fail lamentably in its designed role of interceptor fighter with the USAAF, and to be rejected entirely by the RAF after a brief operational test. The

Ilyushin Il-2 ground attack aircraft, or '*Shturmovik*'. This is the initial single-seat version, first employed in numbers on the Moscow front during late 1941.

Russians on the other hand valued this aircraft more highly than most other types sent, for it fitted exactly into their concept of a tactical fighter.

Returning its best performance at the lower altitudes at which the fighting in the East took place, it would perform creditably for many months as a dogfighter with some of the Red Air Force's top fighter units. It was its ability to double as an extremely effective ground attack aircraft which particularly endeared it to the Russians' hearts however, for apart from six machine guns, two of them of .50 in calibre, it featured a 37 mm cannon firing through the hub of the propeller. Because of its unusual design, featuring the heavy nose cannon, and the only tricycle undercarriage employed by a single-engined production aircraft during the war, the engine was situated behind the pilot, driving the propeller by means of a long extension shaft. In this position it was considerably less vulnerable to ground fire than in the usual nose position, where instead armour plate had been installed. Against most ground targets the 37 mm cannon with its relatively large explosive shells was a most deadly weapon. Designed as a bomber-destroyer however, this gun featured a relatively low muzzle velocity, and as a result was still not able to pierce the armour of the average tank or heavy armoured car. Powered by an Allison V-1710-35 inline engine of 1,150 hp, the Airacobra reached a maximum speed of 360 mph (the later versions improved upon this to 376 mph); 30 rounds were carried for the 37 mm cannon, and the aircraft could carry a single bomb of up to 500 lb weight beneath the fuselage.

It was on the Il-2 that the Soviets pinned their salvation above all other aircraft, and production of these machines was pressed ahead as a supreme priority. Joseph Stalin personally appealed to the workers in factories turning out *Shturmoviks* that they were "as essential to the Red Army as air and bread", imploring them to use every endeavour to speed up production. They rose to the moment with a will, and indeed more Il-2s were to be produced than any other single aircraft type of any nation during the war; one out of every three Soviet aircraft built was to be a *Shturmovik*.

To make good some of the aircraft's early deficiencies, production began during 1942 of the improved Il-2m3. In this version the forward-firing 20 mm cannon were replaced by a pair of much more effective high-velocity 23 mm VYa cannon, against which only the armour of the larger tanks was proof. A rear gun position was also fitted behind the pilot's seat, the gunner being provided with a heavy BS or UB 12.7 mm machine gun. To prevent an unacceptable loss of performance caused by the substantial increase in all-up weight, a more powerful AM-38F engine of 1,750 hp was installed. The first of these new machines appeared over the front in August 1942, the

An armourer prepares 100 kg bombs for loading into the wing racks of an Il-2, on which a fitter is still at work. *Passingham/-Klepacki Coll.*

unexpected presence of the gunner catching many German fighter pilots unawares at first; losses to fighter attack were at once reduced dramatically.

Following their early experiences, the *Shturmovik* units were now modifying their tactics. Instead of a horizontal approach at 50 metres, a shallow dive was found to be more effective, whereby the full weight of fire-power and offensive load could be directed with greater concentration and accuracy. This also proved to have a greater

Ilyushin Il-2m3 *Shturmovik*. Note the area of extensive armour protection around the engine and crew compartment and the gun armament — 2 x 23 mm VYa cannon and 2 x 7.62 mm ShKAS machine guns in the wings, and 1 x 12.7 mm Beresin machine gun in the rear cockpit.

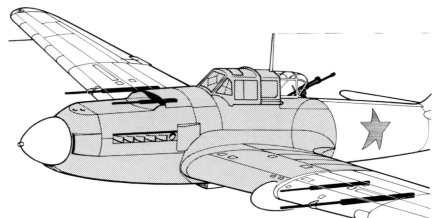

Ilyushin Il-2m3 'Shturmovik': armament alternatives

a) 8 x RS-82 or RS-132 rocket projectiles
b) 4 x 100 kg bombs on internal racks
c) 2 x 250 kg bombs on external racks
d) 6 x 50 kg bombs: 4 on internal, 2 on external racks
e) Four canisters of small fragmentation bombs

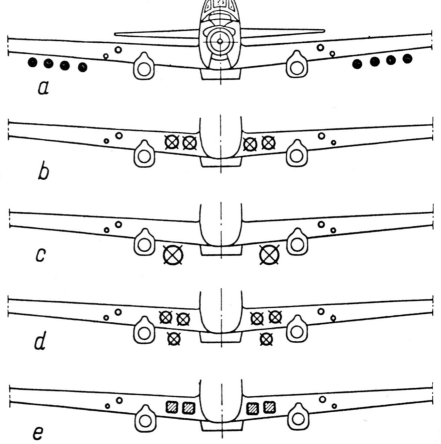

Ilyushin Il-2m3
'*Shturmovik*':
details of armament
installations

a) Under (left) and
head-on views
(right) of the port
inner wing panel,
showing the main
undercarriage unit
nacelle and 1 x 100
kg bomb in posi-
tion in the inner
bomb cell, with the
outer cell empty.
b) Section (left) and
head-on view
(right) of the inner
wing panel, show-
ing a canister of 2.5
kg anti-personnel
bombs in the outer
bomb cell.
c) Head-on (left) and
side view (right) of
250 kg bomb on
external rack under
the inner wing sec-
tion.
d) Under (left), head-
on (centre) and side
views (right) of two
RS-82 rocket pro-
jectiles on
launching rails un-
der the port outer
wing panels. (*Note*:
Normally four
rocket projectiles
were carried in this
position under each
wing).
e) Close up of an RS-
82 (82 mm cal)
rocket projectile on
its launching rail,
showing the elec-
trical activating
wires for firing.

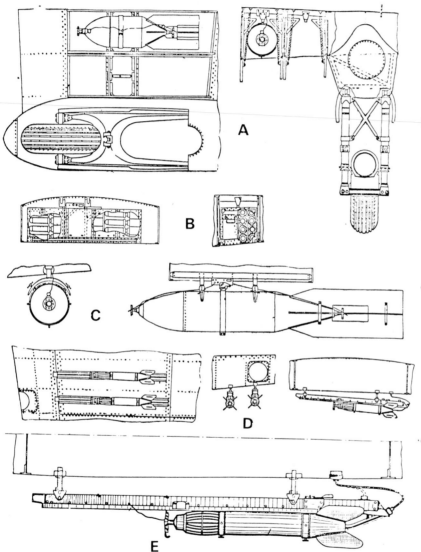

One of the 23-mm
VYa anti-tank can-
non is re-installed
in the wing of an
Ilyushin Il-2m3
after being cleaned
and overhauled.
*Passingham/
Klepacki Coll.*

adverse effect on the morale of the opposing forces, as the aircraft was within sight for a longer period, and its attack was more obviously directed at its target.

The main form of attack became an echeloned assault by from four to twelve aircraft, although a widely used tactic was to despatch Il-2s in pairs or fours on free-ranging armed reconnaissances, to attack targets of opportunity such as small convoys, trains, bodies of marching men, etc., directly behind the lines. On such sorties the aircraft would often make the first attack or two in a shallow dive, and then, with the defences fully alive, would make further attacks horizontally at very low level, using wooded spinneys and such like for cover. These latter approaches were referred to as 'guerilla attacks'. During major offensives designed at achieving breakthroughs in well-defended lines, concentrated attacks would be made in full regimental or divisional strength, or even on occasions in Corps strength of several hundred *Shturmoviks*.

The improved tactics were demonstrated by the veteran 4th ShAP after their re-equipment. The aircraft approached at a height of about 800 metres, flying at 300 km/h. It was positioned so that the target was kept on the pilot's left, and he then dived on this at an angle of 30 degrees, firing when in range· and departing in a tight turn after releasing any bombs or rockets he was carrying.

The Soviets had been among the first to attempt close control between ground assault aircraft and a controller with the tanks on the ground. At first this had to be done visually, since the radios installed in the aircraft up to 1941 proved next best to useless. However, better sets were installed during 1942 and late that year a system of very close co-operation was worked out during the Stalingrad fighting, between fighter-escorted Il-2s and the commanders of tank formations. This system was employed and developed with increasing efficiency throughout the rest of the war.

Meanwhile the 4th ShAP, which had moved to the Southern Front during the year, became the first Guards *Shturmovik* regiment, its title being changed to that of 7th Guards ShAP. It was to remain one of the premier Soviet *Shturmovik* units throughout the war.

GERMAN DEVELOPMENTS

The obvious obsolescence of the Ju 87 had not been ignored by the Luftwaffe, and although a cleaned-up and more powerful version, the Ju 87D, was in production and had still to reach the front at the start of 1942, work was underway to find a replacement. During 1939 the prototype of an armoured twin-engined ground attack aircraft, of basically similar concept to the Il-2, had flown — the Henschel Hs 129A. Test of a small batch by II(Schlacht)/LG 2 had rejected it for service, due mainly to its unsuitable Argus engines. Not until early 1942 were production versions of an improved model, the Hs 129B, becoming available for service; this version was powered by captured French Gnôme Rhône 14M radial engines.

Like the Il-2, the centre section and cockpit area of this aircraft were constructed mainly of welded armour plate. Integral armament included a pair of 20 mm MG 151/20 cannon and a pair of 7.9 mm MG 17 guns, all mounted in the fuselage. Alternative versions could carry either a bombload (two SC 50 bombs, or two canisters each containing 48 x 4½ lb SD 2 anti-personnel fragmentation bombs, or a single SC 250), or under-fuselage gun packs carrying either four additional MG 17s or a single 30 mm MK 101 cannon with 30 rounds. The latter installation was to be the most widely used in service.

II(Schlacht)/LG 2 had withdrawn to rest at the end of 1941, and was used during early 1942 as part of the basis of a new two-*Gruppen Schlachtgeschwader* 1. In May 1942 the new unit moved to join *Luftflotte* 4 in South Russia, to take part in the summer offensive in the Crimea, aimed at the capture of the Caucasus. II(Schlacht)/LG 2 had been incorporated into II/SchG 1, while I/SchG 1 introduced the Hs 129B in its 4. *Staffel*, the other *Staffeln* operating Bf 109Es and Hs 123s like II *Gruppe*.

Messerschmitt Bf 110E-2 '*Zerstorer*', or heavy fighter, which was employed with good effect for general ground attack duties on the Eastern Front during 1941-42. This is an aircraft of 13(Z)/JG 5, which operated from Kirkenes on the Arctic coast during summer 1942. It was flown by Lt Hans-Bodo von Rabenau.

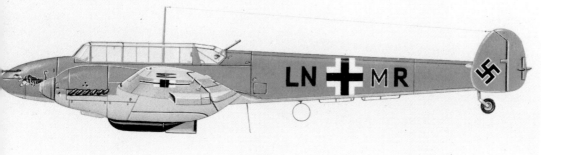

The German answer to the Il-2, the Henschel Hs 129B, entered service with the new SchG 1 in summer 1942, seeing its debut during the advance into the Caucasus. The aircraft seen here has a 30 mm MK 101 cannon in a fairing under the fuselage. It also appears to be carrying clusters of SD 4 hollow-charged bombs beneath the wings. *Bundesarchiv*

Involved in the battle for Sevastopol, the new *Geschwader* was to undertake much close support work, including anti-tank operations. The new Hs 129 suffered almost at once from engine trouble due to dust injestion, but even when in the air failed to achieve any notable results against the Soviet tanks with its cannon armament. This was finally traced to lack of familiarity with the MK 101 gun, and in September the unit was withdrawn for firing practice. During this period more success was gained using the new SD 4 bomb, a small hollow-charge projectile of some 9 lb weight, which featured good penetrative qualities when dropped on the thinner top armour of the tanks. Aiming accurately remained the major problem with the weapon however.

Henschel Hs 129B of 8(Pz)/SG 1 during April 1943. This aircraft was flown by one of the top Luftwaffe 'Panzerjägern', Oblt Rudolf Heinz Ruffer, *Staffelkapitän* of this unit. Ruffer ended the war credited with the destruction of 72 Soviet tanks.

During 1942 II/SKG 210 had reverted to its original designation of II/ZG 1, while I/SKG 210 had become a new I/ZG 1, since the duties in which these units were involed were so clearly those of the *Zerstörer*. These units moved to the command of *Luftflotte* 4 during the year, whilst I and II/ZG 26 were disbanded, and the *Zerstörergruppe* in Norway shrank to a single *Staffel* and became a part of *Jagdgeschwader* 5. *Luftflotte* 4 also now had control of four of the *Stukagruppen*, while *Luftflotte Ost*, which had replaced *Luftflotten* 1 and 2 in control of the air units supporting Army Groups North and Centre, retained three. A new Hs 129 *Staffel* was

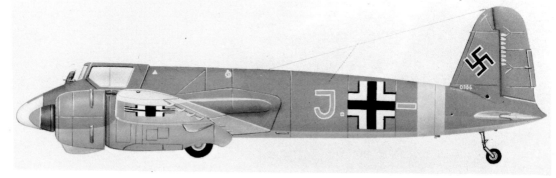

Junkers Ju 87D dive-bombers were introduced to service in the Soviet Union during 1942, these aircraft operating not only with the Luftwaffe, but also with the air forces of Hungary and Rumania on this front. Here Rumanian ground crew are completing the attachment of a pair of SC50 bombs to the auxilliary underwing racks of one of these aircraft.
Squadron/Signal Archives

formed in September 1942 to support Army Group Centre, and was attached to *Jagdgeschwader* 51 as *Panzer Jäger Staffel*/JG 51. It was now planned to re-equip the elderly Bf 109Es in the *Schlacht* units with *Jabo* versions of the Focke Wulf Fw 190A fighter as soon as possible.

During late 1942 one *Gruppe* of SchG 1 operated from the airfield at Morozovskaya, from where part of the giant airlift to the encircled 6th Army at Stalingrad was taking place. The presence of the unit, together with StG 2 and JG 3 was to protect the base against any Soviet attack by land or air. Following a Soviet breakthrough on the

1942 saw the introduction of the first examples of the Focke-Wulf Fw 190A *Jabo* to service. This particular aircraft has an unusual load comprising no less than 8 x SC 50 bombs, four beneath the fuselage and two under each wing.
Franz Selinger

This German photograph of a crash-landed LaGG-3 fighter shows well a typical fighter installation of three RS-82 rocket projectiles under the wing.
Passingham/ Klepacki Coll.

Efforts by the Luftwaffe to produce a viable anti-tank aircraft during 1942 led to the fitting of large-calibre, high-velocity guns to a number of aircraft types. All were tested operationally with a *Versuchskommando für Panzerbekämpfung* early in 1943, and amongst the types on hand were some of these Junkers Ju 88P-2s, fitted with a pair of 37 mm BK 3,7 guns in a massive fairing under the fuselage. In the background is a Junkers Ju 290 four-engined transport aircraft.
IWM

Stalingrad front, such a threat did indeed develop at dawn on December 24, 1942, when an armoured force was spotted from the air approaching over the open steppe. *Schlacht*, Stukas, fighters and bombers all attacked repeatedly throughout the day, causing the Soviets to abandon their thrust after suffering heavy losses, and retreat. This secured the base until it was evacuated the following month.

By this time heavier German and Soviet tanks — PzKw VI Tigers on the one side, KV Is and IIs on the other — were appearing at the front. Both combatants had already found bombs of dubious value against heavy tanks, whilst these new armoured monsters were proving impervious to the 30 mm guns of the Luftwaffe and the 23 mm weapons of the Red Air Force. Both therefore strove to introduce a more effective aerial weapon, and each was to reach the same basic solution at about the same time.

Henschel Hs 129B
fitted with a
higher-velocity
30 mm MK 103
cannon beneath the
fuselage. This
weapon was to
prove considerably
more effective
against Soviet tanks
than the earlier
MK 101.
Bundesarchiv

During 1942 development was carried out in Germany to fit a variety of aircraft with larger-calibre anti-tank weapons. The latest Bf 110G was fitted with a BK 3.7 gun of 37 mm beneath the fuselage, the normal pair of 20 mm MG 151 cannons in the lower fuselage being deleted. A pair of similar weapons were fitted beneath the wings of a Ju 87D, to become the Ju 87G, while a Ju 88A-4 was converted to carry a 75 mm KwK 39 gun in a large fairing beneath the forward fuselage in place of the normal bomb-aimer's position. A small

Henschel Hs 129B
'*Schlacht*' aircraft
of the Luftwaffe,
which was con-
structed on similar
premises to the Il-2.
Note the forward
fuselage is formed
almost entirely
from heavy armour
plate, in this case
including the firing
tubes of the fixed
armament of two
20 mm MG 151/20
cannon and two
7.9 mm MG 17
machine guns.

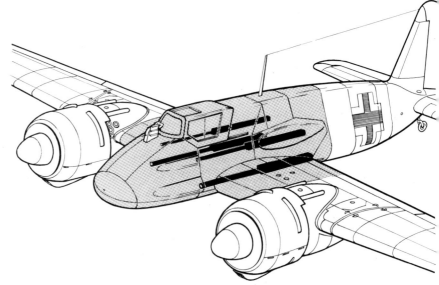

production batch was produced as the Ju 88P-1, the gun being
replaced by a PaK 40 anti-tank gun of similar calibre. A later
development as the P-2 featured a pair of 37 mm BK 3.7s as an
alternative. The Hs 129B was also adapted to carry either a BK 3.7, a
50 mm BK 5, or a 30 mm MK 103 (a development of the MK 101 with
higher muzzle velocity). One was also tested with the heavy PaK 40.

To test the Bf 110 and Ju 88 anti-tank aircraft in action, a
Versuchskommando fur Panzerbekämpfung was formed early in
1943, seeing action in the Crimea during the spring. By this time all
available Bf 110G production was required for the night fighter force,
while the Ju 88P suffered from several shortcomings. The 75 mm
gun was hand-loaded, thus offering a very low rate of fire, while the
massive fairing and long barrel of the gun rendered the aircraft
unwieldy and slow, making it an easy target for ground fire and
fighters.

While the Ju 87G was also slower and less manoeuvrable than the
standard D model, it was both available in quantity for conversion to
the anti-tank role, and featured a rate of fire from its two
automatically-fed guns far superior to that of the Ju 88P. The up-
gunned Hs 129B-2 was also satisfactory, these two types thus being
selected to equip an increased *Panzer Jäger* force.

During this period the concern over the superior Soviet armour
appearing at the front led to the creation of the post of *Führer der
Panzer Jager*, under whose control came the five Hs 129B Staffeln
now available (4 and 8/SchG 1, 4 and 8/SchG 2, PzJäg/JG 51
together with the test units — the Ju 87G PzJagStaffel, 1/ZG 1 with Bf
110Gs, and *Staffel* 92 with Ju 88P-1s.

The real tank-killer! The BK 3.7 emerged from the Germans' tests as the most practical and effective air-borne anti-tank weapon for the Luftwaffe. It was fitted to both the Hs 129B, and the Ju 87D (re-designated Ju 87G), seeing service in both aircraft during the massive Kursk battle of mid-1943. Here one of these guns is being serviced beneath the wing of a Ju 87G. *Bundesarchiv*

The Soviets meanwhile had also produced effective 37 mm anti-tank cannons, and had two types available, the N-37 and the 11 P-37. These guns could even pierce the thick armour of a Tiger tank with relative ease, and during the spring of 1943 a further improved version of the Il-2m3 began to appear from the production line featuring two of these guns in place of the 23mm., while it also introduced an improvement in its defensive armour.

KURSK

On July 5, 1943 Germany staked all on a last great offensive in the East. A massive 'pincer' operation had been planned to nip off a Russian salient in the line near Kursk. Unfortunately for the Germans, Soviet Intelligence was well aware of these plans, while delays in the implementation of Operation *Zitadelle* had allowed the Red Army to complete the construction of defences in unprecedented depth.

What followed was probably the decisive battle of the war; it was certainly the biggest tank battle of all time; but also, it was the occasion on which anti-tank aircraft played a major role for the first time. The German Panzer IVs and Tigers were reinforced by the latest PzKw V Panthers, and by small numbers of the giant Ferdinand self-propelled guns. The Soviets fielded vast numbers of T-34s, KV-1s and IIs. The first days of the offensive saw savage air fighting, whilst the Russian forward defences reeled under the power of the onslaught as the Panzer spearheads bit deep into them — deep, but by no means deep enough.

The Soviets waited three days for the Germans to feed in their

For the Kursk battle the Soviets had also improved the anti-tank capabilities of their *Shturmoviki*. This Il-2m3 features the long-barrelled 37 mm N-37 gun, which was to prove as effective against the German Tigers and Panthers as was the BK 3,7 against the T-34s and KV-1s. Note also the RS-82 rockets on their launching racks. *Jean Alexander via Passingham/Klepacki Coll.*

reserves, and for the edge to be taken off the attack. On the third day their new 37 mm-armed Il-2s appeared over the tank spearheads in greater numbers than ever before, employing their 'Circle of Death' tactics. Formations of *Shturmoviks* flew past the advancing Panzers, slightly to one side, then circled to attack from the rear in shallow dives. The rear of the tank was always its least well-armoured area, incorporating engines, fuel tanks, radiators etc. Following the initial attack, the Il-2s climbed away to circle the area and attack again — a grotesque 'Merry-go-round' of fire and tungsten steel that could be maintained for anything from 15 to 30 minutes. On that terrible July 7 9th Panzer Division lost 70 tanks in 20 minutes in this manner, according to Soviet accounts; 3rd Panzer Divison suffered two hours of almost continuous attack, at the end of which some 270 tanks were out of action and 2,000 casualties had been suffered. Finally 17th Panzer Divison suffered the longest agony of all; following four hours of Il-2 attack, the division was practically wiped out. Of its 300 vehicles with which it began the day, only some 60 remained when the assault was at last over.

Next morning the Soviets threw in a counter-attack west of Bjelgorod, aiming at the flank of II SS Panzer Corps. This was spotted by a section of Hs 129s on patrol, and following their report, all available *Schlacht* units were thrown in to break up the impending attack before it could develop. I and II/SchG 1 were available with two *Staffeln* of Hs 129Bs and four newly-equipped with Fw 190s. 4 and 8/SchG 2, recently arrived from Italy, were also under the overall

command of *Hauptmann* Bruno Meyer of SchG 1, a veteran *Schlacht* pilot. Each *Staffel* had 16 Hs 129Bs operational on this day, and they attacked in turn, one unit taking up the assault while that which had gone before returned to the base at Mikoyanovka to refuel, rearm and return. Meanwhile the Fw 190 *Jabos* swept in to rain SD 1 and SD 2 anti-personnel cannisters on the infantry supporting the attack, and to strafe them with 20 mm cannons. After an estimated 50 tanks had been put out of action, the attack broke up in confusion, and fell back.

The *Schlacht* units had already been heavily involved in the fighting from the first day of the offensive, but this was the first occasion on which the Luftwaffe was able to employ its *Panzer Jäger* in such concentrated strength. The Stukas at this time had been employed in attacking communications, though both StG 1 and 2 each now included a single Ju 87G *Panzer Jäger Staffel*. Initially these had operated independently, but in small numbers and with their low performance they were vulnerable to ground fire, and had not achieved much success. At this stage the indomitable *Hauptmann* Rudel of StG 2 employed one of these aircraft to achieve real success, whereupon all the Ju 87Gs were at once gathered under his command. Rudel's approach was like that of the Il-2s — from the rear, and carried out at an altitude of 15-30 feet. Unlike the Soviet aircraft, his machines lacked both speed and protective armour, but he overcame these disadvantages by employing supporting bomb-carrying Ju 87Ds to suppress the Soviet light anti-aircraft defences.

The Soviet counter-attack of July 9 was but a tiny taste of what was

Il-2m3s played a major role in the Kursk battle, taking a heavy toll of German armoured divisions. This formation is led by a presentation aircraft, bearing the legend 'Avenger'. *Passingham/ Klepacki Coll.*

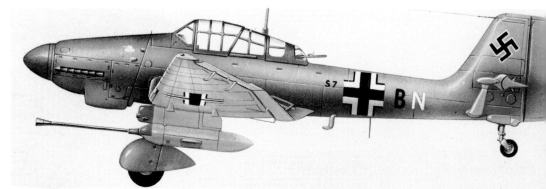

Junkers Ju 87G *'Panzerjäger'* of 10(Pz)/SG 3 late in 1943. These aircraft were introduced to service earlier in the year, seeing considerable action at the Battle of Kursk.

to come however, for on 11th the Red Army launched a mighty counter-offensive of their own to the north and east of Orel. This tore a hole in the German line, necessitating a premature end to the *Zitadelle* operations in order to stabilize the line here, lest a terrible repetition of the Stalingrad encirclement be achieved on an even larger scale.

As Soviet armour broke through to threaten the only reinforcement route to the Germans — the Bryansk-Orel railway — the Luftwaffe was thrown in in force. Practically every Luftwaffe unit in Russia joined in a three day assault in which the Stuka and *Schlacht* units played a major role. It was the last occasion in the East on which the Germans were able to achieve a real concentration of air power, and the results justified the effort. A major armoured breakthrough was halted and driven back by air attack, allowing the Wehrmacht to redeploy, seal off the rupture in the line, and fall back in good order.

REORGANIZATION

As autumn fell a complete reorganization and rationalization of the Luftwaffe ground attack units took place. Unil this time the *Stukageschwadern* had come under the control of the Bomber Inspectorate, whilst the *Schlacht* units had come under the wing of the fighters. Since in fact their role was so complimentary it was a logical step to bring them together under their own *Waffengeneral der Schlachtflieger*, and at this stage all such units became *Schlachtgeschwadern*, abbreviated not as before to SchG, but to a more simple SG. By this time all four *Stukageschwadern* had each added a 10 (*Panzer*) *Staffel* of Ju 87Gs, but it had already been established that all Ju 87-equipped *Gruppen* would be re-equipped with Fw 190s as quickly as production allowed.

A number of *Störkampfstaffeln* had been formed with elderly aircraft to copy the Soviet practice of carrying out night nuisance raids. These were all now to be enlarged into *Nachtschlachtgruppen* (12 in all), and were to receive the Ju 87s as these were replaced in the SGs by the Focke Wulfs.

As part of the re-organization, all five Hs 129B *Staffeln* were formed into IV(Panzer)/SG 9 under Bruno Meyer, but the concentration so initiated was illusory, since the various *Staffeln* were scattered all along the front, as were other Luftwaffe units of all kinds. The other units involved in the re-organization were:—

Stukageschwader 1 became *Schlachtgeschwader* 1 (Soviet Union)

Stukageschwader 2 became I and III/SG 2 (Soviet Union)

Stukageschwader 3 became *Schlachtgeschwader* 3 (Italy and Balkans)

I/StG 5 became I/SG 5 (Norway)

Stukageschwader 77 became *Schlachtgeschwader* 77 (Soviet Union)

The *Jabo* part of II/SchG 2 became I/SG 4 (Italy)

II/SKG 10 became II/SG 4 (Italy)

The *Jabo* part of I/SchG 2 became III/SG 4 (Italy)

The *Jabo* part of SchG 1 became II/SG 2 (Soviet Union)

III/SKG 10 became I/SG 10 (Italy)

IV/SKG 10 became II/SG 10 (Italy)

The Fw 190 series which replaced the Ju 87 were superb aircraft, being a direct adaptation of one of the best all-round fighter aircraft of the war. The initial version was a conversion of the Fw 190A-4 fighter, fitted to carry an SC 250 bomb beneath the fuselage. Later versions of the A model for the *Schlachtflieger* could carry SC 500 or even SC 1000 (2,200 lb) bombs beneath the fuselage, or an SC 250 beneath the fuselage and four SC 50s under the wings. In these versions the armament was restricted to a pair of 20 mm MG 151 cannon in the wing roots and two 7.9 mm MG 17 machine guns above the nose. The normal fighter version carried a further pair of 20 mm cannon further outboard in the wings.

Two specialized close support versions of the A model were also produced, which featured outboard cannon of the 30 mm MK 103 type. Subsequently the Fw 190F and G models were produced specifically for the *Schlacht* units. The G, which appeared first, was a fighter-bomber capable of carrying an SC 1000 bomb, while the F, which featured additional armour to the engine cowling and underside of the fuselage, carried one SC 250 and four SC 50s, with an armament of two 20 mm and two 7.9 mm or 13 mm machine gunns. This typical Fw 190 *Jabo* achieved a maximum speed of 394 mph at 18,000 feet and 342 mph at sea level on the 1,700 hp of its BMW 801D radial engine.

With such a performance the aircraft remained a potent fighter, well-able to look after itself in the hands of a competent pilot. There lay the rub however, for losses in the ranks of the Stukas had been far from light, while pressure of operations and lack of fuel prevented anything more than a rudimentary conversion for the ex-Ju 87 pilots, who received virtually no training in air-to-air gunnery, aerobatics or fighter tactics.

Junkers Ju 87G
Panzerjäger in
flight.
Bundesarchiv

Conversion went ahead apace however. I/SG 5 in the far North received the first Fw 190s in January 1944, followed by II/SG 2 the next month. Other *Gruppen* followed at the rate of about one every six weeks, although Rudel and some of his III/SG 2 were to retain their faithful Ju 87s to the end of the war.

There was now little doubt that the Soviets hated and feared the *Panzer Jägern* above all other Luftwaffe aircraft, just as the Germans loathed the *'Zementer'* ('Concreter') or Il-2. Red Army tank units went to considerable lengths to mislead their attackers as to the results of their fire, often attaching smoke cannisters to the tanks, which were fired when under attack to give the impression that the vehicle had been destroyed. The German pilots soon learned to distinguish this ruse from the real thing, being satisfied only when they saw a burst of flame. An indication of how effective these aircraft could be in the hands of an expert is given by *Hauptmann* Rudel's record; he was credited with the personal destruction of 519 tanks by the end of the war — though this was the highest total by far for any pilot.

However the Soviet light flak — always effective at low level — was steadily increasing in intensity as production allowed gun establishments to be increased, and by mid 1944 the *Panzer Jäger* units were frequently suffering 20% casualties. Undoubtedly the gun carrier proved the most effective aerial weapon of the war against tanks, far surpassing in accuracy the various rocket projectiles favoured by the Allied nations other than the Soviet Union.

Following the battles of 1943, the next major fighting in which *Schlacht* units were deeply involved was over the Crimea and Black Sea coast, where in spring 1944 a major Soviet offensive was launched. SG 2's new Fw 190Fs and Gs took a big part in this fighting, and due to shortage of fighter aircraft, frequently became involved in aerial combats, the *Geschwader* claiming 247 Soviet aircraft shot down during the first six months of the year. Untrained for such duties,, the *Schlachtflieger* threw up the occasional gifted pilot who possessed the attributes to excel in such circumstances, the most notable of whom was SG 2's *Leutnant* August Lambert. He personally accounted for more than a third of the unit's total claims at this time, having made 90 claims by mid-May, 70 of them in just three weeks at the height of the battle. Flying numerous sorties every day he claimed more than ten in a day on several occasions whilst still undertaking his normal ground support duties. In this same period he was also to claim over 100 vehicles and guns destroyed.

The greatest tank killer of them all — the Ju 87G flown by Major Hans-Ulrich Rudel of SG 2. Maj Rudel's claimed personal score amounted to 519 destroyed Soviet tanks by the end of the war. The aircraft is seen here in the Krivoi Rog area in October 1943. *Franz Selinger*

Such activities were the exception however, for the normal tactic of the Fw 190 *Jabos* was to avoid combat wherever possible. Formations of the aircraft would approach the target at relatively low level — an average of about 7,000 feet — splitting into two separate formations of approximately equal numbers as they came up. One formation would then bomb in a 60-70 degree dive, releasing at about 1,000 feet, and following up with a low level strafe. These aircraft would then regain altitude to cover the second formation, which then made a similar assault. Normal reaction when intercepted was to jettison any bombs or auxiliary fuel tanks, and go flat out for home at zero feet.

Increasing weight of USAAF daylight bombing attack on the Reich during 1943 and early 1944 had already led to the withdrawal of some fighter units from the Eastern Front, but the invasion of Normandy on June 6, 1944 resulted in even more such withdrawals, leaving only some half dozen *Jagdgruppen* in the East. The *Schlacht* units were forced as a result to carry an even greater burden of responsibility, while chances of enjoying the luxury of a fighter escort became slim indeed. Now the Fw 190Fs and Gs had frequently to escort the remaining Ju 87s — particularly the *Panzer Jägers*.

On June 22, 1944, exactly three years after Operation 'Barbarossa' had opened the war in the East, the Soviets launched a massive offensive on the Centre of the front, supported by no less than 6,000 aircraft. Many of these were Il-2s and Pe-2s, which operated virtually without interference, as did the fighters, which descended in droves to join as never before in the general strafing attacks. For the first time

Soviet armourers servicing and re-arming the 20 mm ShVAK wing cannon of an Il-2. Passingham/ Klepacki Coll.

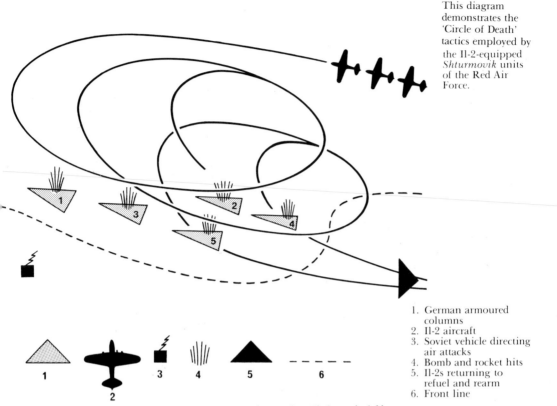

1. German armoured
   columns
2. Il-2 aircraft
3. Soviet vehicle directing
   air attacks
4. Bomb and rocket hits
5. Il-2s returning to
   refuel and rearm
6. Front line

Soviet aerial superiority was overwhelming, the Il-2s winkling out guns, tanks, anti-tank guns, observation posts, machine gun nests, and every available other taarget. The Pe-2s had now developed dive-bombing to a fine art, some experienced pilots being referred to as aerial snipers, for their ability to destroy pinpoint targets such as observation posts with great accuracy. Indeed it was said that some of these pilots could plant their bomb 'right down a factory chimney'. These aircraft saturated German airfields and communications with bombs, also attacking artillery, mortar batteries and troop concentrations.

After the shock of the initial onslaught, the Germans attempted to counter-attack during mid-July, but here the Red Air Force played the role that the Luftwaffe had undertaken in similar circumstances the previous year. On 15 July one such attack came under a continuous five hour air assault from 2,000 aircraft. So great was the concentration of attack that at one point 1,000 aircraft were over the front at the same moment — all of them Soviet!

While still employing their 'Circle of Death' when sufficient Panzers were engaged to warrant it, the Il-2s employed their other tactics to a larger extent now — either a low level run, firing almost horizontally into the target (such attacks were effective against troops

Presentation Pe-2FT dive-bomber, with its pilot, Lt Ilya Presnyakov and his crew at the time of the Kursk fighting in 1943. This view shows well the dorsal gunner's 12.7 mm BS machine gun. *Novosti via Passingham/ Klepacki Coll.*

Growing numbers of Fw 190 *Jabo* aircraft steadily replaced the Ju 87Ds during 1944, and before the year was out this had become the most important German ground attack type on the Eastern Front. Here *Schlachtflieger* confer before a mission, their aircraft hung with SC 250 bombs. *Bundesarchiv*

and 'soft-skinned' vehicles); or against pill-boxes and othe individual targets, a dive attack was employed, with guns firing, an bombs or rockets being released at the same time.

Newer weapons employed included larger RS-132 rockets of 13 mm calibre, featuring either hollow charge heads for use again armour, or a solid head for demolishing buildings. Anti-personne fragmentation bomb cannisters, similar in concept to the Luftwaffe SD 1 and SD 2 containers, were also used, though to the end the gu armament remained the Il-2's most effective form of attack.

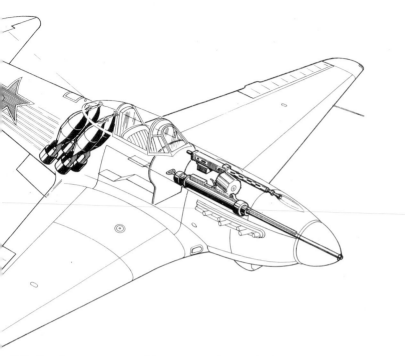

While the presence of large numbers of *Shturmoviks* and the ever-present Luftwaffe fighters during the early years of the war had prevented much use of Soviet fighters as fighter-bombers, as Soviet numerical superority increased, thought was once again given to this possibility. Yakovlev was requested to provide underwing bomb racks on his Yak-9 fighter, but revolted against such an idea as an aerodynamic abomination. To show that such a measure was not necessary, he re-designed the fighter to carry four 100 kg bombs *internally* behind the pilot. Stowed at an angle and released tail-first, this arrangement allowed the carriage of an unusually high bombload for an aircraft of this size and power; it was put into limited production as Yak-9B. For ground strafing other versions of the Yak-were built with the standard 20 mm nose gun replaced by a weapon of 37 mm or 45 mm calibre, while tests were even undertaken with a 57 mm gun.

Lavochkin's last fighter design to see widespread service before 1945, the La-7, could carry up to 200 kg (440 lb) of bombs on more conventional underwing racks.

Harried from East, West and South, the Luftwaffe was now in appalling trouble. Between June 1 and August 31, 1944 an incredible 1,074 aircraft were lost on all fronts by the Germans, including 1,345 *Schlacht* types. Coupled to this, fuel shortages were beginning to be seriously felt; these would soon become critical following the loss in September 1944 of the Rumanian oilfields, and of 'ersatz' oil production facilities to USAAF air attacks.

Fw 190A-3/U3 of a *Schlachtgeschwader* on a snowy Eastern Front airfield. The aircraft carries a single SC 250 beneath the fuselage, the wing racks remaining empty. *Bundesarchiv*

Henschel Hs 129B *Panzerjäger* with BK 3.7 gun, seen here on a snow-clad Luftwaffe airfield. *Franz Selinger*

By late 1944 most *Schlachtflieger* had converted to the Fw 190 including the Hungarian 102/1 squadron, which had previously operated Ju 87Ds. There was no longer much they could do however but make the occasional nuisance raid. Several units were withdrawn to the West during 1944, though most returned East before the end of the war. At this time production examples of the Hs 129B-3, carrying a 75 mm BK 7.5 gun beneath the fuselage appeared, whilst at last German rocket projectiles were fitted to some Fw 190s in October. These were 88 mm *Panzerschreck* missiles, converted from an infantry 'bazooka'-type weapon; six were carried by each aircraft. Two months later the doubly-powerful *Panzerblitz* of the same

Introduced by the Soviets during the last weeks of the war was the Ilyushin Il-10, a new *Shturmovik* developed from the Il-2, but of smaller and cleaner configuration, and with a substantially better performance. These aircraft feature long-barrelled 37 mm cannon in the wings, and carry two large rockets beneath each wing — probably RS-132 missiles. *Passingham/ Klepacki Coll.*

A Hs 129B-2 captured by Allied troops in May 1945 fitted with the experimental SG 131A *'Förstersonde'.* This novel anti-tank weapon consisted of a battery of six oblique downwards-firing rocket launcher tubes mounted behind the cockpit. The missiles were triggered automatically by a magnetic anomaly detector device, but this weapon proved rather unreliable during firing trials. *Franz Selinger*

alibre was tried, but in the event little use was made of either weapon.

During 1945, as the Allied armies moved further East and West, the rea of territory remaining in German hands steadily decreased, ringing all sectors under more frequent air attack from every side. chlachtflieger now frequently faced savage strafing attacks on their ases by long-range American P-51 Mustang fighters, and losses rose eeply, many *Staffel* and *Gruppe* leaders being killed at this stage. In larch 1945 a substantial proportion of the remaining gdgeschwadern were returned to the East, being thrown in to take art in the ground strafing. By now however, pilot quality was very w, and these units also suffered heavily. When fighting ceased in early May 1945, the *Schlachtgeschwadern* had almost ceased to exis

During the final year of war, the Soviet ground attack units ha
been able to develop the level of ground support given to the troops t
a very high degree, thanks to their being largely free of the Germa
fighters at last. In February 1945 an improved version of th
Shturmovik, the Ilyushin Il-10, entered action. Developed from th
Il-2, this was a slightly smaller and considerably cleaner aircraf
though every bit as heavily armoured. Powered by a 2,000 hp AM 4
engine, the aircraft in its standard form carried two fixed wing
mounted 23 mm NS-23 cannon and two 7.62 mm ShKAS machin
guns, as had the Il-2. The gunner however, sat in much close
proximity to the pilot, and was armed with a 20 mm cannon for rea
defence. As an alternative two 37 mm guns could be fitted in the wing
for anti-tank duties, or four NS-23 guns could be incorporated. Due t
the greater all-up weight in the latter case, the gunner's 20 mm wa
replaced by a lighter 12.7 mm UBT machine gun. The greater powe
and better aerodynamics of this aircraft offered a considerabl
increased performance, maximum speed rising to 315 mph. The mai
undercarriage members retracted backwards, turning through 9
degrees to lie flat in the underside of the wings in a manner similar t
that employed in the Curtiss P-36/P-40 Hawk family of fighters. Th
Il-10 was to continue in service long after the war, serving with man
other Communist air forces besides that of the Soviet Union. A sa
note late in the war however was the loss in action on February 1
1945 of their father of dive-bombing, Ivan Polbin. Twice made a Her
of the Soviet Union and promoted Major General at the head of th
1st Guards Bomber Air Corps, Polbin had continued to f
operationally throughout the war, an inspiration to his men. H
sacrifice had not been in vain.

5 Western Developments

The start of 1941 found ground attack and fighter-bombing activity ɔ all intents and purposes at an end in Western Europe. While the ₹AF was making the first tentative steps towards an air offensive cross the Channel, the Luftwaffe was planning no resumption of its ay offensive on Britain. While the bombers continued their 'Blitz' by ight, the Stuka units were gradually dispersed to the Mediterranean, ɪe Balkans, and to East Prussia and Poland, ready for the new assault n the Soviet Union. The *Zerstörergeschwadern* were either converted ɔ night fighting, disbanded, or accompanied the Stukas.

By the early summer of 1941 most of the bombers had gone too, ·aving in Western Europe under *Luftflotte 3*, five *Gruppen* of ɔmbers — four of them anti-shipping units — two *Jagdgeschwader*, single *Zerstörergruppe*, and a variety of reconnaissance *Staffeln*. In ·ermany itself were mainly night fighters, although two ɪgdgruppen protected North-Western Germany and the Baltic ɔast. A few more units in Norway provided the necessary air defence ɪ that country's seaboard.

To bring the Luftwaffe fighters to battle during the spring, the AF had flown a number of large fighter sweeps, together with some ɔmbing raids by small formations of light bombers with large .corts. Pairs of fighters flew 'Rhubarbs' — low-level nuisance raids ɪ conditions of reasonable cloud cover, designed to keep the defences ·yed up, and to strafe targets of opportunity. Following the invasion ˸ Soviet Union in June 1941 these activities were increased in an fort to pull back Luftwaffe units to the West — an aim in which they ɪanifestly failed.

To face attacks of this kind, the Luftwaffe *Jagdgeschwadern* had ɔerated locally in the interceptor role, requiring no offensive ɔplication of their *Jabostaffeln*, which in most cases reverted to ɔrmal fighter activity — in particular once re-equipped with new Bf ·9Fs. No British fighters at this time were even fitted for bomb rrying, although tests were being made with a view to the feasibility ˸ such activity by the Hurricane IIA, which was now appearing from ·e production lines. The Series 2 version of this fighter was provided ɪth underwing attachment points for 44 gallon long-range tanks,

First RAF fighter-bomber in Western Europe was the Hawker Hurricane IIB, which began operations in October 1941. Second unit to equip with this modification of the aircraft was 402 Squadron, RCAF, one of whose machines is seen in flight here, fitted with a pair of underwing 250 lb bombs.
IWM

which could also be used for the attachment of 250 lb General Purpose bombs.

Most of these aircraft were going direct overseas in mid-1941 however, while many squadrons were resting following the events of 1940, converting to Spitfires, providing air defence of more distant areas of the country, or being involved in the night defence of the South-East. Others were being posted to the Mediterranean in relatively substantial numbers.

At this time two further versions of the Hurricane II began to reach the squadrons, these being the Mark IIB, fitted with 12 x .303-in Browning machine guns, and the Mark IIC, with four 20 mm Oerlikon cannons — later changed to Hispano guns of the same calibre, but better reliability and muzzle velocity. Both these models of the aircraft were fitted for bomb-carrying with strengthened wing attachment points built-in right from the production line. When actually fitted with bomb racks, the Mark IIB usually had two of its machine guns deleted. The power of the Mark IIC's armament made it an ideal strafing aircraft, and it was issued to several units for use against shipping, or on 'Rhubarbs'. Two units particularly — 1 and 3 Squadrons — received the aircraft for night intruding missions during which they hunted German bombers over their own airfields and strafed targets of opportunity.

Two further squadrons were now equipped with the twin-engined Whirlwind, and while doubts about the suitability of this aircraft as a dogfighter were being expressed, its propensities for ground strafing with its four-cannon nose battery were beyond doubt. The first such mission was carried out by 263 Squadron, which strafed Luftwaffe airfields at Maupertus and Querqueville on June 14, 1941.

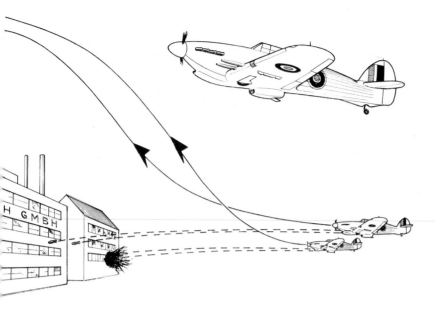

Hurricane IIB fighter-bomber tactics for attacking buildings used during the 1941-43 period.

Development of tactics for the Hurricane IIB as a fighter-bomber were undertaken by the Air Fighting Development Unit during the late summer, and by the autumn two squadrons had been prepared for this new role. The tactics devised were to become classic for the next two years' cross-Channel operations. The aircraft would approach the French or Belgian coast, flying at zero feet, climbing at the last moment to cross the coastline at 6,000 feet. Flight to the target would continue at not more than 18,000 feet. Initially the Hurricanes would attack in pairs, and when buildings were their targets, would dive down to approach them in level flight just above the ground, pulling up at the last moment, while releasing the bombs, so that they continued to move directly forward into the target.

Later, with larger numbers available, and with German flak defences in a greater state of readiness, a more subtle approach had to be made. In a typical attack on an airfield, sections of four aircraft flying in line abreast would approach their target at right angles, turning through 90 degrees to begin their attack dive, preferably from out of the sun. Ideally further sections also began their dives at the same moment from slightly different directions, in order to split the flak defences. The dive was usually made at 65-70 degrees, the steady aiming part of this being kept down to about 10-12 seconds. Bomb release took place at between 5,000 and 12,000 feet, all aircraft then turning in pre-arranged directions. Escorting fighters meanwhile went down in shallow dives to circle the target whilst the fighter-bombers completed their attacks.

Hawker Hurricane IIC, showing the installation of an underwing 250 lb bomb. The first RAF fighter-bomber, the IIC were employed in this role over Western Europe, in North Africa, from Malta, and in Burma.

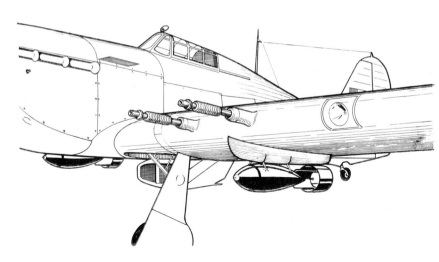

Bombing-up a 402 Squadron Hurri-bomber.
The Public Archives of Canada

The first RAF fighter-bomber attack in Western Europe was undertaken on October 30, 1941 by Hurricanes of 607 Squadron which attacked a transformer station at Tingry. Next day 402 Squadron, RCAF, sent eight aircraft to raid the airfield at Berck-sur-Mer. By the end of the year the Hurricane IIB was cleared to carry a pair of 500 lb bombs, though generally only the 250 lb weapon was used by these aircraft.

The possibility of making similar attacks was being investigated by the Luftwaffe during this period, and within a month of these first British attacks, a new *Staffel*, 10(Jabo)/JG 2 was added to *Jagdgeschwader* 2, equipped not with the older Bf 109E, but with the Bf 109F-4B, which carried a single SC 250 bomb beneath the fuselage. The Bf 109F was already beginning to be superseded in the two *Jagdgeschwadern* of *Luftflotte* 3 at this time by the first examples of the new Fw 190A. Within a few weeks a second such unit, 10(Jabo)/JG 26, had been formed in the other *Jagdgeschwader*, with similar equipment.

Attacks were initially made on various targets along the South coast of England — mainly port installations. Before long however, the favourite prey of the *Jabos* became coastal shipping, and during the first half of 1942 10(Jabo)/JG 2 claimed the sinking of 20 vessels totalling an estimated 63,000 tons. 10(Jabo)/JG 26 claimed only six vessels, but concentrated more of its attacks on inland targets such as railway stations, factories and gasometers. Indeed by this time the latter unit had just re-equipped with some of the precious new Fw 190A-4s — the first to be used for *Jabo* operations — and by September both *Staffeln* were flying this type, which with underwing drop tanks could carry their bombs nearly twice as far as the Messerschmitts.

An assault on German coastal shipping had been carried out throughout 1941 by Bomber and Coastal Command light bomber aircraft under the codename 'Channel Stop', but these operations had resulted in severe casualties. With the appearance of the first fighter-bombers this duty was largely handed over to Fighter Command at the end of 1941, pending the re-equipment of Coastal Command units with more appropriate Beaufighter and Mosquito aircraft. It

The first fighter-bomber examples of the Focke-Wulf Fw 190A-4 saw service in France with 10(*Jabo*)/JG 26. While carrying the same SC 250 551 lb. bomb of the unit's earlier Messerschmitt Bf 109Fs, the fitting of underwing auxiliary fuel tanks affectively doubled the range of these aircraft. *IWM*

was a costly business as the Hurricane units soon found out. During
February 1942 however, 607 Squadron was posted overseas, but it
aircraft and several of its pilots helped form 174 Squadron, which
became operational on 28 March as a fighter-bomber unit with an
attack on Berck-sur-Mer airfield.

1942 was to be a year of considerable expansion for the RAF, no
least for Fighter Command. Whilst more Spitfire units were formed
to continue the succession of sweeps and bomber escorts, which wer
flagging somewhat under the assault of the superior Fw 190s, the
fighter-bombers were not neglected. 175 Squadron was formed for
this role with Hurricane IIBs in April, while 1 and 3 Squadrons wer
joined in their cross-Channel intruding at night by 32, 43, 87, 247 and
a newly-formed 486 (RNZAF) Squadron. Several squadrons of Arm
Co-operation Command were also re-equipped at this time with
new long-range reconnaissance-fighter, the North American
Mustang I, which would be used on 'Rhubarb'-type operations befor
the end of the year. However during March 402 Squadron exchange
its Hurricanes for Spitfires, and resumed pure fighter duties.

The first concerted use of ground support aircraft over Wester
France at this time by the RAF, occurred on August 19, 1942, when
large-scale landing was made at Dieppe by a substantial force. 17
Squadron operated in the fighter-bomber role, whilst 3 and 4
Squadrons strafed with their cannon Hurricanes. The Germans wer
under the impression that a full-scale invasion had begun, and threw
in everything they had. Against flak and fighters, RAF losses wer
high, 174 Squadron alone losing five aircraft. In opposition the *Jab*
aircraft of JG 2 and 26 were very active throughout the day, attackin
ships and landing craft.

Shortly after the Dieppe raid the Whirlwinds were cleared to carry
pair of 250 lb bombs each, this load later being increased to two 50
pounders. 263 Squadron began this new duty during September, an
137 Squadron the following month. The Anglo-American landing
in North-West Africa took away several units at this time, includin
32 and 43 Squadrons, but a new fighter was entering service at th
time which was soon to become the most important weapon in th
RAF's ground attack armoury.

Designed as an interceptor, the Hawker Typhoon proved a failur
in this role due to its poor high altitude performance. Powered by
massive Napier Sabre engine of 2,180 hp, and armed with four 20 m
cannons, it had made a good showing at low altitude, and soc
proved to be the best answer to the Fw 190 *Jabos* which wer
appearing with increasing frequency over the South-Eastern counti
as the year wore on, and were extremely difficult to intercept.

The first unit to convert to these aircraft was 56 Squadron, followe
in April by 609 Squadron, and by 486 in July. The aircraft suffere

substantial teething troubles, the new power plant giving many problems, whilst a weakness in the rear fuselage had to be remedied following several fatal crashes. By the end of the year many of these problems had been resolved, and during the last quarter of 1942 seven new Typhoon units were formed — 181, 182, 183, 193, 195, 197 and 198 Squadrons. At the same time 184 Squadron was formed to equip with the Hurricane IID, the anti-tank aircraft which had already seen service in North Africa. Following early experience in the Desert, an additional 386 lb of armour plating had now been added to these aircraft.

Meanwhile, with the build-up of Allied bombing attacks on Europe, the *Jabo* element remained the main offensive effort of the Luftwaffe for the time being, joined by some small night bombing raids by Do 217s of KG 2. One particularly successful raid at this time was made by 30 *Jabos* escorted by 30 Bf 109 and Fw 190 fighters. Canterbury was the target, on a busy October Saturday afternoon. A similar raid on London on January 20, 1943 was met by a strong force of Typhoons and suffered nine losses, though substantial damage and many casualties were caused in the East End.

Operations against Allied shipping in the Bay of Biscay were becoming more costly to the Luftwaffe at this time, due to the appearance of growing numbers of Coastal Command long range fighters. Ju 88C-6 heavy fighters, and a few Bf 110Gs had managed to achieve little, so a unit of Fw 190 *Jabos* was felt more likely to be able

A year after the first Hurribomber sorties were made, the Westland Whirlwind fighter, two squadrons of which were serving with the RAF in England, were cleared for fighter-bomber operations, and during early 1943 these were to undertake a large part of the RAF's raids of this sort. Here an aircraft of 263 Squadron is seen being bombed-up from a train of 250 lb bombs. *Central News Agency*

to look after itself. As already mentioned in Chapter 3, III/ZG 2 in North Africa had become III/SKG 10 at the end of 1942, and early in 1943 it was decided to form two further *Gruppen* under this designation, to raise *Schnellkampfgeschwader* 10 to full *Geschwader* strength. Consequently a *Geschwader Stab* (Headquarters Flight), I and II *Gruppen* were formed in February 1943, all equipped with Fw 190A-4/U8 aircraft.

Unfortunately for the Luftwaffe, the Fw 190 proved to have insufficient range for the task, and during the early spring these units were replaced by the remaining *Gruppen* of ZG 1, the last *Zerstörer* unit at that time still operating in the Soviet Union, which now moved to the Brest area to undertake these new duties. Meanwhile the two new Fw 190 *Gruppen*, led by Major Günther Tonne, moved up to the Channel area to join in the assault on Southern England and the coastal shipping.

On arrival 10(Jabo)/JG 26 — which had been redesignated 10(Jabo)/JG 54 in February — and 10(Jabo)/JG 2 were redesignated 14 and 15/SKG 10, forming a new IV *Gruppe* for the *Geschwader*. This brough *Luftflotte* 3 to its peak *Jabo* strength since the Battle of Britain, with some 127 Fw 190A-4/U8s on hand. Several more attacks were made on Southern England targets, some of them at night, but the offensive was short-lived. In June 1943, with an invasion of Sicily or Sardinia threatening in the Mediterranean, *Stab*, II and IV/SKG 10 were transferred to Sicily to join III *Gruppe*, only I *Gruppe* remaining in France with about 50 aircraft.

With the RAF, the main weight of fighter-bombing at the start of 1943 was being borne by the two Whirlwind squadrons, backed up by 174 and 175 Squadrons' Hurricanes. Both Whirlwinds and Typhoons were now flying night intruder sorties as well, railway locomotives being the main prey of these flights; the latter fell easy victims to these aircraft's four 20 mm cannons. The night intruder Hurricanes had now ceased to operate, and all such units still in the United Kingdom were converting to Typhoons.

These powerful aircraft had been cleared to carry two 500 lb bombs underwing now, and were slated to become the main fighter-bombers during the year. The first bombing sorties were carried out during March 1943 by 181 and 182 Squadrons, followed in April by 183. Others soon followed, including 174 and 175 Squadrons which converted to these aircraft from their Hurricanes during the spring, continuing their bombing activities from June/July onwards.

A final model of the Hurricane also became available during 1943 — the Mark IV — and this aircraft was to introduce into action an important new weapon during the year. The Hurricane IV had a 'universal' wing which could be fitted with cannon or machine guns and could carry beneath it bombs, 40 mm anti-tank runs, or rocke

The first use of rocket projectiles by the RAF was against shipping targets during 1943. They became available for use by fighter-bombers for ground attack purposes during that year, and the first such aircraft to carry them was the Hurricane IV. A test installation on a tropicalized aircraft is shown here, depicting clearly the four-rail launcher which was to remain standard for RAF aircraft in Western Europe for the rest of the war. *Crown Copyright*

projectiles. The latter had first been tested on a Hurricane II late in 1941, six being fitted beneath the wings on long launching rails. A very crude weapon, the rocket consisted of a 3-in diameter cast iron pipe fitted with lugs to connect to the launching rails, and a set of small cruciform fins for in-flight stability. Filled with a solid propellant charge, it was fired from the front end, the burnt charge being exhausted through a central orifice. This somewhat complicated system was necessary to prevent too great a change in the centre of gravity, which would result if tail firing were employed, burning all the propellant at the rear end of the missile first. A warhead was screwed on the forward end, consisting of either a 60 lb high explosive charge or a 25 lb armour piercing shot. Alternatively a concrete practice head could be fitted. In service the 60 lb head became standard after 1943.

The ballistic characteristics of this missile left much to be desired, as it suffered badly from trajectory drop, making accurate aiming difficult except in a very steep dive. The long and cumbersome launching rails were non-jettisonable, and inflicted a fairly substantial performance loss on the aircraft, so that a high level of air superiority was desirable before they were put into wide use. Against large, slow shipping targets they were extremely effective however, a salvo of eight rockets being said to have the striking power of a broadside from a destroyer's guns. It was on anti-shipping operations that they were first used operationally during 1942, being fired from Royal Navy Swordfish and Coastal Command Liberators.

First use of the
powerful Hawker
Typhoon as a
fighter-bomber was
made late in 1943,
this aircraft carry-
ing two 500 lb.
bombs with ease.
Here one of these
missiles can be seen
in place beneath
the battery of
20 mm cannon in
the wing.
IWM

By the end of 1942 they had been satisfactorily tested on the Typhoon, but it was the Hurricane which was first to use them over Europe, carrying four beneath each outer wing. These could be electrically fired, either in pairs or as an eight-rocket salvo.

164 Squadron had converted from Spitfires to Hurricane IVs in January 1943, flying these aircraft initially fitted with 40 mm anti-tank guns. 184 Squadron, which had seen no action with its Mark IIDs, also received Mark IVs, while 137 Squadron handed its remaining Whirlwinds to 263 Squadron in June, and also received these new aircraft.

This unit flew the first Hurricane IV sorties on June 23, 1943, though with 40 mm cannon rather than rockets. The big gun's brief debut in Western Europe involved train strafing, rather than anti-tank operations. Six days later however 184 Squadron made Fighter Command's first operational rocket strike, Hurricanes under a Typhoon escort attacking coastal shipping with eight 60 lb missiles each. A similar attack on 20 August by 164 Squadron brought all three units into action. The first concerted rocket attack followed on 2 September, when 164 and 137 Squadrons, again escorted by Typhoons, attacked the Zuid Beveland lock gates at Hansweert, Holland. One lock gate was destroyed, although several losses were suffered. A few days later Abbeville airfield was well rocketed, and the missile had become fully operational.

A month later on October 22 the last attack by Whirlwinds was made, when twelve of these fighter-bombers bombed Cherbourg harbour. In November 263 Squadron gave up these aircraft for Typhoons. During October 181 Squadron had made the first rocket attacks with these latter aircraft. As the year approached its end Allied ground support aviation in Western Europe was just about to come of age. With an invasion of France now firmly in the planning stage, a substantial tactical air force, modelled on that operating in Italy, was about to be formed. For this purpose the RAF brought home many experienced officers from the Mediterranean to form the new 2nd Tactical Air Force, while the USAAF shipped the complete Headquarters organization of their 9th Air Force to England from the

Soon to be the main 2nd Tactical Air Force fighter-bomber and anti-tank aircraft for the invasion of Normandy, Typhoons of 198 Squadron are seen here on Manston airfield. The aircraft in the foreground was flown by Sqn Ldr J.R.Baldwin, who later became commander of one of the Typhoon Wings, and was also top-scoring pilot on this type, with 16½ aerial victories.
R.A. Lallemant

same area. These new air forces would have the benefit of the experience of the Allied Tactical Air Force in Italy to call upon, and would be able to put straight into effect many of the systems and tactics laboriously worked out in the crucible of action by the latter's units.

To provide the initial equipment of these new forces, the RAF had 18 squadrons of Typhoons with two more about to form, three squadrons of Hurricanes, several army co-operation Mustang units, a Group of light day bombers, and a large number of Spitfire squadrons. The USAAF had four medium bomber groups (equivalent each to an RAF Wing), a fighter group, a reconnaissance group, and four more groups of fighters on the way.

At the same time as this mighty new force was forming, the nemesis of the Luftwaffe *Jabos* in Western Europe had just about been reached. Allied fighter interceptions had made losses too heavy for day raids to continue. Unlike the Allied fighter pilots, most pilots of SKG 10 were ex-Stuka men, untrained for fighter operations, and consequently ill-equipped to look after themselves when attacked. Consequently morale had fallen low, and only night sorties could be flown. The 'Baby Blitz' was by then in full swing — a series of reprisal attacks in return for Bomber Command's depredations over Germany. It was as an adjunct to these raids that I/SKG 10 was operating as the year drew to a close.

Also entering RAF service in growing numbers during 1943 was the Mark VI version of the De Havilland Mosquito — the first fighter-bomber variant of this versatile aircraft. A 250 lb bomb is just being winched into place under the wing, but additional bombs were also carried internally in the fuselage bomb-bay. *De Havilland via Chaz Bowyer*

6. Sicily, Italy and the Balkans

Following the Axis surrender in North Africa, Allied air power reigned almost totally supreme over the Mediterranean. The fighter-bomber units of the RAF and USAAF had come a long way since the haphazard days of mid 1942, but their employment and tactics still rested on a very 'ad hoc' basis. Despite their telling involvement at the critical moment in the Mareth battle, they were still not closely geared to the requirements and needs of the ground forces, expending much of their effort in interdiction work against the enemy's lines of supply and communication.

Some rationalization of equipment took place before operations across the Mediterranean commenced. The Curtiss P-40 Warhawk/Kittyhawk was to be the main Allied fighter-bombing type, the Hurricanes and Airacobras with their lesser performance were to remain behind in Africa for coastal and convoy patrol and protection duties. Those Spitfire units which had begun carrying bombs over Tunisia were to be released from this duty for the time being, returning to their time-honoured duty of air superiority fighters, and escorts to the Curtiss types and other bombers. The USAAF's P-38 Lightnings would be involved mainly in escorting the heavy bombers of the 9th and 12th Air Forces, but could when necessary, double as fighter-bombers. The Americans however were about to introduce into action a new close support type — the North American A-36A 'Invader'.

Following the Battle of France the USAAF had ordered land versions of Navy dive-bombers in the light of the achievements of the Ju 87. The A-24 — a version of the Douglas SBD — had been the first delivered, but performance in the South-West Pacific area had proved disappointing. Deliveries of the Curtiss A-25 (SB2C) and Vultee A-35A Vengeance did not begin until the superiority of the single-seat fighter-bomber had become obvious, and neither type saw active service with the USAAF.

Before these early disappointments had been fully realised a requirement for a powerful single-seat dive-bomber/strafer was formulated, and in October 1941 the Brewster XA-32 was ordered. This large aircraft carried a wing armament of four 37 mm

Introduced to action in the Mediterranean just before the invasion of Sicily in July 1943, the North American A-36A took part in the pacification of the fortified Italian island of Pantelleria. Developed from the early versions of the P-51 Mustang as a dive-bomber, the A-36A proved more successful as a fighter-bomber, in which role two full Groups of these aircraft were to give sterling service until mid-1944. *American Official via IWM*

cannons, an internal bombload of 3,000 lbs, and achieved a maximum level speed of 311 mph at medium altitude. However, production delays due to Naval orders for Brewster products and to factory mismanagement, led the USAAF in desperation to order the A-36A, a dive-bomber version of the North American P-51 Mustang, which was in production in its early fighter-reconnaissance form for the RAF.

Ordered in August 1942, the A-36A began rolling off the production lines within a month, and by early 1943 two fighter-bomber groups of three squadrons each were equipped with the aircraft; one of these had already arrived in North Africa. Armed with six .50-in machine guns, four in the wings and two in the underside of the nose, the aircraft carried two 500 lb bombs on underwing racks, and reached 356 mph on its 1,325 hp Allison V-1710-87 engine. Although fitted with dive brakes, these were

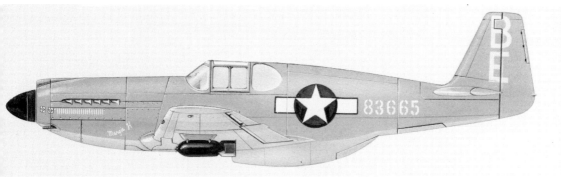

usually wired shut in practice, the aircraft operating as a normal fighter-bomber — a role which it filled most adequately.

Further development of specialized attack aircraft in the States included the mighty Vultee XA-41, a 23,000 lb monster with a 3,000 hp engine which reached 353 mph with a fixed armament of four 37 mm cannon *and* four .50-in machine guns, plus an internal bombload of 7,000 lbs. The twin-engined Beech XA-38 strafer featured a nose-mounted 75 mm cannon, together with machine guns. The USAAF had by then become convinced of the superior flexibility of the fighter-bomber, or of the light bomber converted for strafing, and no production order followed.

The first A-36A sorties were flown over Sicily on June 6, 1943 by aircraft of the 27th Fighter-Bomber Group, while later in the month this unit joined P-40 fighter-bombers of the USAAF in attacks on the fortified Italian island of Pantelleria. An assault by bomb-dropping aircraft of all types on this island led to its surrender to invading forces without a fight, while the nearby island of Lampedusa also surrendered after only one days' air attack.

Preliminary bombardment of Sicily was then left mainly to the level bombers, whilst the fighter-bomber units prepared themselves to support the ground forces once the invasion had commenced. For this purpose the various units moved to airfields on Malta, Gozo and Pantelleria by the beginning of July, from where air support could be easily furnished. Available for these activities were four US Fighter Groups (33rd, 57th, 79th and 324th) with three squadrons each of P-40s, two US Fighter-Bomber Groups (27th and 86th) with three squadrons each of A-36As, and one RAF Wing (239) with five squadrons of Kittyhawks. Another P-40 Group, the 325th, would on occasion join the fighter-bombing, though its main duty involved escorting the bombers of the Allied Strategic Air Force, a task which it shared with three P-38 groups.

The variety of loads carried by the P-40s and Kittyhawks at this stage was wide, including 20 lb and 40 lb fragmentation bombs,

North American A-36As were developed from the early versions of the P-51 Mustang to provide the USAAF with a viable dive-bomber when the purpose-built air-craft of that type currently in production and service proved to have too restricted a per-formance for front-line service. Employed mainly as a normal fighter-bomber, the A-36A enjoyed a successful, if rather brief career in Italy and Burma. This is an aircraft of the 522nd Squadron, 27th Fighter-Bomber Group of the US 12th Air Force, flown in Italy by Lt Lawrence W.Dye.

During the defence of Sicily the Italian *Regia Aeronautica* employed a variety of fighter-bombing types, one of which was this adaptation of the Fiat G-50bis fighter. Employed by the 50° *Stormo Assalto*, the aircraft achieved little success, many being put out of action on the ground by Allied bombers, as has been the case with this captured example. *IWM*

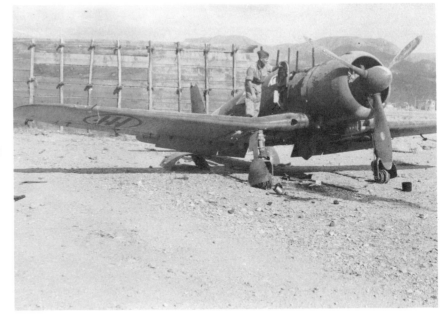

A Reggiane Re 2002 Ariete fighter-bomber of the 239° *Squadriglia*, 102° *Gruppo*, 5° *Stormo Assalto*. These aircraft entered service just before the invasion of Sicily in July 1943, seeing two months' action before the Italian armistice of 9 September. They were subsequently employed over the Balkans by the Italian Co-Belligerent Air Force.

250 lb GP bombs — one or two beneath the fuselage, one beneath each wing, or one under each wing and one under the fuselage — a 500 lb bomb, or on occasions a 1,000 pounder — a load pioneered by the 325th Fighter Group.

In Sicily the fighter-bombers were to be mainly concerned with attacks on lines of communication once more, attacking convoys on the island's narrow roads to deny supplies to the Axis troops and delay deployment of armour or reinforcements.

Facing the Allies at this stage were a number of German and Italian units, many of them equipped with various types of ground attack aircraft. This collection could barely be called an air force, since the two national components operated separately with very little liaison between them. The units in Sicily itself had already suffered heavy losses of aircraft on the ground during the pre-invasion bombing raids, while the early warning system was almost breaking down.

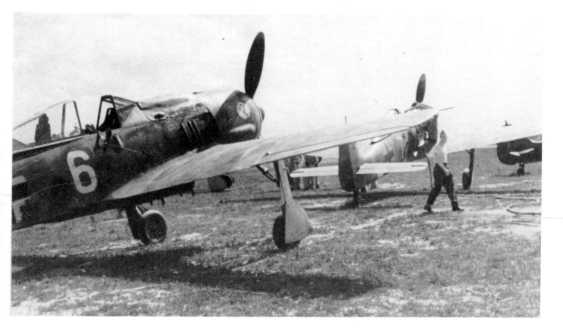

In Sicily were *Stab*, II, III and IV/SKG 10 with Fw 190A-4/U8 fighter-bombers, *Stab*, II and IV *Gruppen* having only arrived from Western France the previous month. The similarly-equipped *Stab*, I and II/SchG 2 were based on Sardinia, but were in the process of making a move to Sicily when the invasion began. In South and Central Italy, with the bomber and reconnaissance units, were the Ju 87Ds of StG 3, joined by the Bf 110s of *Stab*, III and 10/ZG 26. III/ZG 1 with its Me 210s had recently returned to Germany, but the Messerschmitt Bf 110-equipped II/ZG 1 had arrived in Sicily from the Brittany coast of France to take its place. The Stukas were not to be committed to the battle for Sicily however, whilst ZG 26 was in the main retained for bomber interception duties over Italy.

Just before the invasion began the *Regia Aeronautica* moved to Southern Italy a *Gruppo* of Macchi C.200s fitted for fighter-bombing, and two specialized ground attack units, 5° and 50° *Stormo Assalto*. The latter unit was flying elderly Fiat G-50bis fighter-bombers, whilst awaiting re-quipment with a new type. This latter had recently entered service with 5° *Stormo*, and was the Reggiane Re 2002 Ariete. Powered by a 1,175 hp Piaggio P.XIX R.C.45 Turbine-B radial engine, this aircraft was armed with two 12.7 mm Breda-SAFAT machine guns, and two 7.7 mm guns; it could carry up to 1,433 lbs of bombs, and achieved a maximum medium altitude speed of 329 mph.

As soon as the invasion began on July 10, 1943, further units were rushed to the area, mainly from Sardinia. To join the units in Southern Italy went 159° and part of 158° *Gruppo Assalto* with the

Over Sicily, Salerno, Anzio, and during the drive on Rome, the main German riposte by day was offered by the Fw 190A fighter-bombers, elements of which were present in Italy until mid-1944. These aircraft of I/SG 4 are seen on a Central Italian airfield early in 1944.
Bundesarchiv

Although used in small numbers in Tunisia as fighter-bombers, the first large scale use of the Supermarine Spitfire in this role was made by 7 SAAF Wing during the invasion of Italy in September 1943. Here tropicalized Spitfire VCs of 2 SAAF Squadron, each carrying a single 250 lb bomb under the fuselage, patrol over the Sangro River at evening during the Autumn of that year. *IWM*

G-50bis, 121° *Gruppo Tuffatori*, and half 103° *Gruppo Tuffatori*, both recently re-equipped with Ju 87Ds, while the rest of 103° *Gruppo*, together with one gruppo of 15° *Stormo Assalto*, the latter equipped with CR 42s, moved to Sicily itself.

In the fierce fighting which followed the Axis ground attack units were committed almost entirely against the Allied shipping armada, which was anchored off the coast, unloading men and supplies. In the face of an overwhelming fighter 'umbrella' they suffered fearful casualties, achieving very little. Among the losses were the commander of the Luftwaffe's SKG 10, Gunther Tonne, killed in a take-off accident, and *Colonello* Nobili, commander of the *Regia Aeronautica's* 5° *Stormo Assalto*. The new Re 2002s of this unit were slightly more successful than other Italian aircraft, sinking the transport *Talambra* on the first day, and claiming a hit on a British battleship on July 13. Heavy bombing raids on Axis airfields destroyed many of those aircraft which survived the shambles in the air, and by mid July Axis aerial resistance by day had all but ceased.

Allied fighter-bombers met little interference from opposing fighters during this period, and were able to operate virtually at will, moving to landing grounds in Southern Sicily as soon as these had been secured by the ground forces. Ground fire was heavy however, and losses to this cause were by no means light, the two A-36A groups losing 20 aircraft between them in as many days for example.

After much initial Allied success in Southern and central Sicily, the fighting centred on the North-Eastern corner of the island during the final fortnight of the campaign. Here the main target for thee fighter-bombers became the vital Straits of Messina, across which all Axis supplies had to flow. The narrow Straits carried a mass of shipping of all types, defended by one of the heaviest Flak concentrations yet encountered. As a result attacking aircraft were often prevented from pressing home their assaults, and the German divisions on the island were both kept supplied, and subsequently evacuated with most of their equipment.

After a pause for regroupment, 8th Army units crossed to the 'toe' of Italy on September 3, 1943, supported by 239 Wing, RAF, and by the US 57th and 79th Fighter Groups. During the next four days the advancing troops were subjected to some small-scale strafing attacks by Re 2002s of 5° *Stormo Assalto*, but these were the last offensive sorties of the war for the *Regia Aeronautica*.

A large landing by Anglo-American forces went ashore at Salerno just to the south of Naples, on September 9, on which day an armistice with Italy came into force. The new invasion area was at maximum range for Allied fighters, and as a result no fighter-bomber support was initially forthcoming. Luftwaffe reaction to the new attack was made mainly by the Fw 190s of SKG 10, which were now operating from the Foggia area in Eastern Italy. Still weak in numbers after the Sicilian debacle, these *Jabos* made small-scale attacks by day on Allied shipping, and on the build-up of supplies ashore. They had to run the gauntlet of patrolling Allied fighters during these attacks, and these continued to take a toll of them. By this time SchG 2 had gone, as had the *Zerstörergruppen*, all recalled to Germany, together with several other Luftwaffe units.

As German counter-attacks against the beachhead built up, the longer-ranging A-36As, which had operated briefly in the fighter role, resumed their bomb-carrying activities, dive-bombing roads leading to the Salerno area, and strafing German convoys. Their efforts were responsible for slowing down the arrival of at least one Panzer column. Meanwhile units supporting 8th Army's advance in the south were moving to newly-captured airfields on the mainland, and these too flew north to add their weight to the assault.

As the beachhead expanded, airstrips were constructed by combat engineers with all speed, and at the earliest possible opportunity — within four days of the landings — the 33rd, 86th and 324th Groups had moved in, together with RAF and USAAF Spitfires.

With the 8th Army advancing from the south, and the beachhead secure, the Allies were able to press on, and the Germans began to

Still the main Desert Air Force fighter-bomber during 1943 and much of 1944, the Curtiss Kittyhawk continued to give faithful service to the end of the war in Italy. This Mark III carries a 1,000 lb bomb under the fuselage, another such missile being seen in the foreground. It is an aircraft of 5 SAAF Squadron, serving with the RAF's 239 Wing.
IWM

retreat. Naples fell on October 1, while British landings were made at Bari and Termoli on the East coast, speeding the occupation of all Southern Italy. Amongst the prizes was the airfield complex around Foggia, which would become an important Allied air base area for the rest of the war. The necessity of evacuating Foggia had forced the removal of Luftwaffe units from there to the Rome area, and as a result few German aircraft were seen during the rest of 1943. It was at this stage that the Luftwaffe ground attack units were re-organized, II/SKG 10 becoming II/SG 4, whilst III and IV *Gruppen* became I and II/SG 10.

During the advance through Southern Italy, 8th Army's supporting air units, now known as Desert Air Force (DAF), had been joined by a further fighter-bomber wing, 7 SAAF Wing, which had now re-equipped with Spitfire Vs. A remaining Kittyhawk squadron was transferred to 239 Wing, bringing that formation to six-squadron strength, while the South African unit fielded three squadrons of the new fighter-bombers — many of which carried four 20 mm cannons instead of the usual two — plus a single unit of Spitfire IX fighters to provide cover. The Mark Vs initially carried a single 250 lb bomb under the fuselage.

With the capture of Foggia the two RAF wings and their supporting US Fighter Groups (57th and 79th) moved in with other DAF units to support the continued advance in the east. In the west, under the control of XII Tactical Air Command, the other two P-40 groups and the two A-36A units provided support for the US 5th Army, advancing towards Rome. Together the DAF and XII TAC formed Mediterranean Allied Tactical Air Force, comprising light bombers, fighter-bombers, fighters and tactical reconnaissance aircraft for the direct support of the armies in the field. However weather was now deteriorating and the Germans entering strong positions in an unbroken line across the country in the area between Naples and Rome. Here the advance gradually ground to a halt for the winter.

It was at this stage, as the fighting became more static, that the system of forward control for ground support activities which was subsequently to be employed throughout the Anglo-American tactical air forces, was formalized and perfected. Known as the 'Rover system', a liaison headquarters referred to as 'Rover Tentacles' was attached to each Army Corps, which made the necessary arrangements for the level of air support to be provided during periods of major ground activity. A pre-arranged number of aircraft would be allotted, which would keep 'Cab Ranks' of fighter-bombers overhead at all relevant times. It became the practice of the US XII TAC to commit the whole agreed force the night before, while DAF practice was to retain a percentage uncommitted for sudden emergencies. In the air 8th Army support formations operated under the codename Rover Paddy, while those operating in support of 5th Army became Rover Joe.

Actual control from the ground was exercised by a Forward Control Unit, codenamed Rover David. Rover David was in contact with the various Corps, and received their requests regarding specific bombing attacks. It was also in touch with tactical reconnaissance aircraft over the front lines which reported appropriate targets. On receipt of such information, the controller passed it to the 'Cab Rank', which was on station for up to half an hour at a time, over direct VHF/RT. The target was identified by reference to a special gridded map of the area — usually based on recent air reconnaissance photo overlaps — which all pilots carried.

This map was to a scale of 1/100,000, and was divided into squares 500 metres by 400 metres. These small squares were lettered A-Z horizontally across the map, and numbered vertically. Each block of 26 x 26 squares was then given a larger Grid letter (see diagram). Thus an order for an attack would begin with the map reference, for instance "Grid B, C25..." prefacing the description of the target. The need for speed and clarity in the system was great, due to the limited time on station of each 'Cab Rank'. Occasionally the fighter-bombers would rendezvous with a tactical reconnaissance aircraft, which would then lead them to the target, although this system was not always favoured as it resulted in a dilution of direct control.

The initial equipment of a typical 'Rover David' included:—
    1 SCR 522 VHF R/T set and a spare
    1 No.19 HF Army (W/T) set
    2 No.9 HF Army (W/T) sets
    2 No. 22 HF Army (R/T) sets
    Battery charging units and telephones
Vehicles required to carry this equipment:—
    1 Quad tractor for the large sets
    2 White Scout cars
    1 Armoured car
    2 Jeeps with trailers
    1 Standard Utilicon truck
Personnel:—
    1 Army Major (Army Liaison Officer)
    1 RAF Officer — Controller (a pilot resting from operations, usually of Flight Lieutenant rank)
    26 Other Ranks

Methods of attack were also becoming more formalized as a result of experience. For instance it had become apparent that for attacks on airfields large numbers of small fragmentation bombs could be expected to achieve better results than fewer heavier bombs. Extension rods fitted to the nose fuse of 250 lb bombs to cause their explosion slightly above the ground greatly improved the fragmentation effect, but when aircraft were dispersed in pens it was necessary in the majority of cases to achieve a direct hit to be certain of inflicting more than minor damage.

Fighter-bombers in Italy were to operate in a dive to a much greater degree than in Western Europe, due to the basically mountainous topography of the country. It became the normal practice to operate in sixes, approaching the target area in a tight 'box' of two threes, line abreast:—

+ + +

+ + +

From 7-8,000 feet above, the aircraft would move into line astern, slightly echeloned, just before the attack, and then dive as steeply as possible to the lowest practicable altitude — bomb release frequently took place as low as 1,000 feet. Often the flight leader would attack alone whilst the rest circled the area, then climbing up to direct the other five's attack in relation to his own bomb burst. However if flak defences were heavy, four would orbit to draw off the fire of the guns while the leader and his No.2 went in.

When the line was static the Flak could often be kept down by counter-battery fire from Allied artillery, but of course this was only possible when the target attacked was fairly close to the lines. Aiming allowances in the dive were generally left to each pilot's personal experience. No theoretical basis was worked out, but the results achieved were remarkably good. However the manner in which the leader frequently made the initial attack resulted in a rather high loss rate of more experienced pilots.

If strafing was to follow the bombing, the six aircraft generally reformed first to test for any awakening of the Flak defences. However the mountainous nature of the terrain meant that — particularly when attacking moving motor transport — it was necessary to open fire at a substantially greater range than had been the case in the Desert, or in France. Despite this pilots learned quickly to allow sufficient forward deflection for moving lorries, while also making a considerable allowance for bullet drop. Gunnery standards reached in Italy became very high — particularly in 7 SAAF Wing.

No sooner had the various units settled into their more permanent bases than two important events took place. Firstly, fighter-bombers from Eastern Italy flew across the Adriatic Sea to attack targets in Southern Yugoslavia and Albania, in support of partisan forces there. This area was to become of increasing importance from an operational point of view to the ground support units as time went on. Secondly, during early November,

A favourite Allied ground attack type in the Soviet Union, the Far East and the Mediterranean, was the Bell P-39 Airacobra. This aircraft was particularly suited to these duties due to the presence of a heavy 37 mm cannon in the nose, which is seen here being loaded. The aircraft shown here is serving with the Italian Co-Belligerent Air Force in Southern Italy, which employed the Airacobras to strafe targets in Yugoslavia and Albania as a part of the Allied Balkan Air Force.
Stato Maggiore

The Americans introduced the Republic P-47D Thunderbolt to fighter-bomber operations late in 1943, and this aircraft steadily replaced all others in the ground support role with USAAF units in Italy. During 1944 some of these aircraft were fitted with underwing clusters of Bazooka-type rocket-launching tubes. Three of the 4.5 in missiles for these new weapons can be seen (minus their nose fuse caps) standing in front of the port tube cluster, whilst a crewman is inserting one into a launcher in the starboard cluster. *Republic Aviation via W.N.Hess*

the US 57th Fighter Group began re-equipping with Republic P-47D Thunderbolts. These large, heavy and powerful aircraft had been employed only as long-range bomber escorts before, but were now to become the chosen USAAF fighter-bomber, steadily replacing all other types in this role. With 2,300 hp provided by the Pratt and Whitney R-2800-21 engine, the 13,500 lb Thunderbolt carried a very heavy fixed armament of eight .50-in machine guns in the wings, while shackles beneath the wings and fuselage permitted the carriage of one, two or three 500 lb bombs, two 1,000 pounders, or a pair of 500 pounders plus a drop tank. This was virtually the same weight-carrying capability of a twin-engined light bomber, but in this case the pilot also had available a formidable fighter with a top speed of 433 mph. The aircraft was also extremely tough, and with its large air-cooled radial engine was to prove much less vulnerable to ground fire than the smaller P-40s, A-36As and Spitfires, with their liquid-cooled power plants.

During the winter, with the front fairly quiet, the fighter-bombers were mainly involved in interdiction missions against road transport, railway bridges and rolling stock, or on targets in Yugoslavia. In an effort to break the deadlock which had developed in Italy without resorting to an expensive frontal attack, a further major seaborne landing was planned, this time at Anzio, a small town on the coast just to the South-West of Rome.

To support this new venture, a number of DAF units were moved to the West to operate with XII TAC. Included were 7 SAAF Wing and the 79th Fighter Group. The landings took place of January 2, 1944, taking the Germans completely by surprise tactically — although strategically they had been expecting such a move to be made. At the same time an assault was launched on the West side of the German line in the Cassino area, in an effort to join forces with the spearheads from Anzio. However the defences at Cassino held, while delays in exploiting from the Anzio beachhead allowed the Germans to concentrate sufficent forces to form a perimeter, and then to counter-attack.

Throughout these operations Allied air power was supreme, fighter-bombers supporting all the fighting while weather allowed, and particularly taking an active part in breaking up German counter-attacks at Anzio. During the same period Luftwaffe Fw 190 *Jabos* attacked the beachhead repeatedly, although in small formations.

Approaching the area usually in sixes, and covered by Bf 109 fighters, they dived steeply on their targets, before making a low level run for their home airfields. The units taking part were I and II/SG 4, the latter having been recently reinforced by a *Staffel* of aircraft from Norway, which had previously been 14(Jabo)/JG 5. Losses were severe at this time, caused by both defending fighters and Allied AA fire. Indeed at this stage the units in Italy were taking virtually the whole flow of replacement *Schlacht* pilots from the training schools, so much higher were their losses than among those units on the Eastern Front.

With the relatively limited opposition being met in the air over Italy during the latter part of 1943, a number of units, both RAF and USAAF, had been withdrawn and posted to the Far East, while others moved back to Africa to rest and re-equip. This did not at first affect the ground support elements, but in February 1944 the US 33rd Fighter Group was posted to India. Its P-40s were left behind, and because of a shortage of replacement A-36As, which were no longer in production, these were passed to the 27th Fighter-Bomber Group. To make good this loss of fighter-bomber strength in the west, the 57th Fighter Group moved its P-47s over from the east the following month, although shortly afterwards the Spitfires of 7 SAAF Wing moved back to the latter area, where they were to be very active over Yugoslavia, now carrying two 250 lb bombs beneath the wings of each aircraft.

Meanwhile during March the 79th Fighter Group began replacing its P-40s with P-47s, followed soon after by the 27th, which changed its designation from Fighter-Bomber to Fighter Group, though its duties remained unchanged. By mid summer the 86th and 324th

March 1944 saw the introduction to service with the Desert Air Force of the North American Mustang III, the Merlin-engined air superiority P-51B. Employed by the RAF in Italy as a fighter-bomber, this superb aircraft is seen here carrying two 1,000 lb bombs under the wings — a load similar to that carried by many light bombers of the period. It is an aircraft of 260 Squadron, the first unit to use the Mustang III in Italy.
F.F.Smith

Groups would have followed suit, all US XII TAC fighter-bomber units then having Thunderbolt equipment on strength. Meanwhile in March 260 Squadron in the RAF's 239 Wing had received the latest P-51B Mustang III aircraft. This, the supreme long-range bomber-escort fighter of the war, was also an effective fighter-bomber. Not quite so strong and indestructible as the P-47, and with only half the fixed armament, it could nonetheless carry up to 2,000 lb of bombs, though on most occasions its favoured warload was to be two 500 pounders. With these aircraft the Wing was to achieve one of its most notable successes of the war on May 5, 1944, when a force of Mustangs and Kittyhawks, all carrying 500 lb bombs, burst the wall of the Pescara Dam, this mission being accomplished without the loss of a single aircraft.

Many RAF fighter units were leaving Italy at this time to join 2nd Tactical Air Force which was being set up in England, and a considerable number of DAF's top leaders had also gone to aid in the formation of this new force. However, during May 1944 a part of 8th Army, together with 239 Wing, was moved across the country to aid in a new offensive to burst through the German line at Cassino.

During these operations fighter-bombers made attacks on strongpoints and gun positions which were frequently in heavily-defended mountain territory, and losses to German light Flak concentrations rose alarmingly. The collapse of the defences, coupled with a breakout at Anzio led at last to an Allied advance on Rome. No sooner had the Holy City been entered than the news began coming through of the landings in Normandy, and thereafter the Germans

First rocket projectiles to be used by the RAF units operating from Italy, were employed over the Adriatic Sea and Yugoslavian coast by Hurricane IVs of 6 Squadron. For these missions the Hurricanes carried an asymetric load, comprising a 45 Imp gallon auxiliary fuel tank under the port wing, and four 60-lb HE rockets under the starboard.
IWM

fell back to their Gothic Line defences North of Florence. With the situation both in France and the Soviet Union critical by late June virtually all remaining Luftwaffe units withdrew, fighters going to the West, while the remains of SG 4 moved to North Russia. Only a single *Nachtschlachtgruppe*, NSGr 9, remained to support the ground forces, equipped with Ju 87s.

American attention now turned to an invasion of Southern France and for this purpose most of the USAAF units moved to Corsica, from where they could attack either targets in Southern France, or in North-West Italy. At the same time a number of French *Groupes de Chasse*, newly-equipped with P-47Ds, joined the XII TAC units here as did three RAF Spitfire Wings. When Operation 'Dragoon' was launched on August 15, 1944, the forces in Italy lost altogether the support of XII TAC, and Desert Air Force became responsible for the whole Italian front at a time when a major offensive was about to be launched by the weakened Allied armies remaining in that country; their objective was the Gothic Line.

However 7 SAAF Wing now included five squadrons of Spitfires, all of which were soon to be equipped with Spitfire IXs, while due to the almost total lack of opposition in the air, the air-superiority Spitfire VIIIs of the four squadrons of 244 Wing had begun dive bombing and strafing sorties after the end of June.

GROUND ATTACK ACTIVITIES ELSEWHERE IN THE MEDITERRANEAN AREA

Whilst the Italian battlefront had seen the greater part of the close support operations in the Mediterranean area, there had been other activity of note elsewhere. In the Western Mediterranean, several squadrons of RAF Beaufighters had undertaken strafing operations albeit against surface shipping rather than ground targets. During 1944 these units moved to Sardinia, from where they continued to attack such targets in the area off the Southern coast of France, and that of North-Western Italy. In this they were joined by US P-39s and bomb-carrying French Spitfire Vs, together with a few specially converted North American B-25G and H Mitchell medium bombers which had been fitted with a 75 mm cannon and a number of .50-in machine guns in a special 'solid' nose.

Following the landings in Southern France on August 15, 1944 shipping targets disappeared, and while several units were disbanded, or posted away, some of the Beaufighters moved to Eastern Italy to operate over the Adriatic and Yugoslavia.

In the Eastern Mediterranean ill-fated British landings on the Aegean islands of Kos, Leros and Samos, beyond the range of adequate air and naval cover from Egypt and Cyprus, had brought out the Luftwaffe in force, and had seen the last successful daylight

On occasions escort fighters of the US 15th Air Force were employed on longer-ranging fighter-bomber duties in addition to their strategic missions. Here a Lockheed P-38 Lightning of the 96th Squadron, 82nd Fighter Group, carrying five aerial victory tallies on its nose, releases two of four 500 lb bombs during a level-flight bombing attack. *D.Weatherill via W.N.Hess*

dive-bombing operations in the West by the famed Ju 87s, StG 3 being moved to the area from Italy. The islands were soon invaded by the Germans with substantial British loss.

A long air and Naval war in the Aegean followed, strafing attacks being made on German-held islands, and on shipping supplying them. During November 1943 603 Squadron became the first unit in the Mediterranean theatre to be supplied with rocket projectiles. Carrying four beneath each outer wing on the squadron's Beaufighters, initially 25 lb missiles were employed with success against shipping, and against German radar stations — particularly on Crete and Rhodes.

The number of Beaufighter units in the area quickly rose, and by mid-1944 attacks were being made by five squadrons — three carrying rockets, while the other two strafed in the Flak-suppression role. By the latter part of the year targets in the area declined considerably as the Germans withdrew from Greece and Southern Yugoslavia, only a few island garrisons being left stranded. Two rocket-Beaufighter units moved to Italy, one to the Far East, and one was disbanded.

During October the remaining unit, 252 Squadron, together with two RAF and two Greek fighter squadrons, moved to Greece and undertook fighter-bombing attacks on German columns evacuating the area. These formations were later employed against Greek Communist guerillas, following their attempt to take control of the newly-liberated country.

Meanwhile, following the initial attacks on Yugoslavian targets by DAF units late in 1943, elements of the Allied Coastal Air Force became engaged in these duties also, and by the start of 1944 some five squadrons of RAF Spitfires were undertaking strafing and bombing sorties over the area, together with Italian Co-Belligerent units, which had been equipped with P-39 Airacobras.

These attacks, together with those by DAF, played a major part in reducing the effectiveness of substantial German operations which were launched during early 1944 against the growing partisan elements in Yugoslavia.

March 1944 saw the arrival in Italy of 6 Squadron, the old 'tank buster' unit of the African campaign. Now equipped with Hurricane IVs, this unit was once again pioneering, introducing the rocket projectile to the Italian theatre. These were employed initially against shipping targets in the Adriatic, although they were later used over the coastal areas of Yugoslavia — particularly when attacks on buildings were made.

During June 1944 Balkan Air Force (BAF) was formed, including 6 Squadron and several ex-Coastal Air Force Spitfire squadrons, some Italian units, and a squadron of a dozen Soviet Yak 9 fighters. The following month the force was strengthened by the arrival of two SAAF Beaufighter RP squadrons from Egypt, and a Mustang unit. Operations over Yugoslavia and the Adriatic continued for the rest of the war, with attacks on German convoys, army posts, rail transport and some very successful airfield strikes. Forward airfields on the offshore island of Vis were secured, and operations were frequently undertaken from here. Two Greek and two Yugoslav fighter squadrons flew with BAF, one of the latter with Hurricane IVs. The Greek units moved to their homeland late in 1944, where they were the only Spitfire units during the war to carry rockets, two being fitted under each wing of their aircraft.

Widest use of the rocket projectile in the Mediterranean area by RAF aircraft was made by Bristol Beaufighters, which operated with these weapons against targets of all types — land and sea — in the Aegean and Adriatic areas, and over Yugoslavia. *IWM*

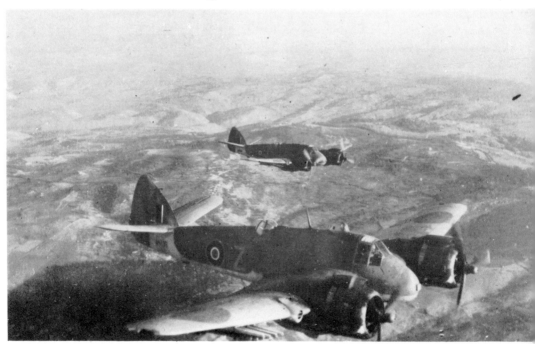

Against their targets the rocket-carrying Hurricanes and Beaufighters flew in fours, sixes or eights. They attacked in dives, firing at 800-1,000 yards, their relatively low speeds preventing their flying into the explosions of their own weapons. They met little Flak during such attacks, and losses were generally light. Over central Yugoslavia however, the Spitfire fighter-bombers were meeting concentrations of light Flak of growing intensity, and their losses rose towards the latter part of the war.

For aiming the rockets, BAF pilots preferred the Mark IIL gunsight, which featured an adjustable reflector screen. Limited availability meant that only about 20% of aircraft were fitted with these, most using the Mark IIG*. This latter was in fact preferred to 2nd TAF, since no adjustment was necessary before use of the aircraft's cannon armament could be made. In Italy these sights were generally harmonized for rocket release at 800 yards' range.

FINAL ACTIVITIES IN ITALY

Due to bad weather and shortage of infantry reserves, the Allied attack on the Gothic Line was only partially successful, and no breakout from the mountains onto the North Italian Plain was accomplished before winter set in. The complete success of the landings in Southern France, and the German withdrawal from that country during the autumn allowed many of the Allied air units which had moved from Corsica to bases in France, to be returned to Italy. In France XII TAC moved under the command of the US 9th Air Force, and a new Tactical Air Command, XXII TAC, was formed for Italian operations. During September and October four US P-47 groups (27th, 57th, 79th and 86th) returned to Italy, together with the three RAF Spitfire wings; a fourth Coastal P-39 group was re-equipped with P-47s, and joined XXII TAC. At the end of October a Brazilian Air Force unit, 1° *Grupo de Caca*, joined this group (350th) as a fourth squadron — also with Thunderbolts — and undertook fighter-bomber operations.

There was now so little need for Spitfire fighters that two of the returned Wings were disbanded, while the third (324 Wing) was trained for dive-bombing and strafing activities. A second SAAF wing had been formed during September however, also intended for ground support and equipped with two RAF Spitfire IX squadrons, one similarly-equipped SAAF unit, and a new SAAF Kittyhawk squadron. 239 Wing meanwhile received more Mustangs, so that four of its six units were so equipped.

On their return, the P-47 units initially rejoined the DAF units in attacks on strongpoints and artillery positions in the Gothic Line while the army's assault continued. They also hit the usual communications targets to the rear. Introduced at this time was another new weapon — the USAAF's version of the rocket. This consisted of the tubes of three infantry-style bazookas strapped together and slung beneath each wing. These fired 4.5-inch projectiles, each of which was reputed to have "the hitting force of a 105 mm howitzer shell".

First used during October 1944, they were found to be particularly useful for attacks on buildings which had been converted into strongpoints. Tactics were fairly standard — a low level approach, shallow dive, and release at 1,000 yards' range. So accurate was Allied target identification by now that fighter-bombers were working to a bomb-line only 1,000 yards ahead of the forward troops. Despite the introduction of the rocket, bombs and guns remained the favoured weapons in Italy. Bombs most in use at this time were the British 20 lb and US M-41 23 lb fragmentation bombs, the US 100 lb, British 500 lb and US 250 lb general purpose bombs, the two latter backed up by supplies of US 500 lb and British 250 lb missiles, and the US 1,000 pounder. Both tactical air forces used whichever was available most readily at the time.

New types of close support had also been evolved — the 'Rover Frank', whereby a 'Rover Tentacle' was attached to the artillery, directing fighter-bombers on counter-battery work was one example. Counter-battery operations against the hated Flak sites were known as 'Apple Pies'. Another tactic — usually employed only at the start of a major offensive — was Operation 'Timothy'. An area designated for an infantry attack on a limited objective some 1,000 yards ahead of the assault troops, was marked with coloured smoke shells — blue in the centre, white on either side and red on the flanks. Aircraft then appeared in sixes at ten minute intervals to bomb, strafe and rocket a square 1,000 yards deep beyond the smoke line for 30 minutes. At the end of this time the infantry moved forward, and the bomb-line was moved ahead 1,000 yards for the attack to continue, this process being repeated as often as was necessary. An example of the effectiveness of such attacks can be observed when considering one such operation where a brigade was enabled to advance 1,400 yards in a heavily-defended area, taking 60 prisoners at a cost of only 13 casualties.

When Rover David 'Cab Rank' operations were not being undertaken, a request for air support by a unit at the front usually took about 75 minutes to fulfil — as follows: Army unit to Army/Air HQ, 9 minutes; Wing HQ to Army unit, arranging estimated time of arrival over target, 12 minutes — 21 minutes so far. Writing messages, briefing pilots and consultations at Army/Air HQ, 34 minutes; flying time to target, 20 minutes — 75 minutes in all. On occasions this could obviously be improved upon, but was a typical average. It was slightly shorter than was normal in Western Europe during the Winter of 1944/45.

Once the fighting on the Gothic Line had become static, the fighter-bombers returned to interdiction on a large scale. The High Command in Italy considered that this type of operation probably contributed more in the long run to the army's success than direct battlefield support by the tactical air forces. Now the fighter-bombers attacked not only the lines of communication immediately to the rear of the front lines, but also strayed much further afield to attack rail and road bridges — particularly those over the River Po — rail targets and transport of all types in the Southern end of the Brenner Pass — the main supply route from Germany. For these attacks bombs were favoured over rockets, as the latter had proved to be rather inaccurate against small moving targets, and of little effect on bridges.

Operations of this nature continued throughout the winter, rising to a peak in March 1945, as the weather improved. This was despite the departure to France once more (and permanently this time) of the 27th and 86th Fighter Groups. Late in 1944 8 SAAF Wing, the new South African unit, had moved to join XXII TAC, since the 79th Fighter Group had rejoined DAF in the east on its return from France.

On March 18, 1945 the Americans joined with 239 Wing on one of the most outstanding fighter-bomber operations of the war. A supply vessel had reached Venice from the north shore of the Adriatic, and was seen by aerial reconnaissance in harbour. A strike was ordered, but was christened Operation 'Bowler Hat', as any senior officer could expect premature retirement (his 'bowler hat', in RAF parlance) if any of Venice's historic buildings were to be damaged or destroyed.

No 260 was the only RAF Squadron of Desert Air Force to use the rocket for ground attack duties in Italy early in 1945. Note that the Mustang carries a different form of launching rail to that employed by other RAF types, with the rockets in pairs, one above the other.
IWM

Led in by an experienced fighter pilot, Wing Commander George Westlake, 48 Mustangs and Kittyhawks bombed, sinking the vessel, the *Otto Leonhardt*, and hitting other vessels and warehouses, while another squadron of Mustangs and two squadrons of 79th Fighter Group P-47s strafed forty-three Flak positions. Not a bomb fell outside the harbour, and only one aircraft was lost, the pilot being picked up out of the sea at once by an accompanying air-sea rescue amphibian.

Around this time 260 Squadron in 239 Wing had become the first and only RAF squadron in Desert Air Force to be equipped to fire rockets. Its Mustangs were fitted with a new type of launching rail, only two of which were carried beneath each wing. Each rail mounted two 60 lb RPs, one above and one below. A further arrival was the first Napalm — known initially as fire-bombs, or 'blaze-bombs'. These consisted of auxiliary fuel tanks filled with highly-inflammable petroleum jelly, together with a fused igniter. The jelly proved more effective than ordinary petroleum, due to its ability to cling in fair quantities to its target while burning.

On the afternoon of April 9, 1945 a final offensive was opened by 8th Army, pressaged by an aerial bombardment of unprecedented proportions by all types of aircraft. 'Timothys' abounded, and the first use of the new fire bombs in Italy was made as well. Close support operations followed, and tremendous progress was made. A similar onslaught on 14th marked the start of 5th Army's offensive in the West, and within a few days the German armies were en route. All fighting ceased on May 2.

During these last months of war the remaining Luftwaffe unit NSGr 9, had attempted to attack Allied troops by night during the Gothic Line fighting, but the Ju 87s had suffered heavily to night fighters. In early 1945 the unit was re-equipped with Fw 190s, but these were few in number and could achieve little. They too suffered casualties to night fighters, since Mosquitos had begun operating over this front at about the same time as the Focke Wulfs had appeared.

At the close of hostilities fighter-bomber strength at the front and elsewhere in Italy was:—

Desert Air Force
239 Wing: four squadrons of Mustang IIIs and IVs, two squadrons of Kittyhawk IVs
244 Wing: three squadrons of Spitfire VIIIs, two squadrons of Spitfire IXs
324 Wing: four squadrons of Spitfire IXs
7 SAAF Wing: four squadrons of Spitfire IXs
79th Fighter Group: three squadrons of P-47Ds

XXII Tactical Air Command
57th Fighter Group: three squadrons of P-47Ds
350th Fighter Group: three squadrons of P-47Ds, one Brazilian *Grupo* of P-47Ds
8 SAAF Wing: three squadrons of Spitfire IXs, one squadron of Kittyhawk IVs
Balkan Air Force
281 Wing: three squadrons of Spitfire Vs and IXs, two squadrons of Hurricane IVs
283 Wing: one squadron of Mustang IIIs, one squadron of Spitfire IXs, two squadrons of Beaufighter Xs

Italian fighters and fighter-bombers had been active over Yugoslavia from late 1943 onwards with the Co-Belligerent Air Force. Initially the remaining Re 2002s were operated, escorted by Macchi MC 202s and 205s. In 1944 P-39 Airacobras were supplied, together with some Spitfire Vs, and these, together with Macchi fighters, made frequent strafing attacks as part of Balkan Air Force right up to the end of the war. At that time the Italians were maintaining in Eastern Italy three *stormi* of fighters, each with six *squadriglie* in three *gruppi*. 4° *Stormo* was equipped with P-39s, 5° *Stormo* with MC 202s, and 51° *Stormo* with one *gruppo* of Spitfires and two of MC 205s.

7. The Conquest
of Western Europe

As mentioned in Chapter 5, November 1943 saw the official birth of the new tactical air forces for the forthcoming invasion of Europe, formation of which had actually been put in train the previous spring. The new air forces would have four primary duties:-

a) Air defence by day and night of the armies and their lines of communication and rear area bases.
b) Direct and indirect close support by fighter-bombers of the armies in the field.
c) Tactical medium bombing.
d) Tactical reconnaissance, both photographic and visual.

It is the second of those duties with which we are concerned here.

On the appropriate day the RAF's 2nd Tactical Air Force was in fact a force in being; the US 9th Air Force was not. Initially three of the former's four Groups continued to operate under Fighter Command control, the fourth not becoming operational until just before the invasion began. As the latter's units became operational they came temporarily under the control of the US 8th Air Force.

Two 2nd TAF Groups each combined duties a), b) and d), 83 Group being intended to support the British 2nd Army, and 84 Group to support the Canadian 1st Army. 2 Group controlled the medium and light bombers, and 85 Group would be responsible in due course for rear area defence. 83 Group initially possessed two wings each of three squadrons of Typhoons, and a single squadron of RP Hurricanes together with ten squadrons of Spitfire Vs and IXs in four wings. 84 Group as yet had no Typhoons, but incorporated 12 squadrons of Spitfires in five wings. To date only the Hurricanes and Typhoon were equipped and trained for fighter-bomber activities. The new air force as a whole enjoyed a particularly high proportion of experienced leaders right down to flight commander level.

During the next seven months more Typhoon units were posted in to both groups, all going in turn to Armament Practice Camps to be initiated into the mysteries of rocket-firing and bomb-dropping. Several of the Spitfire IX squadrons also attended these camps to undertake training in dive-bombing, and more would follow. A number of units with North American Mustang IIIs (P-51Bs) were

also allocated, these also being trained for fighter-bombing; these excellent aircraft were capable of carrying two 1,000 lb bombs.

During the period leading up to the invasion an increasing number of fighter-bomber sorties were flown, particularly by the Typhoons and increasingly by the Spitfire IXs from March 1944 onwards. Targets included the railway system in North-Western Europe, bridges, airfields and radar stations. Another target of increasing importance was the growing number of launching sites being prepared for the V-1 flying bombs, which had not yet made their appearance over England. As a foretaste of what was to come, losses to the accurate, efficient, and increasingly dense German light automatic Flak were relatively heavy during this period, and a number of experienced pilots were lost before the invasion had even begun.

While 2 Group was mainly equipped with medium bombers at this time, it had in November a wing of three squadrons of De Havilland Mosquito VI fighter-bombers, which had recently entered service. These fast twin-engined aircraft carried a forward-firing armament of four 20 mm cannons and four .303 in machine guns, an internal bombload of 1,000 lb, and additionally a 500 lb bomb under each wing. With a considerable range of up to 1,650 miles, and a top speed of 380 mph, they were an extremely valuable addition to the tactical force.

Initially they operated as medium bombers, attacking their targets in medium-level formations, but occasionally they carried out special high-accuracy fighter-bomber attacks on individual targets, as on

By 1944 the US 9th Air Force in England had become a sizeable tactical force, equipped with a substantial number of fighter-bombers. The majority of these were Republic P-47D Thunderbolts. Aircraft of this type serving with the 509th Squadron of the 405th Fighter Group are seen preparing for take-off with a 500 lb bomb beneath each wing, and a third bomb of lesser weight under the fuselage. *Smithsonian Institute*

Close-up of the underwing rack and bomb shackle on a P-47D, with 500 lb. General Purpose bomb in place. *via W.N.Hess*

February 18, 1944, when 18 of them raided Amiens jail in an effort to free 700 French Resistance prisoners from the clutches of the Gestapo. Many prisoners did manage to escape, though a substantial number were killed in the attack. Group Captain P.C. Pickard who led the attack remained to inspect the damage, and as a result his was the only Mosquito to be intercepted and shot down on this occasion.

Meanwhile the US 9th Air Force had come into being with a nucleus of B-26 bomber groups from the 8th Air Force, and a single operational fighter group — the 354th. This latter was the first to take the P-51B Mustang into action, and was operating with 8th Air Force on long-range bomber escort missions only at this time. Another P-51 group was due, but at this stage it was decided to concentrate all available Mustangs into the 8th for bomber escorts, and to rely on the more rugged P-47D Thunderbolt for fighter-bomber duties. A P-47 group due to join the 8th was 'swapped' for the 9th's second P-51 unit, and by the end of the year three more had been allocated.

Three of these new groups became operational during February 1944, but only in a bomber escort role initially. At this stage 9th Air Force organization was similar to that of the 8th, with separate Fighter and Bomber Commands. Experience in North Africa dictated the setting up of Air Support Commands with the same mixed capability as the 2nd TAF Groups, and this change was instituted during February. In April the new commands were more accurately retitled Tactical Air Commands, and two were initially set up to support each of the US Armies destined to go ashore first in Normandy, the 1st and 3rd.

Meanwhile American fighter-bomber activity at last began on March 15, 1944, when P-47s of the 366th Fighter Group dive-bombed St. Valery airfield with 250 lb bombs. Later in the month five operational groups, including the 'Pioneer Mustangs', were to be involved in dive-bombing similar targets to those attacked by 2nd TAF at this time. The puny 250 lb bombs were soon replaced by 500 pounders, and by May the first 1,000 pounders were being employed frequently. Four more fighter groups had entered action during April, including the first to reach the 9th with P-38 Lightnings.

By the beginning of June both air forces were ready; the main ground attack workhorses were the Typhoon and Thunderbolt, backed by other types. The strengths of the fighter-bomber units within these two forces were as follows:-

2nd Tactical Air Force
2 Group
2 Wings Mosquito VIs (6 squadrons)
83 Group (British 2nd Army)
4 Wings Typhoons (10 squadrons) 4 Wings Spitfire IXs (12 squadrons) 1 Wing Mustang IIIs (3 squadrons)
84 Group (Canadian 1st Army)
3 Wings Typhoons (8 squadrons) 5 Wings Spitfire IXs (15 squadrons) 1 Wing Mustang IIIs (3 squadrons)
Total — *57 squadrons*

Typical USAAF load for attacking airfields — one 500 lb bomb and multiple 23 lb fragmentation clusters under the belly of a P-47D. *via W.N.Hess*

In 1944 the US 9th Air Force also used large numbers of Lockheed P-38 Lightning fighters for the fighter-bomber role. The aircraft in the foreground has been fitted with four 500 lb bombs beneath the inboard wing panels, while a pair of long-range fuel tanks await fitting to the pylons which can be seen between the bombs. Note that the booms of this aircraft have been painted on their underside with black and white invasion recognition stripes, which are becoming somewhat worn. *Lockheed via W.N.Hess*

9th Air Force

IX TAC (US 1st Army)

7 Groups P-47s (21 squadrons) 3 Groups P-38s (9 squadrons)

XIX TAC (US 3rd Army)

5 Groups P-47s (15 squadrons) 2 Groups P-51s (6 squadrons)

Total — *51 squadrons*

Additionally both forces had medium bomber and reconnaissance units, while 2nd TAF also employed a number of squadrons of air superiority fighters and night fighters.

D-DAY, NORMANDY, JUNE 6, 1944

From the first minutes of dawn on D-Day, the tactical air forces were deeply involved, first providing air cover, but then entering into their designed task of close support. Initially, on the British part of the beachhead, Typhoons provided immediate front-line support, proving effective with their battery of rockets and cannon against 88 mm gun sites, *Nebelwerfer* multiple-barrelled rocket mortars, dug-in self-propelled guns, and similar targets. The bomb-carrying Mustang IIIs ranged farther afield, attacking convoys and troop columns on roads leading to the battle area, and German airfields as units of the Luftwaffe were rushed to France. By night Mosquito VIs took up the attack in pairs on the lines of communications, these interdiction sorties making sure that there was no let-up in attacks during the hours of darkness.

During this period the Spitfires were mainly involved in patrolling, although a certain amount of strafing of transport targets

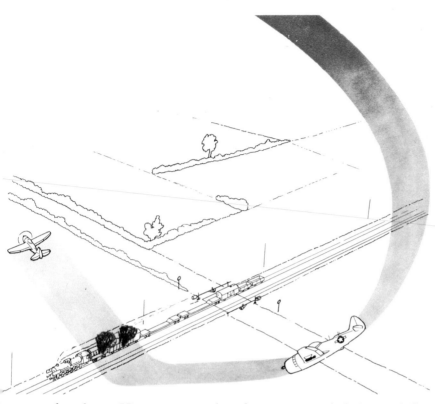

was undertaken. However, no bombs were carried by Spitfire squadrons during the weeks immediately following the invasion.

In the American sector it was much the same story, though at first all attacks were undertaken with bombs and machine guns. Not until July did 9th Air Force fighter-bombers first make use of the US 'bazooka-tube' clusters, and even then rockets were not to be employed to anything like the same extent as was the case with the Typhoons.

On occasions the two air forces co-operated for special operations, as on June 22, 1944 when an assault on the port of Cherbourg was to be launched. Four squadrons of RP Typhoons hit the northern half of the attack area, concentrating on the Flak defences. They were followed by six squadrons of Mustang IIIs, and then by 557 US fighter-bombers, which dropped over 500 tons of 500 lb GP bombs, P-51s and P-38s carrying two apiece, and P-47s three.

As fierce fighting around the beachhead continued, airstrips were constructed as quickly as possible, and before long units of both air forces were moving over to French soil. At this stage however the V-1 assault on Southern England began, and several wings of 2nd TAF's high-performance fighters* were recalled for defensive duties, including 84 Group's Mustang Wing. The Allies had won a high level of air superiority by this time however, and had more than

A typical dive-bombing attack as carried out by Republican P-47 Thunderbolts of the US 9th Air Force during the campaign in Western Europe, June 1944-May 1945.

enough units available over the front. Despite the fitting of rocket rails which reduced the top speed of the Typhoon by some 15 mph, the aircraft still proved itself quite capable of its own defence on a number of occasions. Other Typhoons carrying bombs undertook a number of somewhat unusual operations at this time when they blocked the mouths of rail tunnels with 1,000 lb bombs on several occasions after having observed supply trains entering the tunnel and remaining there to escape attack.

The breakout from the beachhead came to the south, where General Patton's 3rd Army began an armoured thrust into Brittany. In an effort to negate this threat, a German counter-attack — the first since the invasion had begun — was launched on August 7 at Mortain, under the direction of General von Kluge. Avranches was the objective, as the capture of this town would allow Patton to be cut off from the rest of the Allied forces. As the armoured spearheads of the attack threatened a thinly-held sector of the US front, the absence of anti-tank aircraft in 9th Air Force was acutely felt. At once 19 squadrons of 2nd TAF Typhoons were diverted to the area, attacking at dawn with telling effect. Their tactic on finding a column in one of the narrow, embankment-lined Normandy roads, was to attack the head and tail of the convoy first, trapping the rest in between. They would then work their way up the 'sandwich'. In two hours of continual attacks, 81 armoured vehicles were claimed destroyed for the loss of three aircraft, the German thrust being beaten off. They then turned their attention to the Vire area, where British troops were also under attack. During the day a total of 294 sorties were flown by the Typhoons, 2,088 rockets being fired and 80 tons of bombs dropped.

The main Allied anti-tank aircraft in Western Europe was the rocket-armed Typhoon of the RAF's 2nd Tactical Air Force. Here aircraft of this type are readied for action on a forward airstrip in France, the position of the rockets being clearly visible on the aircraft in the foreground.
IWM

Close-up of the business end of the armament on a rocket-Typhoon. *IWM*

What the true cost to the Germans of the Mortain attack by the Typhoons, and other such operations that followed it, is now the subject of considerable controversy. Undoubtedly the rocket projectile was a difficult weapon to use accurately, and many experts hold that against a small moving target such as a tank, it was well nigh useless in the hands of the average pilot. They maintain however that it was cannon fire which destroyed much of the supporting 'soft-skinned' transport carrying the ammunition and fuel required for the Panzers, thus bringing them effectively to a halt for lack of these essentials. The Typhoon was indeed an extremely steady firing platform, which allowed very accurate air-to-ground gunfire to be undertaken. On the other hand, in the narrow Normandy lanes it only required one or two more experienced pilots to achieve accurate or lucky hits to bring a column to a halt, the rest of the formation then being presented with a stationary target of some size. The truth in all probability lies somewhere between the two; it seems unlikely that 81 AFVs were actually destroyed by rockets, but equally it is a fact that these attacks did bring the counter-attack to a halt.

The failure of the German assault, coupled with the success of Patton's breakout to the South, and the general forward movement of the Allied armies led now to a German withdrawal during which much of their 7th Army was encircled in an almost totally-sealed 'pocket'. Only in the Falaise area was a small gap still open, and it was for here that the desperate German columns headed. This situation provided a plethora of targets for the fighter-bombers, and great execution was done by Typhoons, Mustangs, P-47s, P-51s, P-38s and Spitfires with rockets, bombs and guns. Those forces which escaped had still to cross the River Seine, few bridges remaining intact as a result of regular air attack. Consequently much use was made of barges, and these also proved a fruitful target for the fighter-bombers.

August 1944, the month of Falaise, and of the beginning of the Germans' precipitate withdrawal from the whole of France, saw several changes. In mid month the US 7th Army landed in Southern France, supported by XII TAC from the US 12th Air Force — part of Mediterranean Allied Air Forces. This Command, which had previously been operating over Italy, included a number of units of the French *Armée de l'Air*. Towards the latter part of the month 9th Air Force units introduced napalm to action in Western Europe, this ghastly weapon first being used in Brittany during operations for the reduction of the defences around the port of St. Malo. Another new development was the 'droop snoot' P-38, initiated by the 474th Fighter Group. One P-38 had the nose section, including the guns, removed and replaced by a new, larger nose incorporating a bomb-aimer and bomb sight. This aircraft then carried out the aiming for a whole formation of bomb-carrying Lightnings, which all released their bombs on a signal from this leader.

As the Allied armies fanned out across France, the line lengthened daily. To fill the thinning ranks which resulted, the US 9th Army now moved to the Continent, 9th Air Force being re-organized during September to provide a third TAC, XXIX, with four fighter-bomber groups, to support this army. Initially the newly-arrived XII TAC in the South came under 9th Air Force command, but in November it was put under the control of the new 1st French Air Force, becoming 1st Tactical Air Force. This force included US and French P-47 units, and French Spitfire IXs for air superiority. When several of the US units returned to Northern Italy, three P-47 groups from 9th Air Force were sent to reinforce 1st TAF, although one of these returned to its original parent in February 1945.

ARNHEM AND NIJMEGEN

In an effort to speed a drive by British 2nd Army into North-West Germany, designed to bring the war to an end in 1944, an airborne army was dropped on September 17, 1944, around strategic bridges over the Maas at Grave, the Waal at Nijmegen and the Neder Rijn at Arnhem. Due to the unexpected presence of armoured forces resting near Arnhem, and of bad weather which reduced air support and delayed the arrival of 2nd Army spearheads, the operation failed to secure all its objectives. Whilst the landings at Grave and Nijmegen were successful, that at Arnhem was overrun. Thereafter the Nijmegen bridges became the prime target for the Luftwaffe.

On the day of the invasion, June 6, 1944, I/SKG 10, the sole remaining ground attack unit in the West, had become III/KG 51. This bomber unit's I and II *Gruppen* were in the process of converting to Messerschmitt Me 262 jets from the Me 410, the original III *Gruppe* having been disbanded. While many *Jagdgruppen* from the Soviet Union, Italy, Norway and Central Germany, were rushed to the West, III/KG 51 remained the sole ground attack unit available for some time, suffering heavy losses to Allied fighters.

The first sorties by the new Me 262 jets of KG 51 were made during July and August, but it was late in September that these aircraft began appearing frequently, making repeated attacks on the Nijmegen bridges. Fw 190s and Bf 109Gs of various *Jagdgeschwadern* were also equipped with bombs and thrown in against these targets, as were III/KG 51's Fw 190s, and newly-formed II/KG 200, which had seven Fw 190Fs, equipped to carry large SC 1800 bombs of over 3,000 lb weight, this unit operating as *Sonderstaffel Eindhoven*.

The Messerschmitt Me 262 was a radical new aircraft, designed as an interceptor. Powered by two Junkers Jumo 004B jet engines of 1,980 lb static thrust each, and featuring swept-back wing design, the aircraft had a very high top speed of 540 mph, coupled with a formidable fixed armament of four 30 mm MK 108 cannons in the nose. Much has been made of Adolf Hitler's determination to have this aircraft introduced as his 'Blitz Bomber', and of the resultant delay this had in its introduction as a fighter. Be that as it may, it appeared over the front in both roles at roughly the same time. As a

As on other fronts, the Luftwaffe's main offensive capability rested with the Focke-Wulf Fw 190s of the *Schlacht-geschwadern* by 1944. This unusual-ly-marked Fw 190A-5/U8 taxies out, carrying a 1102 lb SC 500 bomb under the fuselage.
Bundesarchiv

fighter-bomber it carried a pair of SC 250 bombs beneath the forward fuselage, but was otherwise equipped much as the standard fighter. It was however flown by bomber pilots in this configuration, these personnel being basically untrained for the fighter role — as had been the case with the *Schlachtflieger*.

With the failure to secure the Arnhem bridge, and with the onset of autumn, the advance came to a virtual halt, as the Allied armies prepared to secure their lines of communication and supply, and consolidate their gains, before preceeding with a general offensive. Many fighter-bomber units had fallen well behind the front line during the swift advances of August/September, but now moved up to new airfields, and began a campaign of interdiction against German supply lines and defensive positions. 9th Air Force concentrated on barge traffic on the Rhine and on Luftwaffe airfields, employing mainly 100 lb, 500 lb and 1,000 lb GP bombs, and 150 gallon napalm tanks.

For 2nd TAF at this time, targets were more varied. At the end of September the last Mustang IIIs were withdrawn for escort duties to the new Bomber Command daylight offensive, their place being taken by Tempests which operated purely in the fighter role, carrying no bombs or rockets, and only occasionally making the odd strafing attack. The Typhoons, joined by Spitfires, which had once again begun fighter-bomber activities (August in 84 Group, October in 83 Group, which saw a greater amount of opposition in the air), were

By the autumn of 1944 a substantial tactical air force which had accompanied the Allied landings in Southern France, had moved up to the Southern frontier of Germany. This force included several *groupes de chasse* of the French *Armee de l'Air* which were equipped with P-47Ds for fighter-bomber activities. These French Thunderbolts, seen on a snow-clad airfield during the winter of 1944/45, carry small 250 lb bombs beneath their wings. *IWM*

These Fw 190F-8 *Schlachtfliegern* are fitted with bomb canisters containing numbers of small 1 or 2 kg anti-personnel bombs. *Bundesarchiv*

involved in attacks on Walcheren Island and other German defences in the Scheldt estuary. These attacks were in support of operations as the British and Canadians sought to open the channel to Antwerp's port facilities, which was still dominated by the Germans.

At the same time 84 Group aircraft were involved in attacks on German garrisons still resisting in various Channel ports, which had been by-passed during the summer advance. They also attacked V-2 rocket-launching sites in Holland, where these missiles were now being launched against both Southern England and Antwerp. Initially the Spitfires carried single 500 lb bombs, but these were soon joined by a pair of 250 pounders beneath the wings. Late in the year the Spitfire IXs were augmented by growing numbers of the basically-similar Mark XVI, which differed principally in having a Packard-built Merlin engine, and in having the four .303 in machine guns in the wings replaced by two .50 in guns, in addition to the normal pair of 20 mm Hispano cannons.

The Mosquito VIs of 2 Group were now deeply involved in their night interdiction attacks, but still made the occasional special low-level precision raids. On July 14, 1944 a Gestapo headquarters at Bonneuil Matours was hit, while other targets of this ilk included a rest home for U-Boat crews, and another Gestapo building at Aarhus, Denmark, which was attacked on October 31.

The Typhoons also on occasions undertook such special missions. A classic example occurred on October 24, 1944, when 146 Wing of 84 Group, led by Group Captain D.E. Gillam — an officer who had

done much to develop and foster the art of ground attack in the RAF
— attacked a building in Dordrecht where a conference of senior
German officers was reported by the Dutch resistance. Gillam led in
the formatino and personally marked the target with smoke bombs,
whereupon the others bombed with 500 and 1,000 pounders. Two
generals, 17 Staff officers, 55 other officers, and many other ranks were
subsequently reported killed.

To the South, other by-passed ports on the French Atlantic coast
were attacked by elements of the French *Armée de l'Air* and
Aeronavale, squadrons of both operating A-24 and SBD-5 versions of
Douglas Dauntless dive-bomber. They were joined later in the war by
P-47Ds. From England meanwhile a small force of Spitfire IX dive-
bombers flew across the North Sea frequently to attack V-2 sites in
Northern Holland, spotted by reconnaissance aircraft.

WINTER BATTLES

As the hard winter of 1944/45 approached, the Germans planned a
desperate offensive in the West to which their remaining reserves were
to be committed. This was designed to push through the Ardennes
area once again, and to reach Antwerp, splitting the British and
Canadian armies in the North from their American and French allies
in the South. This, it was hoped, would make the war-weary Allies
seek a negotiated peace rather than press on for unconditional
surrender.

A period of bad weather was hoped for during December, which
would cut down the activities of the enormously-superior Allied
tactical air power. To support the assault however,
Schlachtgeschwader 4 was moved to the West from the Eastern front,
where it will be recalled, it had arrived from Italy during July. It
joined *Kampfgeschwader(Jagd)*51's Me 262s, and the first elements of
KG(J) 54 and 76 — bomber units which had also undertaken the
conversion to the Me 262. A number of new *Nachtschlachtgruppen*
had also been formed by now, most with Junkers Ju 87s, but with a
few Fw 190 Jabos as well. III/KG 51 had meanwhile been renamed
NSGr. 20, and another new special Fw 190 unit had been formed. *Stab*
and I/SG 5 from the Norway/Finland area had returned to the Reich
to form the nucleus of III/KG 200 under *Reichmarschall* Goering's
direct control. This *Gruppe*'s Fw 190s were fitted to carry a variety of
special loads, including the BT 200, 400 and 700 anti-shipping
torpedo bombs.

The new offensive began on December 16, 1944 in foul weather
conditions, and at first drove all before it, creating a substantial
salient into the Allied line. Whenever weather allowed Luftwaffe
aircraft appeared in the greatest numbers for many months, but the
situation for them was far from ideal. SG 4 frequently found that no

Designed as an attack bomber, and in this version fitted with a solid 'strafer' nose, the Douglas A-20G Havoc proved too vulnerable for low-flying missions of this kind in Western Europe in 1944, and was employed instead in the medium altitude level bombing role. Note the additional bombs carried beneath the wings. *American Official via IWM*

fighter aircraft were available to escort their *Jabos*, and as on the Eastern front, had to allocate a percentage of their Fw 190s to undertake this duty. Just before Christmas the weather cleared, and Allied aircraft poured into the skies. SG 4 and the various *Jagdgeschwadern* now suffered heavy losses to Allied fighter patrols, whilst Typhoons, Thunderbolts, Mosquitos and medium bombers played havoc with the German columns on the narrow, snow-choked roads of the Ardennes area.

During this period the US 1st and 9th Armies, in whose area the offensive had struck, were put under General Montgomery's direct control for the duration of the battle, this brining IX and XXIX TACs under 2nd TAF direction at this time. With ground units reinforced, and the air forces so active, the Germans were soon brought to a halt, and the salient was reduced before the end of the year.

Despite the losses of the Ardennes offensive, the Luftwaffe was able to build up a big force of some 800 single-engined aircraft to attempt one big blow to end the dominance of Allied tactical air power. At first light on January 1, 1945 Operation 'Bodenplatte' went into effect, Bf 109s and Fw 190s making a series of surprise dawn attacks on Allied airfields throughout North-West Europe. The attacks were generally undertaken by *Jagdgeschwadern*, which made strafing runs, but SG 4 also took part before returning a few days later to the Eastern front. The Me 262s of the various KG(J)s and JGs were not involved.

Whilst the attack succeeded in destroying quite a large number of Allied aircraft — mainly 2nd TAF fighter-bombers — on the ground, these were losses that could soon be made good. Luftwaffe losses were

Maintaining the fighter-bomber attack by night, the Mosquito VIs of 2nd TAF's 2 Group also made occasional daylight precision low-level attacks on special targets. This particular Mosquito of 487 (New Zealand) Squadron carries 500 lb bombs on the underwing racks.
IWM

even heavier, and crippled what remained of the fighter force for some weeks, costing the lives of many pilots, including a number of irreplaceable experienced formation leaders.

The Allies now prepared for the final assault, and as the weather improved, the level of very close support work over the front increased greatly, as minor offensives were launched to prepare for the major operation — the crossing of the Rhine.

Throughout the autumn and winter ground attack techniques had been improved and developed, new weapons introduced, and new combinations attempted. For the Typhoon rocket-firers, the main targets were those in the static line — gun positions, dug-in tanks, observation posts, strong points, concentrations of infantry, etc. On longer-range missions these weapons were employed against barges, trains, store dumps etc. Against bridges however they had proved unsuitable, although against other forms of buildings such as fortified houses, the results were good. For longer-ranging work the Typhoons frequently carried a 45 Imp. gallon auxiliary tank beneath each wing, plus only two of the usual four rocket rails.

The standard 60 lb high explosive rocket heads had been supplemented by a few fragmentation missiles of similar weight, and by 35 lb phosphorus marker-shots. It became practice when dealing with specific targets for the leader and his wingman to each carry eight marker rockets, the main force following in one or more sections of four bomb-carrying aircraft, which dropped 1,000 pounders with a 10-second delayed action fuses.

For direct support missions rockets were generally used by all aircraft, the formation approaching at 6-10,000 feet, and the leader diving first at a 40-45 degree angle to mark. The laid-down attack procedure for the rest was to dive at 400 mph in a 45 degree approach, or at 380 mph at 30 degrees. However, so savage was the light Flak by this time, and so heavy a toll did it take of the Typhoon units, that in practice speeds 20-30 mph higher were generally used.

Using the rockets accurately remained difficult. Only the standard Mark IIG* reflector gunsight was available, which was not really good enough. The pilot needed to allow for both trajectory drop and wind effect. The nature of the target and its defences also played a large part. Against the smaller targets usually attacked in direct support operations, the rockets would usually be 'rippled' in pairs, whilst against some larger targets, such as a barge or train, the whole eight could be salvoed in one go.

Ideally the steeper the approach dive, the less trajectory drop would be encountered — but the steeper the dive, the longer was the aircraft in the Flak gunner's sights. Similarly, if a shallow approach was to be employed, the more slowly it was made, and the closer it was pressed, the better were the chances of success. Again however, the level of Flak defence remained the crucial factor, as also did the determination and aggressiveness of the individual pilot.

Results were very difficult for the pilot to assess, as he was past and gone before the dust and smoke of the explosions had subsided. The cine film seldom helped. It was motivated by pressure on the gun-firing button; thus as the pilot approached the launching point, firing his cannons to keep down the heads of the Flak gunners, the camera operated. As soon as he ceased firing in order to operate the rocket-launching button, the camera ceased to function, providing no evidence of the rocket strikes. Generally it was necessary to await a report from the ground as to results.

New pilots reaching the squadrons were found to be far ffrom proficient in the art, and complaints were made that Operational Training Units were still giving a disproportionate amount of time to air-to-air combat training, rather than in practicing ground gunnery, which now made up 80-90% of the average Typhoon pilot's duties. The result was a definite tendency to undershoot, range and trajectory drop being wrongly estimated; the average error was reported to be 50 yards at a range of 1,200 yards. Levels of accuracy achieved by more experienced pilots who pressed home their attacks to a much closer range, were substantially better. However some 20-30% of rockets fired failed to explode in any event.

Ground control also still left something to be desired, but improvements were on the way, with the introduction imminent of the new SCR 584 radio, which was operationally tested by 2nd TAF. For both the British and Americans a new form of rocket launcher was on the way, which would have less effect on the performance of the aircraft to which it was fitted. This new zero-length launching 'stub' was tested on Typhoons, Spitfires and P-47s, showing no loss of accuracy, but was not widely available before the war in Europe ended, although it would see substantial service in the Pacific area.

For dive-bombing, aircraft of both air forces normally approached the target a dozen at a time, flying in fours. The attack was launched from about 8,000 feet, the fighters turning either 90 degrees or a full 180 degrees from their line of flight to dive and release at 3,000 feet. RAF Spitfires and Typhoons usually followed their leader in quick succession from direct formation, often diving in echelon to attack. US P-47s normally went into a line-astern formation immediately before peeling-off for the assault.

Bombing weapons remained basically unchanged. Typhoons carried 500 lb or 1,000 lb bombs, as did P-47s and P-51s. On occasions the US aircraft used fragmentation clusters, whilst late in the war Typhoons also carried a British-developed canister bomb containing twenty-six 20 lb frags. The 9th Air Force continued to make wide use of napalm, while RAF Spitfires carried one 500 lb and two 250 lb bombs on the majority of occasions. This 1,000 lb bombload frequently proved troublesome to the Spitfire however, 60% of all accidents being caused by burst tyres due to the weight carried.

In 9th Air Force, the P-38 had proved quite a load-carrier. When bazooka-tube rocket launchers were carried, clusters of three could be hung from each inboard wing section. Later when zero-length launchers became available, a special cluster of five could be hung in this position, or eight rockets could be carried beneath each outboard wing section. However the aircraft was fast disappearing from service in Western Europe in early 1945, nearly all 9th Air Force Lightnings being replaced by either P-51Ds or P-47s before the war ended.

Typical bombload for 2nd TAF Spitfire squadrons during late 1944/early 1945; this Spitfire XIV of 412 (Canadian) Squadron carries a 500 lb bomb beneath the fuselage, and one of 250 lb under each wing. Fixed armament is a 20 mm cannon and a .50 in machine gun in each wing.
IWM

Introduced to service too late to have any appreciable impact, the Douglas A-26B Invader was the last aircraft to go into production in the USAAF 'A-Attack' series. Seen here with solid 'strafer' nose, the aircraft saw limited service in France, Italy and the Pacific during the late stages of the war.
American Official via IWM

An American heavy night-fighter, the Northrop P-61 Black Widow, had by now entered service with the 9th, and during 1945 was on occasions to join 2nd TAF Mosquitos in the night intruder role, carrying either bombs or napalm canisters.

Late 1944 had seen another new addition to 9th Air Force's armoury in the form of the Douglas A-26B Invader. The finest American light bomber of the war, the Invader was the last aircraft to go into production in the old 'Attack' category, and was eventually to see wide-scale service after the war, its designation subsequently being changed to B-26 when the last Martin B-26 Marauder was withdrawn from service. Powered by two Pratt and Whitney R-2800-27 engines of 2,000 hp each, the aircraft was available either with a glazed bombardier's nose, or with a solid 'strafer' nose. In the former configuration armament comprised two nose-mounted .50 in guns, while in the latter eight were carried. Both versions featured remote-controlled dorsal and ventral turrets, each fitted with a pair of similar guns. A 4,000 lb bombload could be carried, but as a partial alternative, the strafer could have six more '50s or up to 14 x 5-in HVAR rockets fitted beneath the wings.

In prototype form a 75 mm cannon had been featured in the nose of the XA-26B, but this was not incorporated in production aircraft, which were intended to supplement and then replace the A-20 Havocs. Initially only strafer-nose versions were available, and the first missions made late in 1944 had to be lead by an A-20 with a bombadier nose. The aircraft were first employed as had been the A-20s over Europe, in the standard medium-altitude level bombing role, in which the nose armament was rarely employed. The first low level

During the latter months of the war aircraft of the US 8th Air Force also flew increasing numbers of fighter-bomber sorties, though in their case these were aimed mainly at the Luftwaffe's remaining airfields. This 353rd Fighter Group P-51D Mustang, seen about to take off on a raid in November 1944, carries 'parafrag' bombs under the wings. These were one of the most effective of all weapons against dispersed aircraft on the ground. *USAF via W.N.Hess*

strafing attacks were attempted during January 1945, but so intense was the light Flak over Western Europe that the aircraft were frequently prevented from carrying out their mission, and when they did, casualties were high. After a few attempts, this duty was left to the smaller and less-vulnerable fighter-bombers, the A-26s continuing to supplement the B-26s and A-20s in the standard light bomber role, some also being employed to a limited extent on night interdiction duties. During 1945 these aircraft also began to reach the 12th Air Force in Italy and the 5th in the Philippines, but in both cases were too late to see more than a few standard bombing missions before the war ended. The A-26 undoubtedly possessed an outstanding performance for an aircraft of this type, with a maximum speed of 355 mph, but as a ground attack type in the sophisticated conditions of Western Europe in 1945, it was simply too late.

Whatever the accuracy achieved by fighter-bombers, there is no doubt that their effect on the morale of any but the best troops, was substantial. In the later stages of the war there were frequent examples of large bodies of German troops being captured in a thoroughly demoralized state, and having offered very little fight following a sustained fighter-bomber attack. Their delaying effect on the movement of supplies and reinforcements was also of very considerable value, even when they failed to inflict substantial damage. The continual presence of these irritants at low level played upon the nerves of the troops. Unlike the more impersonal medium or high altitude bomber, the fighter-bomber would hang around, attacking individual cyclists, runners or foxholes, giving the troops on the ground the distinct feeling that whatever they did, the enemy was watching. When the fighter-bombers reappeared by night, attacking anything which showed even a glimmer of light, upsetting rest and keeping everyone 'jumpy', this was often the last straw.

On March 7, 1945, just before a major crossing of the Rhine was planned for the British 2nd Army and US 9th Army, the US 1st Army managed to seize the Ludendorff Bridge at Remagen, and to create an unplanned bridgehead on the East bank. Against this bridge the Luftwaffe's last major efforts were made, Me 262s and Fw 190s, the latter from NSGr 20, III/KG 200 and *Sonderstaffel Eindhoven*, all attacking by day, joined at night by Ju 87s of NSGr 2. Eventually, after continual near misses, the bridge collapsed on March 17, but by then it was too late. Another crossing was made to the south on 22nd, followed by the main crossing on 24th. Massive air support was given, the fighter-bombers concentrating to a large extent on German communications, bringing the railway system to a halt, and generally preventing supply and reinforcement.

Thereafter it was really only a matter of mopping up as the Allied armies poured across Germany to meet the Red Army advancing from the East. By May 8 all resistance had ceased. During this final battle the 9th Air Force alone made 29,216 fighter-bomber sorties between March 25 and May 8, suffering 131 losses, but claiming 13,000 road vehicles, 1,600 railway locomotives and 8,900 trucks, 725 tanks and other armoured vehicles, 1,495 aircraft on the ground, and 240 shot down in the air.

While operations of the two major tactical air forces had been in many ways similar, the major difference had been in the very much greater use of the rocket projectile by 2nd TAF, and of napalm by 9th Air Force. The level of differential in the former case can best be appreciated by consideration of the figures; 9th Air Force fired 13,959 rockets during the war, whilst 2nd TAF fired 222,515, 143,327 by aircraft of 83 Group alone.

Colonel Raymond Lallemant, the famous Belgian fighter pilot who flew Typhoons with 609 Squadron, RAF, and who became one of the most successful 'tank-busters' in 2nd TAF, has provided a detailed synopsis of the problems and methods involved in making rocket attacks, which goes far to removing some of the controversy on this subject.

"Rocket firing did require great experience and skill; do not forget that we had no elaborate gunsight. The best we had was a squadron-level modification of the standard sight made by Roland Beamont when he was commanding officer of 609 Squadron.

Most of the rockets did end up short of the target due to pilot inexperience, and because of Flak. We had to be very low to escape that accurate German Flak! That lead to fear of collision with obstacles on the ground. Don't think the German tanks were silly enough to park in the middle of a field! They knew about camouflage!

I must admit that most of my own lucky shots were the result of a last check in the gunsight — split seconds take you closer to your target very swiftly in a diving Typhoon! But I am convinced of the efficiency of rocket-Typhoons against tanks. All counter-attacks I have known were stopped when the Typhoons were able to deliver their attacks. Unfortuately this was not the case in June 1944 because of lack of communication and training between the Army advanced elements and the pilots giving close support. Air support to be effecive must be immediate, and we proved this later with the development of Air Support Signals Units. These were instituted on the Normandy battlefield with the debut of Visual Control Posts (VCPs). This elementary system could have achieved miracles on the beaches on D-Day had it been introduced sooner.

Training and leadership played a very important part; 609 Squadron was a particularly experienced squadron, and during a Wing attack on a road near Vimoutiers on August 20, 1944, this squadron destroyed 10 of the 13 tanks claimed. One of my pilots, a New Zealander called Harkness, got three of these, two with one pair of rockets, and I got two more, so that two of us had gained nearly half the day's score! I became involved in a sharp argument with the Wing Leader, Wing Commander Dring, over my practise of making a pass at low level before firing in order to pick out the tanks from the 'soft-skinned' vehicles. Dring had concluded that this gave the accurate Flak a double chance to shoot the aircraft down and was therefore undesirable, but I considered it to be essential.

Indeed I had done everything possible to improve the lack of proper means of aiming the rockets. My artificial horizon was marked to show the angle of dive, and a special modification to my radio produced a buzzer noise when I reached a pre-selected height. I also had a special gyro compass fitted to my aircraft.

However the real point was to trace the tanks and kill them before they could run for shelter. When they were in the open a vertical dive was best, but not all pilots could put their aircraft into such a position, since one always gains the impression within the aircraft that the dive is steeper than is really the case. I advised them to do a roll during the dive, since in a shallow dive they would feel uncomfortable when the aircraft was on its back; in a vertical dive no such gravity pull would be experienced.

When a tank was hiding the only way was to go down almost straight and level, holding the aircraft very steady, particularly during the firing of the rockets until they had cleared the long launching rails. But the trick was to go as low and as close as possible. My diagram shows the ideal distances for such an attack:-

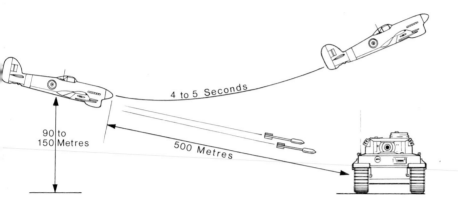

From our experiences we devised a set of basic rules and thoughts however:-

1. The rocket apparatus was heavy and disturbed the aerodynamics of the aircraft. At first we fighter pilots did not like this (Christmas Tree!) so we chose to get rid of the rockets first.
2. We soon learned that there was nothing more disagreeable than firing all our rockets at 'soft-skinned' vehicles, with the result that we then had to attack tanks with 20 mm shells (useless!).
3. So I introduced the rule that we went down first only to find the tanks, so that we could use our rockets on these. On most occasions in such a low approach we could also see other tanks. Pilots as a rule would then attack individually.
4. We had to make up our minds swiftly which tank to choose — usually that one trying to get away to cover under the trees!
5. Those standing still may already have been destroyed — one should never believe one was the first to deliver an attack!
6. When these rules had been observed, the target was selected and was preferably the easiest in sight — i.e. away from obstruction, in the open, on a concrete road, etc.
7. Attack low down and as close as possible. It was necessary however to avoid shrapnel from the exploding rockets, and when low the idea was to start climbing as soon as the rockets left the rails — and like Hell!

8. Many direct hits in such attacks were the result of a last check on aim, the time taken for this bringing you closer to the target. This was the main problem with inexperienced young pilots — fear of the ground or Flak prevented them making this last check on their aim.

9. As for the Flak, this was always very accurate and usually opened up at point blank range. I firmly believe that I avoided many hits by flying at treetop height, and always attempted to achieve an element of surprise. This made a straight approach difficult, for a camouflaged tank was not easy to spot at such low level, and one could only make small last-minute corrections if the rockets were to slide well on their rails (sudden sharp movements would cause the runners to 'bind' in the rails due to the gravity drag). This was one of the reasons why the Typhoon was so good, however, because it was so manoeuvrable and so steady.

10. We delivered vertical attacks usually when a lot of aircraft were attacking a concentration of tanks, or tanks forming up for a counter-attack, and it was necessary for all to attack in a limited time. In such cases we often released our rockets in such a way as to saturate the area, and after this type of attack the pilots never made any personal claims. Such was the case at Montain and Ponteaubault, where considerable success was achieved. (In a vertical dive an experienced pilot could achieve great accuracy with rockets.)

There were occasions when things were made easy for us. I recall on June 8, 1944 east of Mont Picon, we waited while Thunderbolts bombed a concrete road. This brought a line of tanks to a halt, and there they were, black on white, halted close together and obviously hoping for the best! As soon as the Thunderbolts retired, I went down with four Typhoons and in the first attack three 'flamers' were left marking the spot. Of course this was most easy; the tanks were quite close, and the rockets could bounce on the concrete surface until they hit them! I don't remember how many we destroyed that day; I did not note it down — maybe we felt it was too easy a target at the time.

But 609 Squadron was not an average unit. In August 1944 after Falaise, the American military magazine 'Stars and Stripes' was celebrating our success with great excitement. 2nd TAF Headquarters was asked to nominate the best rocket-Typhoon squadron, and to determine this, Air Marshal Leigh Mallory called on his staff to designate the best Group. '84 Group' said Air Marshal Coningham. Air Vice-Marshal L. Brown of 84 Group was called upon to nominate his best Wing, and said '123 Wing'. In turn this Wing's Group Captain, D.J. Scott, who had four squadrons under his control (164, 183, 198 and 609), declared 609 to be his best unit. I was very proud to be with them at the time.

LtCol R.A. 'Cheval' Lallement, the famous Belgian Typhoon pilot whose comments on anti-tank operations are included in this chapter, is seen here in the cockpit of his aircraft when commanding 609 Squadron. Markings include a cock, his squadron leader's pennant, the aircraft's name — a most illustrious one — together with score tallies for his victories over both enemy aircraft and tanks.
R.A.Lallemant

Later, at Christmas 1944 when I was in Halton Hospital being treated for burns which I suffered when shot down in the Arnhem area, friends came to take me out to a restaurant for a celebration. I knew what was going on in the Ardennes in my own country at this time, so I was inclined to refuse, but my friends insisted. I therefore telephoned the Headquarters at Uxbridge to check on the current position and was told that the Typhoons had been flying nearly all day. So I went out and told everyone 'He (Jerry) had had it!', and the next day's papers confirmed my declaration; the tanks had been stopped! This little story illustrates the confidence which I felt in the rocket-Typhoons at that time."

8. The Pacific

The Japanese attack on American, British and Dutch territories in the Far East on December 7/8, 1941 brought a whole new area and a number of new air forces into the war. Initially few ground attack aircraft were involved, although this was a situation which was soon to change.

As mentioned in Chapter 1, the Japanese Army Air Force, like the RAF in 1939, possessed no specialized dive-bombers or attack aircraft whilst its fighter aircraft were not normally fitted for the carriage of bombs. The Navy Air Force had in service substantial numbers of Aichi D3A dive-bombers, which were serving aboard most of the carriers, but while these had seen some early action ashore in China they did not now equip any of the Navy's substantial land-based air force.

On the Allied side the US Navy and Marine Corps had Douglas SBD Dauntless dive-bombers in service, the latter also employing a small number of SB2U-3 Vindicators. Other than this there were a small number of fighters that could be fitted with bombs, but little else.

During the initial strikes, the Japanese Navy's D3As attacked Pearl Harbor and the US military airfields in Hawaii, but all other attacks on Malaya and the Philippines were made by conventional bombers and by fighter aircraft — though Japanese fighter units, both Army and Navy, were always quick to strafe when appropriate, particularly when the target was an airfield.

During the initial fighting, the first operation that might be considered to be a ground attack mission occurred on January 23, 1942, when 20 Dutch Brewster 339 fighters, each carrying a pair of 50 kg (110 lb) bombs under the wings, attacked Japanese shipping sailing through the Makassar Strait to put ashore an invasion force in East Borneo. The next occasion was also undertaken in very similar circumstances. In mid February a Japanese landing force proceeding up the Palembang River, Sumatra, was heavily strafed by RAF Hurricanes, and delayed in coming ashore. With the landing established, USAAF P-40E Kittyhawk fighters from Java attacked the landing fleet anchored off-shore on February 17, each aircraft

Employed in most roles by the Royal Australian Air Force in the Pacific, the Commonwealth Wirraway operated over New Guinea with 4 Squadron in the army co-operation role, undertaking dive-bombing sorties when necessary. One such aircraft is seen here in 1943, armed with a 100 lb GP bomb under each wing.
F.F.Smith

carrying four Dutch 20 kg bombs. Meanwhile during the same month the US carrier *Enterprise* struck at Japanese bases in the Marshall Islands, where naval installations were bombed by SBDs and by Grumman F4F Wildcat fighters carrying a pair of 100 lb bombs each.

The USAAF had attempted to send its first operational group of Douglas A-24 Dauntlesses (the Army version of the Naval dive-bomber) to the Philippines, but they reached the area too late, and after being landed in Australia, one squadron from the 27th Bomb Group (Light) was sent up to Java during February 1942. This unit made just one attack on a Japanese naval force off Java on February 20, seven A-24s claiming a number of hits on a cruiser for two losses. Thereafter the surviving aircraft were withdrawn to Australia before the Indies fell.

In the Philippines few fighters remained after the first few days' fighting, and those that had survived were retained mainly for reconnaissance. However, during the later part of the campaign in these islands, the last four serviceable P-40Es were fitted with 500 lb bombs on March 2 to bomb shipping in Subic Bay. One transport was sunk, but one P-40 was lost, the other three all being unserviceable on return.

Meanwhile the Japanese carrier force struck with its bombers at Darwin in North-West Australia on February 19, then attacking ports on the Java coast. In these attacks the dive-bombers played a major part, creating great havoc and inflicting much damage. In April the carriers entered the Indian Ocean, launching two major raids on

British Naval bases and units in Ceylon, during which the D3As sank the aircraft carrier *Hermes* and two cruisers, *Dorsetshire* and *Cornwall*. They also raided Colombo naval base where they suffered a number of losses to defending British fighters, but also inflicted substantial damage.

Thereafter the war in the Far East resolved itself into a number of connected, but separate struggles, which can most profitably be considered individually.

THE SOUTH-WEST PACIFIC

Following their sweep through the East Indies and Philippines, the Japanese had landed on the North coast of New Guinea by early March 1942, aiming to neutralize the threat of a major Allied base in Australia. Here however, their headlong rush was held. The initial defence was by units of the Royal Australian Air Force on the South side of the island, but soon USAAF elements arrived to join in the fight. The first ground attack was undertaken by A-24s, which dive-bombed Japanese Navy airfields in the Lae and Salamaua area during April, RAAF Kittyhawks also strafing. The following month Bell P-39 Airacobras joined in this duty, soon reinforced by P-400s — an export version of the Airacobra taken over by the USAAF, and differing mainly in having the 37 mm cannon replaced by a 20 mm gun. During June and July, while fighting on the Papuan peninsula was raging, these aircraft provided frequent support to the ground forces, strafing and dropping bombs. After a pause of two months the

Widely used by the Australians for ground strafing throughout the South-West Pacific area, the Bristol Beaufighter was built under licence in that Dominion. This Mark VIC (A19-87) of 30 Squadron, RAAF, is seen heading in to attack targets in the Gasmata region of New Britain on 25 July, 1943. *F.F.Smith*

A-24s went into action again at this time, but on a mission over Buna on July 29, 1942, six of seven were lost to Japanese fighters, and they were thereafter withdrawn from front line service.

The following month an invasion force was seen heading for Milne Bay in South-East New Guinea, and against this on August 25 the first RAAF fighter-bomber sorties were flown, Australian Kittyhawks of two squadrons attacking with 250 and 300 lb bombs. Next day, as Japanese troops landed, the Kittyhawks returned to strafe. Firing thousands of rounds of .50-in ammunition, they played a major part in throwing the enemy back into the sea.

In September 1942 the US air forces in Australia and New Guinea became the US 5th Air Force under General George Kenney, who had under his control also the RAAF elements on the latter island. During this month US P-40s from the Darwin area reached New Guinea and began dive-bombing in the Buna area, with 300 lb bombs, one being carried under each wing. At the same time an Australian Beaufighter squadron arrived for strafing duties — pariculary against shipping. The following month came an Australian squadron of Douglas Bostons to supplement US units with the similar A-20 Havocs, these attack bombers specializing in low-level raids with machine guns and 20 lb fragmentation bombs. An army co-operation squadron of Australian Wirraways also arrived, which supplemented their reconnaissance sorties with strafing and dive-bombing. For this latter duty each carried two 250 lb bombs.

The Papuan Campaign ended in the Allies' favour in January 1943, but by this time New Guinea was being heavily reinforced by elements of the JAAF, the JNAF having meanwhile moved its units to New Britain for operations over the Solomons. Air fighting now became much heavier again, preventing the fighters having much opportunity for ground attack sorties.

The only dive-bomber to be used by the RAF, the American-built Vultee Vengeance, was also employed in fairly large numbers by the RAAF. Here aircraft of the latter force's 23 Squadron are seen preparing for take-off from Nadzah airfield, New Guinea in February 1943. The nearest aircraft is serialled A27-235. *F.F.Smith*

General Kenney, head of the US 5th Air Force in the South-West Pacific, favoured specialized 'strafer' aircraft for attacks on ground targets, and employed particularly specially modified, up-armed A-20s and B-25s for this purpose. The ultimate in this role was undoubtedly the North American B-25H Mitchell, with its massive 75 mm cannon and batteries of eight forward-firing .50 in machine guns.
Smithsonian Institute

General Kenney had strong ideas of his own on this matter however, and was much in favour of attack aviation. At the start of 1943 he had nearly all the A-20s and Bostons converted, their glazed noses being filled in, and fitted with four forward-firing .50-in machine guns, to supplement their four .30-in guns. North American B-25C Mitchell medium bombers were also received and similarly converted to carry four nose .50s, and four more in 'blister' packages on the sides of the nose. The ventral turret and tail guns were removed, and the bomb racks modified to take six 100 lb demolition bombs, and 60 x 23 lb frags. From now on these 'strafers', joined by the Beaufighters, would carry out most ground support operations while the fighters stayed above to battle for air superiority.

Meanwhile from North-West Australia a second Beaufighter squadron joined by a squadron of Vultee Vengeance dive-bombers became operational during early 1943, attacking targets in the Southern East Indies, notably on Timor. In July 1943 RAAF units in New Guinea made a series of attacks on the Gasmata area, Boston and Beaufighters taking part, together with Kittyhawks and Beauforts — the biggest Australian operations yet undertaken involving some 62 aircraft in the first such attack. During these raids the Kittyhawks once more carried bombs, either six 40 lb GP missile each, or two 30 lb incendiaries and four 40 pounders.

In September a second Australian Vengeance squadron was ready for action and moved to New Guinea, but this time the availability of improved US fighters had reduced the scale of air combat, and the Kittyhawk squadrons were somewhat underemployed. Under the prodding of Desert Air Force veterans, fighter-bomber operations were re-introduced on a larger scale, the aircraft now carrying a 500 lb demolition bomb beneath each wing.

Both 5th Air Force and the RAAF were growing fast at this time, and towards the end of 1943 a full group comprising three squadrons of Vengeances, three Kittyhawk squadrons and a unit of new Commonwealth Boomerang tactical fighters, moved to New Guinea to operate over the Nadzab area. For six weeks the Vengeances provided considerable dive-bomber support to the ground forces, often operating in formations up to 36 strong; the escorting Kittyhawks also frequently joined in the bombing. However the superiority of the Kittyhawk for such operations was now obvious — it carried the same two 500 lb bombs, had a far heavier armament for strafing, required a crew of only one, and could take care of itself in the event of fighter attack. Improved American close support types, including a group of P-47 fighter-bombers, were now also becoming available. Consequently early in 1944 the Vengeances were recalled to Australia, and saw no further action.

With less opposition in the air, US fighters were now also frequently carrying bombs, sometimes dive-bombing whilst escorting bomber formations. Considerable fighter-bomber support was provided by both the US and Australian units during mid 1944 when landings on areas of the New Guinea coast still occupied by the

The RAAF was supplied with a number of A-20 'strafers', employing one squadron of these aircraft over the front until late in 1944. Aircraft of this unit — 22 Squadron — are seen here on Noemfoor Island. Both aircraft in the foreground exhibit large totals of mission symbols, indicating the frequent use made of these aircraft. The aircraft coded DU-U carries the serial A28-28.
F.F.Smith

The main RAAF fighter-bomber throughout the Pacific war was the Curtiss Kittyhawk in its various models. Here late-model Mark IVs (P-40Ns) of 80 Squadron, RAAF, are seen flying from Morotai Island in the Southern East Indies in early 1945. Each aircraft is armed with a pair of underwing 500 lb bombs. *F.F.Smith*

Japanese were made, and on islands nearby such as Wakde, Noemfoor and Morotai. P-47s and Kittyhawks played a large part in these operations, in company with the increased strength of B-25 and A-20 strafers, and the Beaufighters. By this time the RAAF was receiving Kittyhawk IVs — P-40Ns — with which they frequently carried three 500 lb bombs.

After September 1944 the 5th Air Force concentrated its attention on the Philippines, moving to these islands after the initial landings in October. The RAAF was left behind with responsibility for the areas of New Guinea, New Britain and the Northern Solomons still in Japanese hands — a responsibility which it was to share with the RNZAF.

SOUTH PACIFIC, AUGUST 1942-SEPTEMBER 1944

Following the halt imposed on the Japanese in New Guinea in March 1942, they proceeded to spread on down the Solomon Islands chain into the South Pacific. When it was noted that an airfield was under construction on Guadalcanal Island, the US High Command decided that it was time to act, and on August 7 the first US amphibious landing of the war was made on this obscure island. It then became the focal point of the war in the Pacific for several months, both sides expending every effort to maintain and improve their respective positions.

The initial landings were supported by US carrier aircraft, but shortly afterwards, with the airfield in US hands, Marine Corps fighter and dive-bomber units were flown in, soon joined by a USAAF P-400 squadron. Subsequently US Navy dive-bombers and fighter squadrons were also to be based on the island. Heavy Japanese air raids followed, but it was quickly apparent that the P-400 was not up to combatting these, and while the air fighting was left to the Marine and Navy pilots thereafter, the P-400s joined the SBDs in September in providing close support to the ground forces, and attacking Japanese seaborne supply convoys trying to reach the island.

Initially each P-400 carried a single 100 lb bomb, but when P-39s arrived during the month, these carried 300 pounders. More P-39 units arrived before the end of the year, but at this stage Japanese Navy D3A dive-bombers began appearing over the island, as Japanese carriers entered the area to do battle with their US counterparts. By the end of the year the island was firmly in American hands, and offensive sorties became possible. In December an airfield under constructon at Munda, New Georgia, was attacked, and by now the P-39s were carrying 500 lb bombs beneath their bellies.

A second USAAF fighter group arrived in January 1943 with P-40s and P-39s, and further reinforcements including an RNZAF Kittyhawk squadron, and some P-38s, were not far behind. The Japanese Navy now brought several of its carrier air groups ashore and sent them down to the main Southern naval base at Rabaul, New Britain. From here in early 1943 they launched a series of heavy attacks on Guadalcanal, the main striking force being D3A dive-bombers. Throughout 1943 the fighting surged back and forth. Further US landings were made on islands in the Solomons to acquire airfields nearer to Rabaul, such landings bringing out the Japanese dive-bombers in force. Meanwhile raids at an increasing intensity were launched on Rabaul by both medium bombers, and by Marine Dauntlesses.

When the new generation of US Navy carriers began their series of attacks on Japanese island bases late in 1943, the Dauntless dive-bomber still made up a major part of their air striking power. Bomb-laden SBD-5s of Bombing Squadron VB-16 from USS *Lexington* are seen heading for Saipan on 15 June 1944. *Smithsonian Institute via R.M.Hill*

Fighter-bombing operations in the Solomons Islands did not commence on any large scale until early 1944, following the departure of the Japanese fighter units from Rabaul. Here US Marine Vought F4U-1 Corsairs are seen en route to the target, each aircraft carrying a 1,000 lb bomb beneath the forward fuselage.
American Official via IWM

Vought F4U-1D Corsair fighter-bomber of US Marine Corps Fighting Squadron VMF-312, flown by Lt Fred M.Borwell. This unit was the first to operate from an airfield on Okinawa in April 1945; USMC Corsairs provided the main support for the forces subduing this island. The aircraft carries 5 in High Velocity Aircraft Rockets (HVARs).

Marine Vought F4U-1 Corsairs first saw action over the Solomon during 1943, and additional RNZAF Kittyhawk units also arrived. In November US landings on Bougainville Island brought further Japanese air reinforcements to the area, while a series of counter strikes by US Navy carriers introduced such new types as the Grumman F6F Hellcat fighter and Curtiss SB2C Helldiver dive bomber to action.

Although P-39s frequently strafed inter-island barge traffic, the intensity of air fighting during 1943 effectively put an end to fighter bomber operations, while dive-bombers played a major role on either side. By early 1944 the Japanese had decided that the cost of maintaining their position in the Solomons was too high, and by February their main air units had been withdrawn. Thereafter the remaining US Marine Corps units, the RNZAF, and the US 13th Air

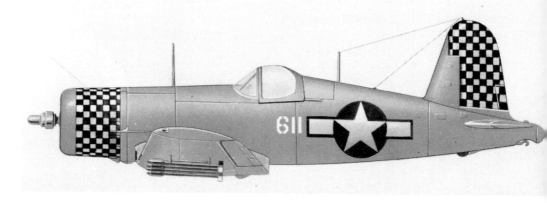

Force spent their time attacking by-passed island garrisons, and pounding the remaining defences at Rabaul. At this time the Marines began fighter-bomber sorties with their powerful Corsairs, these aircraft also gradually beginning to replace the Kittyhawks in the New Zealand squadrons. Most USAAF fighter units had already converted to P-38s, those that had not done so soon following.

The Corsair, soon to become one of the really great fighter-bombers of the war, was powered with the same Pratt and Whitney Double Wasp engine that was fitted to the Thunderbolt, the R-2800-8W in the F4U providing 2,250 hp. It carried a basic armament of six .50-in machine guns in its inverted gull wings, and from the start had been designed like all US Navy fighters with a bomb load in mind. However, it was never to carry its designed load in combat; points had been incorporated in the outer wing panels for the carriage of two 100 lb bombs, while provision had been made for a jettisonable auxiliary fuel tank to be carried under the fuselage centre line, beneath the aircraft's centre section. An adaptor designed by Brewster Aviation made it possible to fit a 500 lb or 1,000 lb bomb to this pylon fitting, and it was with this modification that the Corsair first operated as a fighter-bomber. In the later F4U-1D model, twin pylons were fitted, allowing a pair of bombs to be carried of either weight, while later in the war this mighty load-carrier was making its attacks with a pair of 2,000 lb weapons — the ultimate load for a single-engined fighter-bomber during World War II. Top speed of this fighter was 425 mph.

With the invasion of the Philippines in October 1944, Marine units moved to those islands to provide support for the ground forces. The USAAF units had to wait a little longer to move in, when the 13th Air Force was incorporated into the 5th. The RNZAF remained behind to continue the neutralization of the by-passed garrisons, and to aid with the clearance of New Britain.

THE SOUTH-WEST PACIFIC AREA, OCTOBER 1944-AUGUST 1945

The initial landings in the Philippines were supported by US Navy carriers, resulting in some tremendous air battles, and the appearance of the first 'Kamikaze' suicide attacks by the Japanese. As soon as airfields ashore were available, both US 5th Air Force and Marine Corps units flew in. While A-20 and B-25 strafers, Marine F4Us and SBDs, together with P-47s and P-40s provided close support for the ground forces, P-38s and other P-47s provided air defence as the Japanese sent in wave after wave of aerial reinforcements. Shipping convoys attempting to carry reinforcements from outlying islands were also attacked by combined forces of fighter-bombers. Gradually the weight of air combat subsided, and the fighters were able to give

As the quality of Japanese fighter opposition diminished, US Navy Grumman F6F Hellcats began increasingly to carry bombs and to join in the attack on ground installations. This F6F-5 about to take off from a carrier deck, carries a 1,-000 lb bomb under its fuselage. Note that new zero-length rocket launching rails are also featured beneath the wings. *Smithsonian Institute via R.M.Hill*

increased attention to ground support. Napalm was introduced in February 1945, in containers varying from 75-165 gallons.

Latest versions of the P-38 and P-51 became available in quantity at this time, and during June 49th Fighter Group Lightnings were able to begin attacks on Formosa. Napalm was used in one such raid, while on others dive and skip-bombing attacks were made on railway bridges and other such targets with 1,000 lb bombs, other aircraft dropping fragmentation bomb clusters to silence the AA defences. The fighting in the Philippines and raids on Formosa continued until the end of the war.

Meanwhile the RAAF units on Morotai and New Guinea were titled 1st Tactial Air Force from October 1944, comprising two Beaufighter squadrons, six Kittyhawk squadrons, and various other units, with a further Beaufighter unit and two Spitfire squadrons on the way. Attacks were first made on Celebes in the East Indies, and on other targets in the area. By January 1945 napalm was becoming available, whilst the Beaufighters were being fitted with rocket projectiles, 500 lb bombs and depth charges. 1st TAF had grown ever bigger by April, but had little to do. However, a landing on Tarakan island was ordered, followed by one on Labuan. Having secured bases near Borneo, a landing in the Balikpapan area was then undertaken late in the war, the Spitfire VIII squadrons joining in the fighter bomber operations at this time.

In New Britain and Bougainville meanwhile, Australian Boomerangs moved to join the RNZAF Corsair units, now augmened by New Zealand Dauntless dive-bombers, the little Australian fighter leading these aircraft to bomb specific targets with 500 and 1,000 lb bombs. Operations here were designed to keep the by-passed Japanese quiescent until the end of the war.

INDIA AND BURMA

During the initial retreat from Burma no ground attack aircraft were available to either side. Fighters of both combatants made airfield strafes, but none were fitted for bomb-carrying, and the best that could be done was to carry a few small anti-personnel bombs in the flare chutes of American Volunteer Group Tomahawks.

Towards the end of the retreat the AVG received a few P-40E Kittyhawks, and with these were able to undertake some fighter-bomber sorties against Japanese columns, before withdrawing into the interior of China in May 1942. Some of the first US reinforcements to reach India were P-40s of the 51st Fighter Group, which took up station in Assam to protect the base of the 'Hump' air route into China. These aircraft were soon undertaking fighter-bomber missions against the advancing Japanese, dropping 500 lb bombs in support of this distant Eastern end of the front. In October 1942 the unit withdrew to China, being replaced by the similarly-equipped 80th Fighter Group.

During the 1942 monsoon little aerial activity took place elsewhere, and not until an abortive British offensive was launched in the Arakan Peninsula late in the year did much happen. This 'push' was supported by the first RAF dive-bomber squadron, No 45, which took Vultee Vengeances into action for the first time on November 27. It was joined early in 1943 by three more such units — 82, 110 and 8 (Indian Air Force) Squadrons. Flying in formations of six or twelve aircraft, the Vengeances always operated with fighter escort, diving

The only single-engined fighter unit in Burma to use British rockets was 20 Squadron, RAF. Here armourers are fitting these weapons to the launching racks of two of the squadron's Hurricane IVs. It will be noted that these tropicalized aircraft have no main gun armament in the wings, this allowing them to be adapted speedily for the carriage of underwing 40 mm anti-tank cannon when necessary. *IWM*

steeply to attack their targets with a 1,000 lb bombload, made up of two 500 pounders or four of 250 lb. Hurricanes also strafed in support of the ground forces, usually concentrating on transport targets such as lorries, ox carts, columns of men, or sampans on the many rivers. The first units to operate in this way were 607 and 615 Squadrons, the latter unit having introduced the first cannon-armed Mark IICs to this front. By early 1943 at least four more Hurricane and two Mohawk units were joining in the strafing, while 27 Squadron had entered action withh Beaufighters, ranging further afield to strafe locomotives on the railways, storage tanks, coastal shipping and other such targets.

The monsoon again resulted in a lull in operations during mid 1943, but towards the end of that year the British once more prepared for an offensive in the Arakan, while the Japanese greatly increased their aerial activity over the area, as they too prepared a major offensive, designed to burst into India and cut the 'Hump' route to China. The Allied air forces had been substantially strengthened by this time. Spitfires had arrived for air defence, leaving more Hurricanes free for strafing, and two former bomber squadrons had re-equipped with the Mark IIC version of the aircraft specially for ground-support activities.

A second Beaufighter squadron was now operating, but the first had temporarily re-equipped with Mosquitos, which it operated on the same long-range strafing duties. The USAAF had made available a squadron of P-38s for air superiority work, these fighters also undertaking long-range strafes of Japanese airfields. To support the Chinese-American forces near the Chinese frontier, the 311th Fighter-Bomber Group with North American A-36A Invaders and P-51A Mustangs had arrived and was just entering operations in the ground support role.

North American P-51A Mustang of the US 1st Air Commando Group, which supported Orde Wingate's Chindits on their second expedition. This particular aircraft carries a 1,-000 lb bomb and a rocket tube cluster beneath each wing. *USAF*

During 1944 the main RAF fighter-bomber on the Burma front became the Republic Thunderbolt, these American-built aircraft steadily replacing the remaining Hurricanes. An RAF 'erk' commits his feelings towards the enemy to writing on a 500 lb. calling card! *IWM*

QL61
YOU'VE HAD IT
CHUM

While the Americans were thus receiving a fair degree of fighter-bomber support, the British army was still reliant mainly on the Vengeances, and on strafing Hurricanes. The first RAF fighter-bombers in Burma, rather strangely, were the sole remaining Curtiss Mohawks of a single squadron, which now began dropping 20 lb Armour Piercing, 30 lb incendiary, and 40 lb GP bombs, moving to Imphal to support the forces there in this role.

The availability of Spitfires, and of additional Hurricane squadrons, coupled with a withdrawal of part of the JAAF strength from Burma early in 1944, allowed the diversion of Hurricanes to fighter/dive-bomber duties — particularly as several more Blenheim bomber units had recently converted to the aircraft for this very purpose.

The British Arakan offensive late in 1943 was met by a Japanese counter-offensive, following which, early in the New Year, the latter's attacks on Kohima and Imphal heralded the start of one of the major land battles of the Far Eastern war. Now however the British did not retreat as before, but dug in, relying on air power for supply and support. Much more became available, for during the early weeks of the year five additional squadrons of Hurricane IICs began strafing operations, while three other units of these aircraft and one with Hurricane IVs, began dive-bombing with 500 lb bombs. A new Beaufighter unit, 211 Squadron, introduced the 25 lb and 60 lb rocket projectiles to the theatre, employing these mainly against rivercraft during long-range strafes. US P-40N Warhawks of the 80th Fighter Group also lent a hand, while the Vengeances were extremely active.

Up to four squadrons were available much of the time, operating often with a bomb line very close to the forward troops.

During April 1944 for example, 110 Squadron flew 542 sorties, making 55 separate strikes and dropping 2,319 bombs with a total weight of 703,000 lb. When the last Vengeance operations ceased in June, the aircraft had given splendid service on the Burma front. In 18 months of almost continuous action — much of it when Japanese air power was still extremely evident, they had not suffered a single casualty to air attack, and only a relatively small number to ground fire.

Just before the Japanese advance up the Imphal Valley had begun, Orde Wingate's Chindits had been air-landed in territory behind hostile lines to cut communications and generally create havoc. For their support a special new American formation, subsequently called the 1st Air Commando Group, had arrived in January, equipped with a balanced force of P-51A Mustangs, B-25 bombers, transport, glider and light liaison aircraft. The P-51A squadron entered action in February, just before the Chindit operation began, becoming the first Mustang unit to drop 1,000 lb bombs. During March it also introduced the American bazooka-tube clusters to action over Burma. Initially these P-51As undertook a number of very successful long-range airfield attacks, on occasions carrying a drop tank under one wing and a 500 lb bomb beneath the other. Ground support sorties in aid of the Chindits were flown until the latter returned in May, the unit then withdrawing to India to replace its Mustangs with P-47Ds.

Meanwhile during December 1943 the first Hurricane IIDs to reach the area had gone into action with 20 Squadron. Lack of Japanese armour meant that most sorties here were flown against road and river craft. Against these however the solid shot of the 40 mm Vickers 'S' guns proved somewhat ineffective, and it was some weeks before supplies of adequate high explosive ammunition was available. A detachment was sent to operate from the besieged Imphal area, and here during June a few Japanese tanks were at last encountered. Against these the 40 mm proved very effective and all of 12 seen were put out of action for the loss of one aircraft. By the end of the month the squadron had also destroyed 501 sampans, 348 dugouts and many other targets.

After the raising of the Imphal siege an interesting test was carried out against a number of captured tanks. Hurricane IIDs fired 128 rounds at them, gaining 33 hits, while Hurricane IICs of 11 Squadron fired 680 rounds from their quadruple 20 mm cannons, gaining only 19 hits.

So little opposition was met in the air during mid 1944, that four squadrons of air superiority Spitfire VIIIs at time descended from their patrolling to undertake some strafes. However new fighter-bomber equipment was about to make its appearance, as large quantities of Thunderbolts were being supplied to the RAF by the United States. The first of these entered action with 261 Squadron during September 1944, and before the end of the year seven squadrons were strafing, dive-bombing with 500 lb bombs, and on occasion dropping canisters of the new napalm. In addition the US 80th Fighter Group was also equipped with these aircraft, as was part of another unit, the 33rd Fighter Group. For longer-range operations two squadrons of Mosquito VIs and three of Beaufighter Xs were available, the former carrying bombs and the latter rockets in addition to their heavy gun armaments. Two more squadrons of Beaufighters and one of Mosquitos would join them early in 1945, as would a further four Thunderbolt units, all of which had previously been Hurricane squadrons. The air forces supporting the 14th Army in Burma had now become 3rd Tactical Air Force. As the British forces advanced steadily southwards however, some American units were withdrawn to China, both the 311th and the 1st Air Commando Groups leaving during December 1944.

Operations in Burma were now following closely the pattern in Italy and Western Europe. In February 1945 during the crossing of the Irrawaddy River, and fighting around Meiktila, the Thunderbolts frequently flew 'Cab Rank' operations, joined at that time by P-51D Mustangs of the newly-formed 2nd Air Commando Group. 20 Squadron also joined in these operations, having re-equipped one

The USAAF 51st Fighter Group operated in Assam and then in China, defending the China-India 'Hump' route, and then aiding the Chinese ground forces. Here a 1,-000 lb bomb is being attached to one of the units P-40 Warhawks, marked with the 'Assam Dragon' sabre-tooth tiger nose markings, and the unusual name. *USAF via W.N.Hess*

flight with Hurricane IVs during December, fitted with rocket rails — the only RAF single-engined squadron to use these weapons in Burma.

Shortage of rockets became so severe during February that two of the new Mark IVs were converted to gun carriers. On 19th of that month 13 heavy, medium and light tanks were seen in the village of Paunggadaw, to the south of the Allied bridge-head, and all were destroyed — most by the 40 mm cannons, though a few 60 lb RP hits were also achieved. Subsequently the Mark IIDs hunted motor transport on the roads, whilst the Mark IVs sought rivercraft on the Sittang. When operations ceased in June, 20 Squadron was the last RAF Hurricane unit still in action anywhere in the world.

During the final advance on Rangoon some of the Spitfire VIII squadrons undertook their first bombing sorties, while during the capture of the city in May Mosquitos operated in 'Cab Ranks' as most other fighter-bomber units were based too far away for sustained operations, only the Mosquito enjoying the necessary range. After the fall of Rangoon operations were directed against Japanese troops attempting to escape across the Sittang into Thailand. Many bombing and strafing sorties were flown on these duties until the end of hostilities.

CHINA

After the retreat into China in early 1942, the AVG (American Volunteer Group) P-40s, which formed the basis of the US 23rd Fighter Group in July 1942, were heavily committed to air fighting, which restricted the possibilities of their use as fighter-bombers. On

Only known illustration of a P-40 Warhawk fitted with rocket tube clusters. This aircraft, seen on an airfield in China, also features a long-range droptank beneath the fuselage.
J.Christie via W.N.Hess

occasions bombs were carried, as on October 27 when 500 pounders were dropped on Hong Kong harbour during a joint raid with B-25s.

Arrival of the 51st Fighter Group late in the year allowed a few more ground support missions to be undertaken in aid of the Chinese armies during 1943, when the line stayed fairly static until late in that year. In November 1943 a Japanese offensive led to fairly intensive bombing and strafing duties, and this was repeated in June 1944, when a major Japanese offensive was launched to gain a direct overland route through to Thailand.

The first P-51Bs arrived at this time, and became greatly involved in close support, carrying a wide variety of warloads, including fragmentation clusters, rocket tubes and a selection of heavier bombs. The US air elements in China had become the 14th Air Force during 1943, but they were not really greatly strengthened until the beginning of 1945. At that time the 311th Fighter Group and 1st Air Commando Group with P-51Ds and P-47s respectively, arrived from India, and the P-47-equipped 81st Fighter Group — a veteran of the North African Campaigns — joined the fray, together with a number of P-40 and P-51 equipped Chinese-American fighter groups. These units were all in action until the end of the war.

THE CENTRAL PACIFIC

Following the initial carrier strikes on ground targets, the opposing fleets first clashed in May 1942 in the Coral Sea. In the first major naval engagement fought by aircraft alone, the dive-bombers of both sides were instrumental in achieving the greater part of the destruction inflicted. Again the following month it was the US Navy SBDs which sank four Japanese aircraft carriers, although Marine SBDs and SB2U-3s from Midway Island were less successful and suffered heavy losses.

In subsequent fighting in the Solomons area later in 1942, American SBDs and Japanese D3As attacked not only shipping, but targets ashore as well, during the battle for Guadalcanal. 1943 saw little carrier action however, as both combatants strove to rebuild their shattered carrier fleets and air divisions — a task in which the Americans, with their greater production facilities, achieved a notable advantage.

They returned with a new breed of fast carriers during late 1943, with new aircraft aboard such as the Grumman F6F Hellcat fighter, and the SB2C Helldiver dive-bomber. The latter however was still playing second fiddle to a larger number of improved versions of the older SBD Dauntless. During initial strikes on Marcus Island and Rabaul during late 1943, the dive-bombers and torpedo-bombers played the main striking role, though the Hellcats strafed when air opposition was not in evidence.

By early 1945 the powerful SB2C-4 Helldiver had taken over the dive-bombing role from the Dauntless on most carriers. These aircraft of VB-3 from USS *Yorktown* are heading out over the massed shipping of the Allied fleets off Okinawa in February 1945. Note that they are augmenting the normal bomb-bay load with underwing 500 lb bombs. *Smithsonian Institute via R.M.Hill*

Of these new aircraft the Hellcat was to see by far the wider service. Powered by a 2,000 hp Pratt and Whitney R-2800-10 radial, it attained a maximum speed of 376 mph with an armament of six wing-mounted .50-in machine guns. It would later carry two underwing bombs of either 500 or 1,000 lb weight. The SB2C-1 was powered by a Wright R-2600-8 engine of 1,700 hp, which gave it a top speed of 281 mph. Fixed armament was four wing-mounted .50s, with two flexible .30s in the rear cockpit for defence. A 1,000 lb bomb was carried internally in a fuselage bomb bay. Later models, which entered service in 1944, featured an improved performance with a top speed just below 300 mph, and with the wing-mounted .50s replaced by a pair of 20 mm cannon.

Strikes on island bases in the Gilberts and Marshalls were followed by attacks on the main Japanese naval base at Truk, and then the Marianas in February 1944. At this time the Japanese, as they rebuilt their carrier air groups, were introducing a new dive-bomber, the Yokosuka D4Y. This was a modern monoplane of sleek appearance, with a retractable undercarriage and an Aichi Atsuta 32 inline engine of 1,340 hp. Armament and bombload were virtually identical with the earlier D3A, but the aircraft was endowed with the very high maximum speed of 360 mph.

The new aircraft first saw action during June 1944 when a massive US Navy carrier task force covered and supported a landing on Saipan island in the Marianas. As soon as landing grounds ashore were available, P-47Ds of the 318th Fighter Group from the Central Pacific US 7th Air Force, flew in from a carrier to provide close support for the troops.

By mid-1944 the Hellcats were also carrying bombs for their strikes on airfields and in support of landing troops, a pair of 500 lb GP missiles being the normal load. September 1944 saw the introduction on some carriers of napalm tanks also. Thereafter the Hellcats played an ever-greater part in the offensive operations of the Task Forces in their attacks on the various island targets, and against units of the Japanese Navy. The aircraft was economical of space and crew; it could carry virtually the same bombload as the SBD, possessed a heavier strafing armament, and could look after itself. It also allowed for a greater standardization of spare parts, tool kits and replacement aircraft carried — a very important consideration for the limited space availability in a carrier. The aircraft was also very flexible, being able to undertake either offensive or defensive missions. Indeed, of the economies of concentrating production on one basic type, rather than on several specialized ones, it epitomized the fighter-bomber's multiple advantages over dive-bombers, attack aircraft, or any other types for ground-attack duties, except perhaps in the highly-specialised tank attack role.

At the start of 1945 such large numbers of F6Fs were being carried by some Fleet carriers that it became necessary for administrative purposes to divide them into two squadrons — a fighter and a fighter-bomber unit — although in practice both carried out identical duties. The development of the new zero-length rocket launcher stubs allowed these to be fitted to US Navy fighters early in 1945, supplies of

While US Fleet carriers operated F6F Hellcats and F4U Corsairs during 1945, the smaller escort carriers continued to carry aboard the smaller and older Wildcat in its up-dated versions. Used mainly to give close support to forces once they were ashore, FM-2 Wildcats such as this one operated over the Philippines and Okinawa. Here an aircraft of VC-84 leaves USS *Makin Island* during March 1945 for a sortie over the latter target. It carries three of the new 5-in High Velocity Aircraft Rockets on zero-length launchers, together with an auxiliary fuel tank under each wing. *Smithsonian Institute via R.M.Hill*

the new US 5-inch HVAR (High Velocity Aircraft Rocket) — a slightly larger and more sophisticated weapon than the British 3-inch rocket, becoming available.

With rockets, bombs and napalm the Hellcats covered the initial invasion of Okinawa in late March 1945, then striking at targets on Formosa, the Japanese Home Islands, and various other objectves. With the SB2Cs, which were steadily replacing the remaining SBDs, Hellcats joined in raids which sank most of the remaining major Japanese warships.

Meanwhile the US Marine Corps continued to use its SBDs in the Solomons throughout 1944, but following the departure of Japanese aviation units from this area the Corsair units steadily went over to fighter-bombing from 1944 onwards, squadrons VMF 222, 223 and 224 first introducing the aircraft to these duties. In March 1944 Corsairs of VMF 111 undertook dive-bombing sorties in support of Marine landings on Mille Island in the Marshalls.

Following the invasion of the Philippines late in the year, most Marine Corps units moved to support ground forces in that area, operating almost entirely in the ground support role. Late in the war a few SB2C dive-bombers were taken on charge by the Marines, but most work in the Philippines was undertaken initially by F4Us and SBDs.

'The Sweetheart of Okinawa'. Marine Corsairs provided a high level of close support to the ground forces on Okinawa, using 5-in HVARs, napalm canisters and high explosive bombs. This photograph of an F4U-1A Corsair launching its broadside of eight rockets is believed to have been the first air-to-air shot ever taken from behind a firing aircraft. The blast blew the photographic P-38 onto its right wing, and almost caused it to crash.
US Marine Corps

Corsair fighter-bombers of Marine Fighting Squadron VMF-214 (The Black Sheep) on Okinawa in 1945, preparing for a strike. These aircraft are F4U-4Cs, armed with four 20 mm cannon instead of the usual six .50-in Brownings in the wings. The aircraft taxiing carries four 5-in HVARs beneath each outer wing panel, whilst under the fuselage are a 1,000 lb bomb and a drop tank containing either fuel or napalm. *Smithsonian Institute*

The Okinawa invasion of March 1945 provided a new area of operations for the Marines, who were to employ their greatest concentration of air power of the war on this island. The first Corsair squadrons were flown in during April, and by May some twelve units of these fighter-bombers were available, including some of the very latest F4U-4 models, which possessed an improved performance. While at times carrying two 1,000 lb bombs, or napalm, a typical load for Marine Corsairs at this time was a pair of 500 pounders beneath the centre section, with four HVARs on zero-length launchers beneath each outer wing panel. Providing close support on the 'Cab Rank' principle throughout the fierce fighting leading to Okinawa's subjugation, the aircraft was to be christened by the grateful ground forces "The Sweetheart of Okinawa". The pilots were also frequently in action against the swarms of suicide aircraft sent to attack US and British shipping off the island, a task in which the Corsairs achieved considerable success.

Other Marine Corsairs had gone aboard US carriers at this time to aid in the fight against the 'Kamikazes', whilst some Navy units were also at last equipped with these aircraft. As a result Corsairs were to join in the final series of fighter-bomber attacks on the Home Islands later in the year.

British carrier fighters also operated in the Pacific and the Indian Ocean at this stage of the war. Hellcats, fitted with standard British RP launching rails on special underwing fairings, or carrying bombs, attacked targets along the coast of southern and central

The *Ta-dan* bomb container of the Japanese Army Air Force, introduced to service late in the war, mainly for use by fighter-bombers. This hexagonal container carried 12 small incendiary missiles.

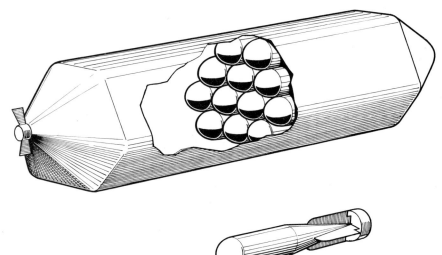

Burma, and in the Andaman Islands, while later British Hellcats and Corsairs, joined by rocket-firing two-seater Fairey Firefly reconnaissance-fighters, took part in the strikes on Okinawa and the Home Islands during 1945.

In this task they were also joined by long-range P-47N fighter-bombers of the 7th Air Force's 318th Fighter Group in the Ryukus, and by the Strategic 20th Air Force's 414th Fighter Group on Iwo Jima — the latter specializing in attacks on Japanese radar stations. The P-47N was able to carry both a 500 lb bomb and a battery of HVARs beneath each wing for these missions.

Final version of the Republic Thunderbolt to see action was the long-range P-47N, which flew a few sorties over the Japanese home islands during the closing weeks of the war. This large and heavy aircraft depicts one of the many varieties of warload it could carry, in this case comprising two 1,000 lb bombs and ten 5 in. HVARs. *USAF via IWM*

To the end of the war Japanese fighters still very rarely carried bombs of any type for ground attack purposes. In Burma Nakajima Ki 43 fighters of the JAAF on occasions carried a pair of 110 lb underwing bombs during 1944 for attacks on British airfields, while the Army also developed the *Ta-dan* late in the war, this being a container bomb with a quantity of small incendiaries inside. Bombs were also carried on a few missions in China and the Philippines by Army Nakajima Ki 84 fighters. However, as by this time the Japanese were generally on the defensive and greatly outnumbered, there were few opportunities to develop this form of attack. The most frequent occasions on which bombs were carried was when fighters were employed on suicide missions, to dive into their targets with their bomb. In these cases a weapon usually of around 500 lb weight was strapped to the fuselage of the aircraft.

Thus by 1945 the ground attack aircraft had gone full circle. Most specialized types — with the major exception of the Soviet *Shturmovik* — had disappeared from service (or were soon to do so in the case of the US Navy's dive-bombers). The main weapon of ground support was once again the bomb-carrying fighter, as it had been in 1918, and as it continues to be to the present day.

Appendix

Major ground attack/support aircraft used during World War II

Type	Service	Operational area/time
Focke Wulf Fw 190A	Luftwaffe, Hungarian AF	Western Europe 1942-45, Eastern Front 1943-45, Mediterranean 1943-45
Fw 190F & G	Luftwaffe	Western Europe 1943-45, Eastern Front 1943-45, Mediterranean 1943-45
Henschel Hs 123A	Luftwaffe	Poland 1939, Western Europe 1940, Balkans 1941, Eastern Front 1942-44
Hs 129B	Luftwaffe, Rumanian AF	Mediterranean 1942-43, Eastern Front 1942-45
Junkers Ju 87B	Luftwaffe, Rumanian, Hungarian, Bulgarian and Italian AFs	Poland 1939, Western Front 1940, Balkans 1941, Mediterranean 1941-42, Eastern Front 1941-42
Ju 87D	Luftwaffe, Rumanian, Hungarian and Italian AFs	Mediterranean 1942-44, Eastern Front 1942-45, Western Europe (night) 1944-45
Ju 87G	Luftwaffe	Eastern Front 1943-45, Western Europe 1944
Ju 88C	Luftwaffe	Mediterranean 1941-43, Eastern Front 1942-43
Messerschmitt Bf 109E & F	Luftwaffe, Hungarian AF	Western Europe 1941-43, Eastern Front 1941-43, Mediterranean 1941-43
Bf 110C & D	Luftwaffe	Western Europe 1940-41, Eastern Front 1941-44, Mediterranean 1941-43
Me 210C	Hungarian AF	Eastern Front 1944-45
Me 262	Luftwaffe	Western Europe 1944-45
Blackburn Skua	FAA	Western Europe 1939-40, Mediterranean 1941
Bristol Beaufighter I & VI	RAF, RAAF	Western Europe 1942-44, Mediterranean 1941-44, Far East 1943-45

Beaufighter X	RAF, RAAF	Western Europe 1944-45, Mediterranean 1943-45, Far East 1944-45
De Havilland Mosquito VI	RAF, RCAF	Western Europe 1942-45, Far East 1944-45
Fairey Firefly I	FAA	Western Europe 1944-45, Far East 1945
Hawker Hurricane II & IV	RAF	Western Europe 1941-43, Mediterranean 1941-44, Far East 1942-45
Hurricane IID	RAF	Mediterranean 1941-43, Far East 1944-45
Typhoon I	RAF, RCAF	Western Europe 1943-45
Supermarine Spitfire IX	RAF, RCAF	Western Europe 1943-45, Mediterranean 1944-45
Westland Whirlwind I	RAF	Western Europe 1941-43
Bell P-39 Airacobra	USAAF, Soviet AF	Mediterranean 1942-43, Eastern Front 1943-45, Far East 1942-44
P-63 Kingcobra	Soviet AF	Eastern Front 1943-45
Curtiss P-40 Kittyhawk/ Warhawk series	USAAF, RAF, RAAF, SAAF, RNZAF, Soviet AF	Mediterranean 1941-44, Eastern Front 1943-44, Far East 1942-44
SB2C Helldiver	USN, USMC	Far East 1942-45
Douglas A-20 Havoc series	USAAF	Mediterranean 1943-45, Far East 1943-45
SBD/A-24 Dauntless	USN, USMC, USAAF, Armee de l'Air, Aeronavale, RNZAF	Mediterranean 1942-44, Western Europe 1944, Far East 1942-45
Grumman F6F Hellcat	USN, FAA	Mediterranea 1944-45, Far East 1942-45
Lockheed P-38 Lightning	USAAF	Mediterranean 1942-44, Western Europe 1943-45, Far East 1942-45
North American A-36A	USAAF	Mediterranean 1943-44, Far East 1943-44

P-51 Mustang series	USAAF, RAF, SAAF	Western Europe 1943-45, Mediterranean 1943-45, Far East 1942-45
B-25 Mitchell	USAAF	Far East 1942-45, Mediterranean 1943-45
Republic P-47 Thunderbolt series	USAAF, RAF, Armée de l'Air, Brazilian AF	Western Europe 1943-45, Mediterranean 1943-45 Far East 1943-45
Vought F4U Corsair series	USN, USMC, FAA, RNZAF	Far East 1942-45
SB2U Vindicator	USMC, Aeronavale	Western Europe 1944, Far East 1943-44
Vultee A-35 Vengeance	RAF, RAAF	Far East 1943-45
Ilyushin Il-2 (BSh-2)	Soviet and Polish AFs	Eastern Front 1941-45, Far East 1945
Il-10	Soviet AF	Eastern Front 1945
Breguet Br 693	Armee de l'Air	Western Europe 1940
Loire-Nieuport LN 411	Aeronavale	Western Europe 1940
LaGG-3	Soviet AF	Eastern Front 1941-44
Petlyakov Pe-2 (PB-100)	Soviet AF	Eastern Front 1941-45
Sukhoi Su-2 (BB-1)	Soviet AF	Eastern Front 1941-43
Yakovlev Yak-9B, -9T	Soviet AF	Eastern Front 1943-45
Commonwealth CA-13 Boomerang	RAAF	SW Pacific 1941-43
Breda Ba 65	Regia Aeronautica	Mediterranean 1940-42
Ba 88 Lince	Regia Aeronautica	Mediterranean 1940-41
Fiat CR.32	Regia Aeronautica	Mediterranean 1940-43
CR.42-AS Falco	Regia Aeronautica	Mediterranean 1940-43
G.50*bis* Freccia	Regia Aeronautica	Mediterranean 1940-43
Macchi MC.200 Saetta	Regia Aeronautica	Mediterranean 1941-43
Reggiane Re 2001 Falco II	Regia Aeronautica,	Mediterranean 1943-45
Re 2002 Ariete	Regia Aeronautica,	Mediterranean 1942-45
Aichi D3A ('Val')	IJNAF	Pacific 1941-43
Yokosuka D4Y ('Judy')	IJNAF	Pacific 1942-45
IAR 81	Rumanian AF	Eastern Front 1943-44

Bibliography

9th Air Force   Kenn C. Rust   *Aero*   1967
Pacific Sweep   William N. Hess   *Doubleday*   1974
Carrier Fighters   David Brown   *Macdonald and Jane's*   1975
Russian Aircraft Since 1940   Jean Alexander   *Putnam*   1975
Luftwaffe War Diaries   Caius Bekker   *Macdonald*   1967
Warplanes of World War II series   William Green   *Macdonald*   Various
American Combat Planes   Ray Wagner   *Macdonald*   1960
The Birth of the Luftwaffe   Hanfried Schliephake   *Ian Allan*   1971
Fighter Squadrons of the RAF   John Rawlings   *Macdonald*   1969
Japanese Bombers of World War II   Rene Francillon   *Hilton Lacey*   1969
Fifth Air Force Story   Kenn C. Rust   *Historical Aviation Album*   1973
Battle Over Britain   Francis Mason   *McWhirter Twins*
Flying Leathernecks in World War II   Thomas E. Doll   *Aero*   1971
Italian Civil & Military Aircraft, 1930-1945   *Aero*   1963
Saga of the Bent Wing Bird   Walter A. Musciano   *Aerofile*
The Soviet Air Force in World War II   Ray Wagner   *Doubleday*   1973
USMC Aircraft, 1914-1959   William T. Larkins   *Aviation History Publications*   1959
The Hawker Hurricane   Francis Mason   *Macdonald*   1962
Air War Against Japan, 1943-1945   George Odgers   *Australian War Memorial*   1957
Stuka Pilot   Hans-Ulrich Rudel   *Euphorion*   1953
Stuka! Junkers Ju 87   Richard P. Bateson   *Ducimus*   1972
2nd Tactical Air Force   Christopher Shores   *Osprey*   1970
Fighters Over the Desert   Christopher Shores & Hans Ring   *Neville Spearman*   1969
Fighters Over Tunisia   Christopher Shores, Hans Ring & William N. Hess   *Neville Spearman*   1975
Mediterranean Air War, Vols 1-3   Christopher Shores   *Ian Allan*   Various

Various Profile Publications, Osprey Aircams and a selection of magazine articles in Air Pictorial, RAF Flying Review and Flying Review International, Aero Album, and AAHS Journal.

Index

Afrika Korps 59, 60, 65
Aichi D3A 'Val' 38, 160, 162, 167, 177
Airacobra — *see* Bell P-39/400
Air Support Signals Units 156
Allenby, Gen. Sir Edmund 13
American Volunteer Group (AVG) 171, 176
'Apple Pie' 132
Arado Ar 65 27
  Ar 81 28

B-25 — *see* North American B-25
Baltimore — *see* Martin
BB-1 — *see* Sukhoi Su-2
Beaufort — *see* Commonwealth (CA)
Beaumont, WgCdr Roland 155
Beech XA-38 115
Bell FM-1 Airacuda 34, 35
  P-39 Airacobra 65, 66, 75, 76, 113, 128, 129, 131, 135, 162, 167, 168
  P-400 162, 166, 167
BETAB-150DS (Soviet rocket projectile) 32
Bf 109 — *see* Messerschmitt Bf 109
Bf 110 — *see* Messerschmitt Bf 110
BK 3,7 cannon 85, 86
BK 5 cannon 86
BK 7,5 cannon 98
Blackburn Skua 37, 41, 45
Blohm & Voss Bv 137 28
Boeing F4B 22
Bohrt, *Major* Roland 61
Boulton Paul Defiant 46
Breda Ba 64 36
  Ba 65 36, 37, 51, 52
  Ba 88 Lince 34, 35, 36
Breguet Br 690 34
  Br 691 45
  Br 693 35, 44
  Br 695 35
Brewster F2A-1 25
  Model 339 160
  XA-32 113
Bristol Beaufighter 34, 35, 37, 55, 56, 59, 60, 63, 105, 128, 129, 130, 131, 164, 166, 170, 172
  Beaufighter X 135, 175
  Blenheim 20
  Blenheim IF 34, 37, 44
  Blenheim IVF 56
  Fighter 13
Brown, Air Vice-Marshal L. 158
BT 200 bomb-torpedo 148
BT 400 bomb-torpedo 148
BT 800 bomb-torpedo 148

'Cab Rank' 121, 132, 175, 181
Caldwell, Sqd Ldr Clive R. 57

Caproni Ca 310 36
'Circle of Death' 75, 88, 95
Commonwealth (CA) Beaufort 164
  Boomerang 165
  Wirraway 163
Conningham, Air Marshal Sir Arthur 158
Consolidated B-24 Liberator 109
Cooper bombs 12
Cornwall, HMS cruiser 162
Corsair — *see* Vought F4U; also Vought O3U
Curtiss A-3 (Falcon) 17, 21
  A-3B 17
  XA-8 (Shrike) 17, 18
  A-12 18
  XA-14 20
  A-18 20
  BFC-1, -2 23, 28
  F8C 21
  F11C Goshawk 23, 26
  Hawk 38, 43
  O-1 21
  OC-1 Helldiver 22
  P-36 Mohawk 172, 173
  P-40 Tomahawk 56
  P-40E Kittyhawk 57, 59, 60, 62, 63, 113, 120, 126, 134, 160, 161, 162, 163, 164, 165, 166, 171
  P-40F Warhawk 53, 64, 65, 113, 115, 121, 124, 125
  P-40N Kittyhawk IV 134, 135, 166, 167, 168, 169, 170, 173, 176, 177
  SBC-3, -4, 23, 24
  SB2C Helldiver 168, 177, 178, 180

D-Day 140
DB-3F — *see* Ilyushin Il-4
De Havilland DH.4 21
  DH.5 12
  Mosquito 105, 134, 139, 149, 153, 172
  Mosquito VI 137, 140, 147, 175, 176
Dewoitine 520 44
Dornier Do 17 20
  Do 217 107
Dorsetshire, HMS cruiser 162
Douglas A-20 21, 153, 154, 163, 164, 166, 169
  A-24 113, 148, 161, 162, 165
  A-25 113
  A-26B Invader 153, 154
  XA-26 153
  Boston 61, 163, 164
  DB-7 21
  SBD Dauntless 25, 148, 160, 161, 167, 170, 177, 180
  O-2 16

Douhet, General Guilio 26
Dring, Wg Cdr 156

Enterprise, USS aircraft carrier 161

Fairey Battle 37
  Firefly 181
  Swordfish 109
Ferdinand heavy SP gun 87
Fiat CR.25 34, 35
  CR.32 28, 37, 51, 52
  CR.42 58, 59, 63, 118
  G.50*bis* 58, 64, 117, 118
Fieseler Fi 98 28
Fiji, HMS destroyer 54
Flambo 40
Focke Wulf Fw 187 34, 35
  Fw 190A 64, 105, 145, 149
  Fw 190 *Jabo* 65, 83, 88, 89, 90, 92, 94, 98, 107, 119, 125, 134, 148, 155
  Fw 190A-4 91, 105
  Fw 190A-4/U8 108
  Fw 190F 91, 93, 94, 145
  Fw 190G 91, 93, 94
Fokker XA-7 17
  C.X 37
  G.1 34, 44
Formidable, HMS aircraft carrier 54

Galland, *Hptm* (later General) Adolf 40
Gilliam, Gp Capt. D.E. 147
Gloster F.9/37 34
  Gauntlet 52
  Gladiator 51, 52
Gloucester, HMS cruiser 54
Goering, *Reichsmarschall* Hermann 148
Graf Zeppelin (German aircraft carrier) 30
Great Lakes BG-1, -2 24
Greyhound, HMS destroyer 54
Grumman F2F 24
  F3F 24
  F4F Wildcat 25, 161
  XF5F 34, 35
  F6F Hellcat 168, 177, 178, 179, 180, 181, 182
  XP-50 34, 35
'Guerilla attacks' (Il-2 tactics) 80

Hanriot NC 600 34
Hawker Henley 37
  Hurricane 37, 46, 48, 52, 54, 56, 160
  Hurricane I 56, 60
  Hurricane II 56, 59, 63
  Hurricane IIA Srs 2 101
  Hurricane IIB 60, 62, 63, 102, 103, 104, 106

Hurricane IIC 57, 102, 172, 173, 174
Hurricane IID 57, 58, 59, 60, 63, 65, 66, 107, 174, 176
Hurricane IV 108, 110, 111, 112, 130, 131, 135, 136, 173, 176
Hurricane night intruder 108
Tempest 146
Typhoon 106, 107, 108, 110, 111, 112, 136, 137, 139, 140-144, 146, 147, 149-151, 152, 155-159
Heinkel He 50 27
He 51 28
He 70 28
He 118 28
Hellcat — *see* Grumman F6F
Helldiver — *see* Curtiss SB2C; also Curtiss OC-1
Henschel Hs 123 26, 27, 28, 29, 40, 42, 54, 67, 81
Hs 129A 81
Hs 129B 63, 64, 66, 81, 82, 83, 86, 88, 89
Hs 129B-2 86
Hs 129B-3 98
Hermes, HMS aircraft carrier 162
Hitler, Adolf 39, 145

I-15 — *see* Polikarpov
I-15*bis* — *see* Polikarpov
I-153 *Chaika* — *see* Polikarpov
Illustrious, HMS aircraft carrier 53
Ilyushin Il-4 (DB-3F) 71
Il-2 (BSh-2) 32, 33, 66, 70, 73, 74, 75, 76
Il-2m3 76, 80, 87, 88, 92, 94, 95
Il-10 100

Jabo — German for 'Fighter-bomber'
Junkers Ju 52/3m 44
Ju 87 27, 28, 39, 41, 43, 46, 50, 54, 56
Ju 87A 29, 35
Ju 87B 29, 42, 51, 53, 63, 67, 68, 71
Ju 87D 59, 64, 65, 81, 89, 117, 118, 127, 129, 134, 148, 155
Ju 87G 85, 86, 89, 90, 92, 94
Ju 87R 42
Ju 88A 33, 34, 41, 54, 67
Ju 88C 35, 59, 61
Ju 88C-6 107
Ju 88P-1, -2 86
Ju 88Z 35
K-47 26, 27

K-47 — *see* Junkers K-47
Kamikaze 169, 181
Kashmir, HMS destroyer 54
'Katyusha' — *see* Rocket projectiles
Kawasaki Ki 45 'Nick' 34, 35
Kelly, HMS destroyer 54
Kenney, General George 163, 164
Kittyhawk — *see* Curtiss P-40
Kluge, General Hans von 142
Königsberg (German cruiser) 41
KV-1, -2 tanks 84, 87
KwK 39 cannon 85, 86

La-7 (Lavochkin) 97
Lallemant, Col. Raymond 155-159
Lambert, Lt. August 93
Langermann, *Oblt* 61
Otto Leonhardt (German ship) 134
Lockheed Hudson 46
P-38 Lightning 34, 35, 64, 113, 115, 139, 140, 141, 144, 152, 167, 169, 170, 172

Loire-Nieuport LN 411 35, 45
LN 42 35

Macchi C.200 58, 59, 63, 64, 117
C.202 135
C.205 135
Mallory, Air Marshal Leigh- 158
Marat (Soviet battleship) 69
Martin B-26 Marauder 138, 153, 154
Baltimore 61
BM-1 22, 23
167 (Maryland) 21
Messerschmitt Bf 109 28, 44, 50
Bf 109E 33, 43, 54, 61, 67, 68, 71
Bf 109E *Jabo* 54, 57, 73, 81, 83
Bf 109E-4/B 47, 49
Bf 109F 54, 57, 61, 71, 74, 101
Bf 109F-4/B 105
Bf 109G 61, 125, 145, 149
Bf 110 34, 44, 47, 48, 49, 53, 54, 56, 59, 67, 68, 70, 73, 117
Bf 110C-4/B 47
Bf 110G 85, 86, 107
Me 210 61, 63, 117
Me 262 145, 148, 149, 155
Me 410 145
Meyer, *Hptm* Bruno 89, 91
Mitchell — *see* North American B-25
Mitchell, Col. William 22
MK 101 cannon 81, 82
MK 103 cannon 86
MK 108 cannon 145
Mohawk — *see* Curtiss P-36
Montgomery, General Bernard 62, 149
Morane 406 44
Mosquito — *see* De Havilland
Mussolini, Benito 15, 51
Mustang — *see* North American P-51

N-37 cannon 87
Naiad, HMS cruiser 54
Nakajima Ki 43 'Oscar' 183
Ki 84 'Frank' 183
Napalm 134, 155, 170, 180
Nobili, *Colonello* 118
North American A-36A 'Invader' 113, 114, 115, 118, 119, 121, 124, 125, 172
B-25 Mitchell 21
B-25C Mitchell 164, 166, 174, 177
B-25G & H Mitchell 128, 169
P-51 Mustang 99, 140, 144, 152
P-51A Mustant I 106, 172, 174
P-51B Mustang III 126, 130, 134, 135, 136, 138, 139, 140, 146, 177
P-51D Mustang IV 134, 152, 170, 175, 177
Northrop Model 2 18
Model 2E 18, 19
8A-1, 8A-2 19
8A-3N 19 44
8A-3P 19
8A-4 19
8A-5 19
XA-13 18
A-17, A-17A 19, 20, 24
A-33 19
Bt-1 24
XBT-2 25
P-61 Black Widow 153
NS-23 cannon 100
Nyeman R-10 31

Operation Barbarossa 67
Bodenplatte 149

'Bowler Hat' 133
Crusader 56
Dragoon 128
Mercury 54
Pedestal 64
'Timothy' 132, 134
Zitadelle 87, 90

P-36 — *see* Curtiss
P-38 — *see* Lockheed
P-39 — *see* Bell
P-40 — *see* Curtiss
P-47 — *see* Republic
P-51 — *see* North American
11 P-37 cannon 87
Pak 40 86
Panzerblitz 98
Panzerschreck 98
Patton, General George 142, 143
Petylakov Pe-2 33, 70, 72, 94, 95
Pickard, Gp Capt P.C. 138
Polbin, Maj. Gen Ivan 72, 100
Polikarpov I-15 28
I-15*bis* 75
I-153 Chaika 75
I-16 28
R-5 30, 75
R-SSS 31
R-Z 31, 73, 75
Potez 63 20
631 34
633 35, 45
PzKw IV 87
PzKw V Panther 87
PzKw VI Tiger 84, 87
PZL P.43 Karas 37
R-5 — *see* Polikarpov
R-10 — *see* Nyeman
R-SSS — *see* Polikarpov
R-Z — *see* Polikarpov
Reggiane Re 2001 64
Re 2002 Ariete 117, 118, 119, 135
Republic P-47 Thunderbolt 165, 166, 169, 175, 177
P-47D Thunderbolt 124, 125, 126, 128, 131, 134, 135, 138, 140, 141, 144, 148, 149, 152, 158, 174, 179
P-47N Thunderbolt 182
'Rhubarbs' 101, 102
Richthofen, General Wolfram von 48
Rocket projectiles —
American:
4.5-in 'Bazooka' type 132
5-in HVAR 180, 181, 182
British: 25lb 129, 173
60 lb 109, 173 etc.
German:
see *Panzerblitz*, *Panzerschrek*;
WfrGr 210
Soviet:
RBS-82 32
ROFS-132 32
RS-82 74, 75 etc.
RS-132 32, 96; also BETAB-150
Rolla-Royce BF cannon 58
Rommel, General Erwin 50, 57, 62
'Rover David' (Forward Control Unit) 121, 122
'Rover Frank' 132
'Rover Tentacle' 132
Rubensdorffer, *Hptm* Walter 47, 48
Rudel, *Hptm* (later *Oberst*) 69, 89, 92

Savoia-Marchetti SM.85 37, 51

SB-2*bis* — *see* Tupolev
Scott, Gp Capt D.J. 158
SD-1 anti-personnel bomb container 89, 96
SD-2 anti-personnel bomb container 81, 89, 96
SD-4 anti-personnel bomb container 82
SE. 5A 13
SE 100 34, 35
Shturmovik (Soviet assault aircraft); usually Il-2
Sigel, *Hptm.* Walter 59
Sopwith Camel 12, 13
Southampton, HMS cruiser 53
Stars and Stripes (magazine) 158
Sukhoi Su 2 (BB-1) 32, 33, 71
Supermarine Spitfire 46, 65, 102, 106, 113, 119, 124, 125, 129, 130, 135, 144, 146, 152, 173
'Spitbomber' 62, 66
Spitfire V fighter-bomber 62, 120, 128, 131, 135, 136
Spitfire VIII 128, 134, 139, 170, 174, 176
Spitfire IX 120, 128, 131, 134, 135, 136, 137, 144, 147, 148
Spitfire XVI 147
Swordfish — *see* Fairey

T-34 tanks 73, 87
Ta-dan Japanese bomb container 183
Tempest — *see* Hawker
Thunderbolt — *see* Republic P-47
Tomahawk — *see* Curtiss P-40
Tonne, *Major* Günter 108, 118
Tratt, *Major* Eduard 69
Tupolev SB-2*bis* 71
Typhoon — *see* Hawker

Udet, General Ernst 26
V-1 137, 141
V-2 147, 148
'Vertushka' 72; *see also* 'Circle of Death'
VCP (Visual Control Posts) 156
Vickers 'S' gun 58, 174
Vultee Model V-11 19
V-11GB 31
V-12, -12C, -12D 19, 20
A-35A Vengeance 113, 164, 165, 171, 173, 174
XA-41 115
Vought F4U Corsair 168, 169, 170, 180, 181, 182
F4U-1D 169
F4U-4 181
O3U Corsair 23
SBU-1 23
SB2U 24, 160, 177
V-156F 35, 45

Wavell, General Archibald 52
Warhawk — *see* Curtiss P-40
Warspite, HMS battleship 54
Westlake Wg Cdr George 134
WfrGr 210 74
Westland Whirlwind 34, 35, 102, 106, 108, 110, 111
Wirraway — *see* Commonwealth (CA)

Yakovlev Yak-9B 97
Yak-9DD 130
Yokosuka D4Y 'Judy' 178

Zelenska, Z 71

Air force formations
Allied:
1st TAF (Tactical Air Force) 144, 170
2nd TAF 111, 126, 131, 136, 138, 139, 140, 141, 142, 146, 149, 151, 153, 155, 158
3rd TAF 175
1st ACG (Air Command Group) 174, 175, 177
TAC (Tactical Air Command) 138
IX TAC 140, 149
XII TAC 121, 125, 126, 128, 131, 144
XIX TAC 140
XXII TAC 131, 133, 135
XXIX TAC 144, 149

American:
US 5th AF 154, 163, 165, 169
US 7th AF 179, 182
US 8th AF 136, 138
US 9th AF 111, 113, 131, 136, 138, 139, 140, 141, 142, 144, 146, 152, 153, 155
US 12th AF 113, 144, 153
US 13th AF 168
US 14th AF 177
US 20th AF 182
27th Bomb Group (Light) 161
27th FBG (Fighter-Bomber Group) 115, 125, 131, 133
86th FBG 115, 119, 125, 131, 133
23rd FG (Fighter Group) 176
33rd FG 115, 119, 125, 175
49th FG 170
51st FG 171, 177
57th FG 63, 65, 115, 119, 120, 124, 125, 131, 135
79th FG 65, 115, 119, 120, 125, 131, 133, 134
80th FG 171, 173, 175
311st FG 172, 175, 177
318th FG 182
324th FG 115, 119, 125
325th FG 115, 116
350th FG 131, 135
354th FG 138
366 FG 139
414th FG 182
474th FG 144
VMF 111 180
VMF 222 180
VMF 223 180
VMF 224 180

Brazilian:
1° *Grupo de Caca* 131, 135

British:
Air Fighting Development Unit 103
Balkan Air Force (BAF) 130, 131, 135
Desert Air Force (DAF) 120, 121, 125, 126, 128, 130, 131, 133, 134
2 RAF Group 136, 137, 139, 142
83 RAF Group 136, 139, 146, 155
84 RAF Group 136, 139, 141, 146, 147, 158
85 RAF Group 136
123 RAF Wing 158
146 RAF Wing 147
233 RAF Wing 60, 61, 125, 128
239 RAF Wing 59, 61, 63, 65, 115, 119, 120, 126, 131, 133, 134
244 RAF Wing 128, 134
281 RAF Wing 135
283 RAF Wing 135

7 SAAF Wing 62, 63, 65, 120, 123, 125, 128, 134
8 SAAF Wing 133, 135
1 Sqn RAF 102, 106
3 Sqn RAF 59, 102, 106
6 Sqn RAF 57, 59, 63, 65, 66, 130
11 Sqn RAF 174
20 Sqn RAF 174, 175
27 Sqn RAF 172
32 Sqn RAF 106
43 Sqn RAF 106
45 Sqn RAF 171
56 Sqn RAF 107
80 Sqn RAF 56, 57, 63
82 Sqn RAF 171
87 Sqn RAF 106
110 Sqn RAF 171, 174
112 Sqn RAF 57, 59
113 Sqn RAF 56
126 Sqn RAF 62
127 Sqn RAF 63
137 Sqn RAF 106, 110, 111
152 Sqn RAF 66
164 Sqn RAF 110, 111, 158
174 Sqn RAF 106, 108
175 Sqn RAF 106, 108
181 Sqn RAF 107, 108, 111
182 Sqn RAF 107, 108
183 Sqn RAF 107, 108
184 Sqn RAF 107, 110, 111
193 Sqn RAF 107, 158
195 Sqn RAF 107
197 Sqn RAF 107
198 Sqn RAF 107, 158
211 Sqn RAF 173
247 Sqn RAF 106
260 Sqn RAF 126, 134
252 Sqn RAF 129
261 Sqn RAF 175
263 Sqn RAF 102, 110, 111
272 Sqn RAF 56
274 Sqn RAF 59, 60, 63
335 Sqn RAF 63
603 Sqn RAuxAF 129
607 Sqn RAuxAF 104, 107, 172
609 Sqn RAuxAF 107, 155, 158
615 Sqn RAuxAF 172
3 Sqn RAAF 52
402 Sqn RCAF 104, 106
486 Sqn RNZAF 106
7 Sqn SAAF 60, 63, 66
8 Sqn Indian Air Force 171

French:
1st French Air Force 144
GBA I/54 44
GBA II/35 45
GBA II/54 45
GC I/5 43

German:
Oberkommando der Luftwaffe (OKL) 29
Luftflotte 1 67, 82
Luftflotte 2 43, 49, 67, 82
Luftflotte 3 47, 101, 105, 108
Luftflotte 4 67, 81, 82
Luftflotte Ost 82
VIII. *Fliegerkorps* 48
X. *Fliegerkorps* 53
ErpGr 210 (*Erprobungsgruppe*) 47, 48, 49, 67, 69
Führer der Panzerjäger 86
Gefechtsverband Sigel 59

Jabogruppe Afrika 61
Legion Condor 28
Versuchskommando für
  Panzerbekämpfung 86
Waffengeneral der Schlachtflieger 90
JG 2 (Jagdgeschwader) 106
10(Jabo)/JG 2 105, 108
JG 3 83
JG 5 82
14(Jabo)/JG 5 125
JG 26 106
10(Jabo)/JG 26 105, 108
JG 27 54
II/JG 27 57
JG 51 47
PzJäger Staffel/JG 51 83, 86
JG 53 61
II/JG 53 57, 61
JG 54 74
10(Jabo)/JG 54 108
JG 77 54
II(JG 77 54, 61
KG 2 (Kampfgeschwader) 107
KG 30 41
II/KG 51 145
KG(J) 51 148
KG(J) 54 148
KG 76 148
I/KG 200 145
II/KG 200 148, 155
LG 1 (Lehrgeschwader) 30
I/LG 1 54
IV(Stuka)/LG 1 47
I(Z)/LG 1 47, 48, 49
2/LG 1 59
I(Jagd)/LG 2 54
I(Schlacht)/LG 2 29, 40, 42, 47, 49,
  54, 67, 69, 81
NSGr 2 (Nachtschlachtgruppe) 155
NSGr 9 128, 134
NSGr 20 148, 155
SKG 10 (Schnellkampfgeschwader)
  112, 118, 119
I/SKG 10 108, 112, 145
I/SKG 10 91, 108, 117, 120
II/SKG 10 64, 91, 108
IV/SKG 10 91, 108, 117, 120
I/SKG 210 67, 82
II/SKG 210 67, 82
SchG 1 (Sclachtgeschwader) 81, 83, 89
I/SchG 1 88
II/SchG 1 81, 88
I/SchG 1 86
I/SchG 1 86
SchG 2 119
I/SchG 2 61, 63, 91, 117
II/SchG 2 64, 91, 117
I/SchG 2 86
I/SchG 2 64, 86, 88
SG 1 91
SG 2 93
I/SG 2 91
II/SG 2 (Jabo) 91, 92
III/SG 2 91, 92
SG 3 91
SG 4 128, 148, 149
I/SG 4 (Jabo) 91, 125
II/SG 4 91, 120, 125
III/SG 4 (Jabo) 91
I/SG 5 91, 92, 148, 149
IV(Panzer)/SG 9 91
I/SG 10 91, 120
II/SG 10 91, 120

Sonderstaffel Eindhoven 145, 155
Staffel 92 80
I/Stukageschwader 162 27
StG 1 39, 89, 91
I/StG 1 41
StG 2 47, 54, 69, 83, 89, 91
I/StG 2 54, 63
II/StG 2 54
III/StG 2 63, 64
StG 3 59, 117, 129
I/StG 5 91
StG 51 47
StG 77 91
Trägergruppe 186 30, 39
ZG 1 (Zerstörergeschwader) 108
I/ZG 1 82, 86
II/ZG 1 67, 82, 117
III/ZG 1 61, 63, 117
III/ZG 2 64, 108
I/ZG 26 54, 67, 82
II/ZG 26 54, 56, 67, 82
III/ZG 26 56, 59, 61, 117
10/ZG 26 63, 117
II/ZG 76 49
III/ZG 76 67

Hungarian:
102/1 Sqn 98

Italian:
158° Gruppo Assalto 117
159° Gruppo Assalto 117
5° Stormo Assalto 117, 118, 119
15° Stormo Assalto 118
50° Stormo Assalto 51, 52, 117
2° Stormo CT 58, 63
103° Gruppo Tuffatori 118
121° Gruppo Tuffatori 118
Italian Co-Belligerent AF 129, 135
4° Stormo CBAF 135
5° Stormo CBAF 135
51° Stormo CBAF 135

Soviet:
4th ShAP (Ground Attack Rgt) 73,
  74, 80, 81
215th ShAP 73
606th ShAP 75
7th Guards ShAP 81
150th Bomber Rgt 72, 73
1st Guards Bomber Air Corps 100

Army units
America:
US 1st Army 138, 140, 149, 155
US 3rd Army 138, 140, 142
US 5th Army 121, 134
US 7th Army 144
US 9th Army 144, 149, 155

British:
2nd Army 136, 139, 144, 155
8th Army 65, 119, 120, 126, 134
14th Army 175

Canadian:
1st Army 136, 139

French:
2nd Army 43

German:
6th Army 83
7th Army 143
II SS Pz Corps 88
3rd Pz Div 88
9th Pz Div 88
17th Pz Div 88

Turkish:
7th Army (WW I) 13